D0340405

American River College Library
4700 College Oak Drive
Sacramento, CA 95841

Liberating Economics

Liberating Economics

Feminist Perspectives on Families, Work, and Globalization

Drucilla K. Barker
and
Susan F. Feiner

THE UNIVERSITY OF MICHIGAN PRESS
Ann Arbor

Copyright © by the University of Michigan 2004
All rights reserved
Published in the United States of America by
The University of Michigan Press
Manufactured in the United States of America
⊚ Printed on acid-free paper

2007   2006   2005   2004   4   3   2   1

No part of this publication may be reproduced,
stored in a retrieval system, or transmitted in any form
or by any means, electronic, mechanical, or otherwise,
without the written permission of the publisher.

A CIP catalog record for this book is available from the British Library.

Library of Congress Cataloging-in-Publication Data

Barker, Drucilla K., 1949–
    Liberating economics : feminist perspectives on families, work, and
globalization / Drucilla K. Barker and Susan F. Feiner.
        p. cm.
    Includes bibliographical references and index.
    ISBN 0-472-09843-8 (cloth : alk. paper) —
    ISBN 0-472-06843-1 (pbk. : alk. paper)
    1. Feminist economics.   2. Women—Employment.
    3. Family—Economics aspects.   4 Globalization
    I. Feiner, Susan.   II. Title.
    HQ1381.B365 2004   2004015058

To our mothers
who shared their hope
that the world could
be different

Contents

List of Figures   ix

List of Tables   xi

Preface and Acknowledgments   xiii

Chapter 1. "Economics," She Wrote   1

Chapter 2. Family Matters: Reproducing the
Gender Division of Labor   19

Chapter 3. Love's Labors—Care's Costs   41

Chapter 4. Women, Work, and National Policies   56

Chapter 5. Women and Poverty in the
Industrialized Countries   75

Chapter 6. Globalization Is a Feminist Issue   95

Chapter 7. Dickens Redux: Globalization and
the Informal Economy   118

Chapter 8. The Liberated Economy   128

Notes   145

Select Bibliography   167

Index   181

Figures

1.1. Two views of gender   12
1.2. Two views of society   14
1.3. Gender and society   15
2.1. Circular flow   37
2.2. Household production   38
3.1. Betty Good Wife advertisement   53
4.1. Changes in female U.S. labor force participation by age   60

Tables

3.1. Maternity/Parental Leave Benefits for Seven Selected
      OECD Countries   47
4.1. U.S. Civilian Labor Force Participation by Sex   58
4.2. Civilian Labor Force Participation by Sex for Ten
      OECD Countries   59
4.3. Gender Wage Gap in Manufacturing for Ten
      OECD Countries   62
4.4. Female Percentage in Major Occupation Groups for
      Ten OECD Countries   64
4.5. U.S. Wage Gap for Females by Occupation   65
5.1. Effectiveness of Welfare State Regimes   81
5.2. Basic Family Budgets   85
5.3. Population in Poverty in Nine Selected Countries   92
6.1. Female Share of Labor Force and Gender Wage Gap for
      Ten Selected Countries   110

Preface and Acknowledgments

As feminists and as economists it is important to begin with context and history—both the personal and the professional. Our vision of economics was shaped by the political and cultural movements of the 1960s and 1970s, including the antiwar movement, the civil rights movement and the women's movement. An important insight of this era is expressed in the slogan "the personal is political." First as graduate students in economics, now as professors in the discipline, we've come to appreciate the relevance of this truth. The decision to study economics, like economics itself, is political. But the politics of economics need not reflect the fear of scarcity or the narcissism of self-interest. Instead, feminist economics rests on a politics of inclusion, the recognition of mutual reciprocities, and social justice.

When we began to study the discipline, no one told us that in its formative years many women wrote and lectured in economics. Here, as in other disciplines, professionalization was accompanied by the exclusion of women. The result was a decidedly androcentric approach, one that accepts male superiority and female subordination as normal and mutually beneficial.

In economics, as in virtually every other academic area, the discovery and recovery of women's contributions to the field did not occur until a critical mass of appropriately credentialed women began to ask new questions and search for their predecessors. In the second half of the twentieth century more and more women earned doctorates in the discipline. This led the premier organization in economics, the American Economic Association, to establish the Committee for the Status of Women in the Economics Profession (CSWEP) in 1971. But in economics, unlike the other social sciences or the humanities, it took another twenty years for a self-consciously feminist community of economists to emerge. It was not until the early 1990s that the International Association for Feminist Economics (IAFFE) was formed and in 1995 the first volume of the IAFFE journal, *Feminist Economics,* was published.

Preface and Acknowledgments

We were motivated to bring the explanatory power of feminist theory to our work as we observed feminist developments in virtually all the disciplines of the social sciences, the humanities, and the sciences. As economists started to view economic theories, institutions, and policies through the lens of gender, they began to question and transform the field. IAFFE provided the intellectual community where this could occur. We have been privileged to be among the founders of this tradition, and we are grateful for the many invaluable conversations, debates, and friendships that brought this new path to economic knowledge into being.

We would like to thank Hollins University, the University of Southern Maine, and the Hawke Institute at the University of South Australia for their support of this project. Through a combination of leaves and visiting appointments we had both the time and the space to work together. Our colleagues in women's studies and economics offered many thoughtful comments on earlier chapter drafts. Thank you. Thanks also to Ellen McCarthy and Raphael Allen, our editors, and to the anonymous readers for their valuable feedback. We also thank our students, whose questions and interests helped us shape our ideas. Special thanks to Jim Kessler for his invaluable and timely assistance with our computers, networks, and file recoveries and also to Kathleen Ingoldsby for her inspired work on the cover art.

Finally, we gratefully acknowledge the loving support of our spouses, who encouraged us even as our work spread over dining room tables, family rooms, and vacations.

1. "Economics," She Wrote

It is the best of times; it is the worst of times. Today, women's contribution to economic well-being is more than matched by the injustices that accompany their work. Virtually all international organizations agree that gender equity is necessary for economic growth and prosperity, yet inequality and exploitation haunt the lives of women and girls everywhere. Today, many women do "men's" work, but the invisible, devalued, and poorly paid work remains "women's" work. In the poor nations women and girls suffer disproportionately from malnutrition and disease, and even in the most prosperous nations women encounter glass ceilings and sticky floors. Women, regardless of geographic location, are especially prone to hardship and poverty.[1]

Unpaid household labor is now recognized as crucial to every economy, yet all over the world unpaid domestic work is still the province of women. Women and men now engage in paid labor in nearly the same proportions, but the responsibility for child and dependent care still falls mainly to women. Women add more to household income than ever before, so women's total work time exceeds men's by at least two hours per day. The unprecedented growth in career opportunities for educated, privileged women is accompanied by rapidly increasing numbers of poor women employed as domestics, caring for the children of the privileged. Globally, women-owned businesses are increasing at a rapid rate; female entrepreneurs are, however, disproportionately located in the informal sector, beyond the reach of labor organizations that could mitigate the harsh exploitation of the poorest of the poor. The formal, political power of women has reached an historic high, and still 70 percent of the world's 1.3 billion poor living on less than one U.S. dollar per day are women. It is a season of hope; it is a season of despair.

Feminist economists explain these facts without romanticizing the existing unequal distribution of resources between women and men, without assuming the naturalness of women's subordinate social status, and without rationalizing the oppression and exploitation of the world's least privileged peoples. Reigning interpretations of economic inequality—by gender, race, ethnicity, religion, and nation—trace social inequalities back to different individual choices, abilities, and resources. Analyses that follow this logic are, in our view, thinly disguised apologies for the existing social hierarchies of gender, class, privilege, and power. Feminist economists reject such essentialist justifications and instead root economic inequality in social processes of inclusion, valorization, and representation.

Our feminist perspective allows us to reframe the criteria for evaluating economic performance. Five criteria are especially important. First, participants in an economic system should insist on a system that is fair. Fairness as we see it is a question that goes beyond opportunity to consider outcomes. For example, when people follow the economic rules—work responsibly at their jobs and contribute to the community through tax payments and volunteer work—will they reap the benefits or will race, class, and gender block their full participation in the economy? Likewise, will people who do not have access to market incomes be able to enjoy a socially acceptable standard of living? Second, we ask whether an economic system is likely to provide an improved quality of life over time. Here we explicitly include in our vision of the quality of life such criteria as leisure, health, education, and the conditions of work so that this metric goes far beyond the traditional market basket of goods and services as a measure of well-being.

A third and closely connected dimension of the economic system involves economic security. Can participants in the economy expect to be able to support themselves and their families? Or, as is the case in the United States today, will the economic security of the many be sacrificed by policies that benefit the few? A fourth concern recognizes the potential wastefulness of economic activity. We can no longer ignore the extent to which production and consumption may waste human and nonhuman resources. Our last question is perhaps the most contentious: To what extent does the economy provide opportunities for work that are meaningful? Is it written in stone that most jobs must involve hateful activities that drain the creativity and humanity out of the people who do them? Or can we envision an economy where work validates the inherent dignity of every human being?

These are not new questions in economics or in any other inquiry into social conditions. This book does not set out answers to these questions but, rather, shows how feminist economists frame them. In so doing, this book demonstrates how a feminist analysis liberates economics.

What Is Economics?

Wait a minute, feminism and economics? Isn't a price just a price? A market just a market? Don't men and women feel the ups and downs of economic activity equally, whether they are black or white, straight or gay? Won't a change in interest rates affect everyone the same way, regardless of gender? To all these questions feminist economists answer, "no." Gender, like race, ethnicity, class, nation, and other markers of social location, is central to our understanding of economics and economic systems. The categories of economic analysis do not express timeless truths. Economic categories and concepts, like the categories and concepts of every knowledge project, are embedded in social contexts and connected to processes of social differentiation.

But what is economics? Let us begin to explain this by asking a simple question: How do we get our daily bread? As individuals we only produce a tiny fraction of the commodities we consume each day. We buy the rest. How is it that ordinary goods and services like bread, soap, and electricity are available for us to purchase, providing we have the cash? A humble loaf of bread, like a bar of soap or a kilowatt of electricity, requires the coordinated activities of thousands of people, in dozens of occupations, scattered around the globe. Farmers grow wheat expecting to sell to millers. Millers process flour to sell to bakers. Bakers produce bread to fill orders from large supermarket chains. And grocers sell us bread so we can make sandwiches for ourselves, our families, and our friends.

Our daily bread depends upon all of these activities, plus those involved in manufacturing farm equipment, transportation, newspaper advertising, and supermarket hiring. Each of these must take place at approximately the right time, in roughly the correct sequence, and in sufficient quantity to keep grocery store shelves stocked. As we widen the scope of our vision to encompass the enormous array of commodities available today—education and health; DVDs and cell phones; art and music; childcare and eldercare; Barbies, books, and bombs—the complexity of modern industrial economies becomes apparent.

The activities necessary to maintain human life take place over and over and over again. What motivates individuals and institutions to undertake these activities? As Adam Smith so famously observed, the farmer, the miller, and the grocer do not act out of altruism or interest in your well-being. In market economies many goods and services are produced in anticipation of profits that may be realized when commodities are sold. The focus on commodity production, sales, and profits has been central to economics since its inception. But what happens to all those loaves of bread once they are sold? Economists since Adam Smith have ignored this question.

Adam Smith, writing in the late eighteenth century, saw that the processes of market exchange worked to coordinate the diverse activities of people who neither knew each other nor knew what the others wanted. Smith argued that self-interest would ensure that individuals would produce the goods society wanted. These insights continue to be valid. Farmers won't grow wheat, automakers won't produce cars, and accounting firms won't hire accountants unless they have a reasonable expectation that they can sell what they've produced. This is what Smith meant when he imagined that the economy was guided "as though by an invisible hand" to serve the social good. The idea that the division of labor works in concert with a self-adjusting market was Smith's brilliant insight. What Smith was unable to see was that much of what happens in markets relies on the vast amount of unpaid labor that takes place in the home.

We agree with feminist economist Julie Nelson that economics is the study of provisioning.[2] This points us to the importance of the production and redistribution that take place in families. Families share their resources with each other, including those members of the family who do not work for pay. Thus, feminist economists extend the economic horizon to analyze the economic activities that take place in households and families without assuming that these activities parallel behaviors found in markets.

Although mainstream economics has evolved since Smith's day, his focus on markets and the mutually beneficial nature of voluntary exchange remains a cornerstone of what is known today as neoclassical economics. For most economists, neoclassical economics is the standard against which all other schools are compared. Neoclassical economists start from premises about the state of nature and the nature of human beings. Nature is parsimonious, so resources are scarce. Human wants, in contrast, are unlimited. These assumptions about the human and nonhuman world allow neoclassical economists to define economics as the science of choice: the study of how societies allocate scarce resources among alternative uses. In this view economics is an objective, gender-neutral, and value-free science that articulates the laws of economics in the same way that physics articulates the laws of physical phenomena.

Neoclassical economics is defined by its reliance on rational choice theory. By rational choice economists mean that individuals can (and do) arrange their preferences (their likes and dislikes) logically and consistently. Then, given their preferences, and the constraints of time and income, individuals make choices that maximize their self-interest (utility). Given this specification of rational choice, the mathematics of constrained optimization can be used to solve many problems, all of which take the same logical form: economic agents maximize their well-being by engaging in activities up to the point where marginal benefits just equal marginal costs. The economics literature is rife with examples: childbearing, marriage, surrogacy, prostitution, drug addiction, and even suicide are said to result from utility-maximizing behavior.

Aside from being simplistic, this framework assumes away personal, familial, and communitarian responsibilities. Individuals exist solely in the sphere of exchange where they contractually interact if and when such interactions promote their self-interest. This rational economic agent is commonly referred to as *Homo economicus,* or Economic Man. For mainstream economists, *Homo economicus* is defined absent gender, race, class, or any other markers of social location. Indeed, neoclassical economists see the universality of rational economic agents as the triumph of their paradigm.

Feminist economists, applying the insights of feminist criticism in literature, psychology, and philosophy of science, argue that just as there is no universal human subject, there is no universal economic agent. Assuming universal economic rationality erases the deep differences among upper-class Egyptian housewives, homeless women in U.S. urban centers, women in refugee camps, and preteen sex workers in South Asia. Neoclassical economics insists on seeing each as essentially the same: they are all rational economic agents seeking to maximize their utility within the dual constraints of time and income. The feminist alternative holds that gender, race, ethnicity, and nation are analytical categories, not mere descriptors attached to rational agents who are in all other regards identical.

Feminists in economics ask questions about the production of individuals: Where do these so-called rational agents come from? Do they spring from the ground like Hobbesian mushroom men? Is all economic activity, absent a gun to the head, or a state commissar's directive, voluntary and mutually advantageous? If so, conflict, power, and exploitation are ruled out *a priori.* In contrast, feminist economics interrogates these questions.

The two major alternatives to the neoclassical tradition are Marxian and institutional economics. One of the remarkable similarities of these paradigms is that their founders (Karl Marx and Friedrich Engels on the one hand and Thorstein Veblen on the other) did initially frame issues central to women's social status in ways that are surprisingly consistent with contemporary feminist analysis. In the 1884 monograph *The Origins of the Family, Private Property, and the State,* Engels argued that women's subordinate economic position derived from the social organization of production rather than biology.[3] Veblen's classic 1899 work, *The Theory of the Leisure Class,* offered similar arguments concerning women's social and economic status.[4] But the feminist insights of the founders of these two heterodox economic traditions were pushed aside as economics became an academic discipline and as the mathematical, promarket ideology of neoclassicism pushed out other practitioners. It was not until the 1960s and 1970s, with the rise of second-wave feminism, that Marxist and institutionalist economists began to rediscover the relevance of gender.

Feminism and Economics

One might suppose that when social science research—whether in economics, history, sociology, or psychology—focuses on issues relating to women, it is feminist. But this is not the case. Social analyses that are distinctively feminist are not only, and not necessarily, about women. Feminist social science questions existing relationships between women and men and among diverse groups of women. Feminists do not assume that these relationships are in any sense essential, optimal, or natural. Rejecting traditional views of women and men shifts our perspective, and from this angle of vision social relations can be seen in new ways. Producing this perspective is the central objective of the feminist economics project.

The foundation for feminist economics was built during the 1970s by scholars working in three different theoretical traditions: neoclassical economics, institutionalist economics, and Marxist political economy. Feminist work in the neoclassical and institutionalist traditions focused on questions about women's labor force participation, the gender wage gap, and occupational segregation. This scholarship took the position that women's participation in the paid labor force, on equal footing with men, was the key to women's emancipation and empowerment.

Feminist work in the Marxist political economy tradition criticized traditional Marxist analyses of women and noted that under patriarchy women faced gender oppression regardless of their class status (although, of course, wealth and income accorded some women more privilege than others) or the dominant mode of production (socialist, capitalist, or feudal). Gender oppression was a result of the sexual division of labor—which under capitalism meant the division between paid and unpaid, productive and reproductive, and domestic and paid labor.

With few exceptions, women's access to resources and opportunities is less than men's, and gender inequality is ubiquitous. We recognize, however, that differences among women arise from hierarchies of race, class, ethnicity, nationality, and heterosexism. These differences create systems of privilege that are antithetical to feminist aspirations for social justice. The tension between talking about the interests of women as a group and recognizing important differences among them is as acute in feminist economics as it is in all other branches of feminism. Women occupy multiple and often contradictory social locations that challenge simple notions of common interest. Indeed, this book explores the many different ways that economic privileges are distributed and analyzes the significance of gender in the distribution of and access to resources.

Gender refers to the social organization of sexual difference.[5] Social roles, responsibilities, privileges, and opportunities are allocated according to gender. The traditional view of women and men divides the world into male and female realms and accords the traits associated with masculinity greater value. The resulting dualisms—reason and emotion, strong and weak, active and passive, knowledge and intuition—are assumed to be given by biology so that women's nature suits them to lives of domesticity and the care of others, while men's nature suits them to competitive achievement in politics, business, and the professions. As a consequence some types of work get coded as masculine, while others are coded as feminine. The former are almost always accorded more status than the latter.

This gender coding is then projected forward and backward in time (remember the Flintstones and the Jetsons?), with the effect that gender roles are seen as unchanging and unchangeable. Feminist scholarship has, however, demonstrated the enormous variation in how societies have organized sexual difference. Recognizing this, gender analysis always needs to be historically grounded. As we show, this masculine-feminine coding also varies by class, race, ethnicity, and nation so that what is appropriate for women or men in one group may not be appropriate for women or men in other groups. For example, the view of women as passive, weak, and lacking sexual appetite only characterized elite, privileged white women. Working-class women and women of color were, in contrast, depicted as aggressive, strong, and sexually voracious.

Feminists argue that the behaviors, attributes, strengths, and weaknesses of women and men are not determined biologically, nor do they follow some overarching design. With other feminists we take Simone de Beauvoir's famous remark "One is not born, one becomes a woman" as a bedrock commitment of feminist scholarship. When gender and sex are social, not natural categories, one must look to social relations to understand both the causes and consequences of women's subordinate economic status.

For centuries, male superiority and female subordination were taken for granted. The resulting asymmetries in, for example, political power, wealth, education, artistic achievement, and religious authority went largely unchallenged. Few women (and even fewer men) recognized or spoke out against the enforced inferiority of women. In consequence, the resulting masculine monopoly on reason, rationality, and wisdom gave considerable support to laws, customs, and day-to-day practices that excluded women from the spheres of life that were seen as important and thus worthy of study.[6] Scientific understanding and scholarly erudition, long assumed to be masculine prerogatives, secured men's historically privileged access to government, commerce, the military, and, of course, the institutions where knowledge was produced.

Feminist scholarship casts a critical eye on these received knowledge projects. A "hermeneutics of suspicion" informs the feminist reappraisal of accepted paths of causality, as well as a reassessment of the forces that play significant roles in social processes. This phrase is widely used in feminist religious studies, a field that employs the interpretive methods traditionally associated with the study of sacred texts (hermeneutics). Feminist theologians and Bible scholars speak of a hermeneutics of suspicion to name their emancipatory project of imagining and reconstructing the stories of the women who are marginalized, devalued, or absent in the Scriptures. The parallel with economics is striking.

Feminist economists read economic texts to discover, name, and valorize the many productive economic activities performed by women and other subordinated peoples. Economic analyses informed by such suspicions are able to uncover what dominant economic narratives repress. Even when women are confined to the household, they still perform the lioness's share of the world's work; the activities of reproduction (both biological and social) and provisioning are incredibly valuable yet are consistently deval-ued. Conflict is as likely to characterize economic processes as are harmony and mutually beneficial voluntary exchange, while power, class position, and status—not the workings of the invisible hand—are key determinants of who gets what.

Insofar as economists construct theories, analyze data, and produce poli-cies within a paradigm that takes existing relationships between women and men as natural, universal, and mutually advantageous, then such scholarship runs counter to feminist economics, especially when the topic of that research is woman. Indeed, much of the early work of feminist eco-nomics was the discovery of the many implicit assumptions about gender embedded in the discipline. At the most basic level, this critical stance changes the activities considered relevant to economics and shifts the gaze of economists away from the public spheres of the market to the private sphere of the home. This is a dramatic change in perspective, as revolu-tionary in economics as was the cinematic shift to the "upward gaze" in sex scenes.[7] But this new focus did not automatically challenge business as usual in economics.

Traditional economists also analyze issues that are central to feminist economics today: male-female wage gaps, valuing unpaid household labor, and women's role in development. When such work does not question the gender division of labor or use gender as a category of analysis, it is not fem-inist.[8] This approach has significant limitations since it studies women within the given normative Western conception of gender roles. In contrast, when gender is a category of analysis and not just a descriptor, features of social life that had been invisible are thrown into sharp relief. Our feminist approach to economics builds on the idea that the visions of masculinity and femininity that circulate in a specific sociohistorical context shape the way people describe and understand their world. Today, high-prestige econo-mists continue to offer explanations of differences in economic outcomes that rest on assumptions about race and gender that are not noticeably dif-ferent from those that circulated in the nineteenth century.

During the Victorian era, in the emerging capitalist industrial societies, women were increasingly defined as subservient to men. Women's subor-dination rested on the belief that insurmountable differences separated the masculine from the feminine. As a result, radically different imperatives were imagined to govern the lives of women and men. Men were to be the breadwinners and rule makers, while white women were instructed to devote all their energies to hearth and home, kith and kin. Laws, editorials, sermons, and scientific research endorsed the view that any woman whose behavior even hinted at autonomous action in the worlds of commerce, politics, religion, or education risked her sanity, her femininity, her fertility, and her very life.[9]

An equally important, self-evident truth of the nineteenth century was encapsulated in the racist euphemism "the white man's burden." This expression rationalized the ruthless exploitation of the peoples of Asia, Africa, and the Americas that took place during the colonial era.[10] Ideas of racial inferiority came to be an integral element of the ideology of the Victorian era, and race was seen to be as determining as biological sex.[11] Today, many scholars, men as well as women, realize that when views such as these are at the foundation of a discipline's approach to its field of study, the knowledge that results is likely to be one-sided and biased against gender equity and social justice.

Feminist economists, following this idea through the labyrinth of two hundred years of economic scholarship, have discovered that gender and race bias, misogyny and racism, are woven through the theories, empirical investigations, and policy prescriptions put forward by economists who, not coincidentally, have been almost exclusively white men.[12] The homogeneity of the economics profession is not without consequence. As feminist philosophers of science have shown, science is not produced by isolated individuals; it is produced in science communities. Theories, hypotheses, and patterns of reasoning—paradigms—are shaped and modified within such communities. To the extent that implicit assumptions and values are shared among the members of a community, they will not be questioned.[13] This is a persistent problem in the economics profession, composed as it is of mainly white, affluent, men.[14] Moreover, graduate training socializes economists to accept the overarching values and norms of the profession.[15]

Economics became a formal, academic discipline, complete with professional societies and journals, in the last decades of the nineteenth century. The men who conducted economic research, measured economic activity, and formulated economic policy were all thoroughly wedded to the Victorian ideology that defined women solely in terms of their childbearing, domestic capacities. This, of course, shaped their views regarding women's proper economic roles, the features of the economy worth studying, and the correct direction of economic policies aimed at women.

Men (but not women or people of color) were viewed as autonomous, self-acting human beings. White women were seen as passive and economically dependent: wives, mothers, and daughters.[16] Because the culturally and ideologically accepted view of woman equated "female" with "dependent" and "mother-homemaker" and since the realm of the home was deemed to be "not the economy" (neither monetary exchange nor commodity production took place there), economists developed their theories without taking women's productive but unpaid roles into account.[17] For the most part economics went forward as if women played no significant economic role despite the millions of women (and children) who worked in factories, mines, agriculture, and domestic service.[18] The view that women's proper place was in the home led economists to advocate restrictive workplace legislation, unequal and lesser wages for women, and outright prohibitions on women's employment.[19] One of the practical effects of this was to mask the very real and adverse conditions facing women and children in the labor force.

A Methodology for Feminist Economics

Traditional scholars insist that the knowing mind can and should be held rigorously separate from the objects of inquiry. But the comforting idea that knowledge progresses through the efforts of scholars untainted by any influences emanating from the society in which they live and think has been thoroughly debunked. Work in the history and philosophy of science has established the impossibility of a "view from nowhere." Every view is a point of view, and every point is somewhere. There is *always* a there there. Claims about disinterested, and value-free science are as outmoded and inappropriate in economics as they are in all other disciplines. As every view is located, each has a perspective.[20] Our perspective views society as a whole, and we take the position that all people, regardless of social location, are fully human.

Despite the Enlightenment ideal that all human beings are created equal, many societies that claim allegiance to such an ideal continue to resist the political, economic, and cultural changes that are preconditions for gender equity and social justice. As we write, social location—race, gender, ethnicity, sexual orientation, nation, and religion—functions to isolate, divide, and deprive. Consider this ironic definition of feminism: "Feminism is the radical idea that women are human beings."[21] This means that women are not objects, commodities, or the "other." Such a view of women, however, rejects notions of biological essentialism and contradicts the view that gender roles follow from nature.

We can use a simple heuristic to illustrate these different understand-

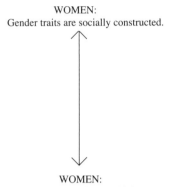

WOMEN:
Gender traits are socially constructed.

WOMEN:
Gender traits are given by biology or nature.

Fig. 1.1. Two views of gender

ings of the category women. In figure 1.1 the feminist view that women are fully human actors whose gender traits are determined socially is placed at the top, while the traditional view of women as biologically destined to lives of domesticity is placed at the bottom.

It will be helpful to understand the relationship between these dichotomous views of women, on the one hand, and similarly dichotomous views of society, on the other. One might suppose that the social sciences—economics, anthropology, sociology, history, and political science—begin with the idea that all aspects of society are interrelated. After all, isn't the very concept of society a reference to a whole and not to its component parts—the schools, governments, families, firms, and other institutions that comprise society? Not necessarily. Some concepts of society are predicated on an "atomistic" worldview, while others are predicated on a "holistic" worldview. In our view, holism is the appropriate approach to feminist economics.[22]

An important difference between atomism and holism concerns agency, that is, the extent to which individuals can shape their existence by exercising control over the circumstances of their lives. In the atomistic view individuals are assumed to be the authors of their beliefs (about society, religion, politics, art, the economy, and, of course, gender). Each person has ultimate responsibility for her or his standard of living since the material conditions of one's life reflects one's choices. People who make good choices will succeed, while people who do not succeed must have made bad choices. Absent political tyranny, dictatorship, or direct coercion, every able-bodied person is assumed to be "free" to live life in conditions of her or his own choosing. Poet William Ernest Henley ably expresses these sentiments, "[I] am the master of my fate, I am the captain of my soul."[23]

Our view builds from very different premises. Individuals do not preexist social relations. Instead, all aspects of individual experience are mediated by society. Individuals gain their beliefs about religion, the economy, and gender roles, for example, through their interactions with the culture. Parents, teachers, television, and popular music all play a role in socializing individuals to the views and behaviors appropriate to their social characteristics of sex, class, nationality, and race.[24] Individuals, their consciousness, their likes and dislikes, are constituted through the social relationships in which they live. Paraphrasing John Donne, no one is an island; everyone is a piece of the Continent, a part of the main.[25]

Although we believe that people are influenced by social processes that are invisible to them, and that they do not control, we are not saying that people are mere automatons, programmed by society to live just this way, think exactly these particular thoughts, and believe precisely these specific ideas.[26] Instead, we believe that individual agency operates within the constraints of culture, politics, and economics.[27] Individuals, in very idiosyncratic ways, often come to recognize the influence of society on their views and beliefs, and in response they often change them.[28] Recognizing that people are shaped by their circumstances does not mean that they have no ability to shape their world. This is in contrast to the atomistic view.

The differences between atomistic and holistic visions of society are of interest not least because these alternative views lead to diametrically opposed political agendas. Many influential political arguments rest on the idea that society is just so many individual parts. Former British prime minister Margaret Thatcher's remark "[T]here is no such thing as society: there are individual men and women, and there are families"[29] expresses the atomistic perspective. Our argument, in contrast, rests on the idea that society is a whole not reducible to its component parts. We agree with the Reverend Martin Luther King Jr., "[I]njustice anywhere is a threat to justice everywhere. We are caught in an inescapable network of mutuality, tied in a single garment of destiny."[30]

Figure 1.2 is another simple heuristic that represents these approaches to social theory.

ATOMISM:
Societies are the sum
of their parts.

HOLISM:
Societies are
structured wholes.

Fig. 1.2. Two views of society

Combining figures 1.1 and 1.2 allows us to bring understandings of gender into relation with understandings of social causation. Figure 1.3 has four quadrants. The two on the top are aligned with the feminist concept of women as human beings with traits that are socially determined, while the two on the bottom are aligned with the nonfeminist (or antifeminist) position that women are defined by biology. The two quadrants on the right are aligned with holistic views of social relations, while the two on the left are associated with atomism. The upper-right quadrant is the only space for economic analysis that is both feminist and holist.

The theoretical positions defined by the upper-left-hand quadrant and the lower-right-hand quadrant are plagued by deep internal contradictions. In the upper-left-hand quadrant, gender is a social construct. At the same time, society is seen as driven by the actions of individuals for whom race, class, and gender don't fundamentally matter since these agents are all essentially the same. It is very difficult, if not impossible, to reconcile these two positions. In the lower-right-hand quadrant, societies are seen as structured by the interaction of the whole. Yet the social totality is viewed with concepts and categories that do not take gender into account. The logic here is just as untenable as it is with respect to the upper-left-hand quadrant.

The quadrant on the bottom left is the space where neoclassical economic analysis is located. Here we find analyses of the family, the male-female wage gap, black-white differences in income, and the uneven impacts of globalization in which the ultimate causes of these outcomes are

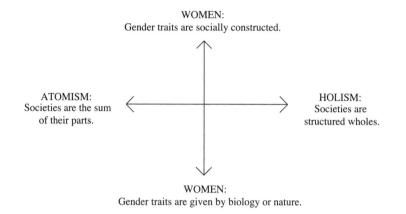

Fig. 1.3. Gender and society

differences in choices, abilities, and resources. Mainstream economics admits no difference between the decision making associated with housework, child rearing, or caring for others and the decision making associated with digging ditches, managing corporations, or deploying armies.

In mainstream economics, discussions of processes as diverse as globalization, environmental protection, nuclear proliferation, and population growth are explained in terms of the rational choices of self-interested actors. When economists observe huge disparities in living standards between rich and poor nations, for example, they argue that these reflect either different choices or different endowments of skills, technologies, and resources. Limiting the analysis of globalization or other complex social processes to rational choice, the nature of constraints, and the mutually advantageous effects of all exchanges equates the behavior of huge, transnational corporations with the behavior of children selling lemonade on a hot day.

From our perspective vast differences in economic outcomes are not only a matter of individual choice. Of course, people make choices, and those choices have consequences for better or worse. But not all choices are equally important, and not everything in life is a choice. Poor people, who are disproportionately women and children, do not choose to be poor. In

15

our view, social processes structure the economy in ways that produce and reproduce the persistent correlation between poverty and femaleness.

Mapping the Terrain

The potential scope of feminist economics is enormous. In writing this book we had to establish priorities and set some boundaries. It was important to go beyond topic areas that were simply "about women." But at the same time, we needed to retain the relevance of gender as a key category. To accomplish this, we decided to focus on topic areas where the economic consequences of the gender division of labor are of particular salience.

We begin in chapter 2 with an examination of the history of the Western family to show the economic, political, and cultural effects of the male breadwinner–female homemaker model of domestic life. In the nineteenth century, feminist economists like Charlotte Perkins Gilman, Harriet Martineau, and Josephine Butler recognized the many ways that the increasingly rigid gender division of labor disadvantaged women. In the twentieth century feminists began to make a direct connection between the subordinate status of women and the assumption of a gendered split in the economy. On the one hand there was the male sphere of public (outside the home) production, and on the other there was the female sphere of private (in the household) consumption. Standard economic theories take the production-consumption divide as a given, and in so doing they reproduce and reinforce the gendered dualisms that shape our understanding of social relationships.

In contrast, our discussion in chapter 3 of the history of gender division of labor lays the foundation for an analysis of the work done in contemporary households. Clean homes and healthy, well-fed children are often attributed to feminine altruism. This view sees caring work as both unskilled and natural. Caring labor does not, therefore, require monetary compensation. Upon closer inspection, we find that this view is antithetical to gender inequality, hides the painful realities faced by low-wage domestic workers, and obscures real differences in interests related to class or privilege. A feminist analysis of caring labor challenges many long-held views about women's work by recognizing its importance on the one hand and its socially devalued status on the other.

In chapter 4 we turn to a discussion of paid employment in the industrialized countries and note that in the United States, as in most other nations, the majority of occupations continue to be segregated by gender. That female workers tend to be concentrated in just a handful of occupations helps to explain persistent disparities in women's earnings, wealth, and career achievements. Many nations have programs and policies aimed at reducing gender segregation in paid employment. But few policy regimes recognize that caregiving and wage earning are equally important dimensions of life. Women's caregiving obligations impinge on their labor market opportunities because earning and caring impose different demands on employees and employers. Until these competing demands are reconciled, and caring labor becomes as much the work of men as it is of women, women will not achieve income-earning parity with men.

As we discuss in chapter 5, the feminization of poverty is a sad reality of contemporary life. Unfortunately, female poverty is more prevalent today than in the recent past. It is important for feminists to be able to explain this turn of events without resorting to myths that either malign the economic contributions of women or romanticize the poor. In our discussion of the gendered aspects of poverty in the industrial nations, we confront directly today's version of "the culture of poverty" hypothesis to demonstrate that the behavior of single mothers is not the cause of their poverty.

Chapter 6 explores the uneven impacts of globalization. Over the past fifty years the willingness of many nation-states to seek market-based solutions to human problems has risen and the pressure for global economic integration has increased. There is a direct connection between the expanding volume of international activity in terms highly favorable to corporations that stand outside or above the laws of all nation-states and the increasing disparity between the rich and poor of the world. The already rich industrial nations have prospered, while the poorer nations of the Global South have seen standards of living fall as their participation in the global economy has grown. Women and men experience these economic changes differently, with a disproportionate share of dislocation and suffering borne by women. They are the preferred workforce for transnational corporations, and structural adjustment policies force them to increase their unpaid labor time. Today, women are the poorest of the poor because these women and their advocates are excluded from the supranational bodies that make global economic policy.

As women's access to traditional sources of livelihood has declined, their participation in the informal economy has increased. This is the focus of chapter 7. Over much of the world, poor women, children, and men eke out an existence on the fringes of the economy. They are street vendors, homeworkers, servants, gardeners, and sex workers working in unorganized and unregulated industries. The rise of the informal sector evokes the worst excesses of nineteenth-century industrialization.

To conclude, chapter 8 shows how representation, discourse, and ideology connect feminist economics and social policy. A feminist economic agenda must begin by acknowledging difference and diversity and must explicitly address questions relating to fairness, quality of life, economic security, wastefulness, and the meaning of work. Shared interests rather than shared oppressions, aspirations rather than fears, and visions of the future rather than calls to the past ground our approach to feminist economics.

Feminists seek to liberate economics from the ideologies that have justified the social relations of domination and subordination central to Western hegemony. We do not simply identify and measure the economic differences associated with different social locations. For feminist economists, differences are analytical as well as descriptive. That is, feminist economists examine the many ways that socially constructed differences affect and are affected by the division of labor, the distribution of resources, and the exercise of power. So armed, feminist economists can uncover and expose the atavistic social values that have shaped economic knowledge. Feminist economists offer an alternative, socially progressive understanding of the economy.

2. Family Matters

Reproducing the
Gender Division
of Labor

A catchy restaurant slogan cheerily proclaims, "When you're here, you're family!" We ask, is our dinner free? Can we wash the dishes instead of paying the bill? Of course not—when you patronize a restaurant, you are a customer not a family member. Families are social units made up of people joined by marriage, birth or adoption, or mutual consent who offer each other economic, social, and emotional support. From an economic perspective, families are places where many of the economic activities relating to production, reproduction, and redistribution occur.[1] Cooking, cleaning, caring for children, and providing for family members without access to market incomes are some examples of these activities. Determining who will do this work and how family resources will be allocated often generates tension and conflict. Indeed, economic relationships within families are characterized by inequality, conflict, and exploitation as well as by support, caring, and cooperation.

The term *family* comes to us from the Latin *famĭlus,* which means "a man and his servants." This translation illuminates the fact that throughout much of the ancient world wives were the property of their husbands.[2] They were expected to serve their husbands by bearing and raising children, cooking, spinning, weaving, and managing the household. The husband was the undisputed head of the household. Even as conceptions of marriage, marital roles, and spousal obligations changed over the course of history, the presumption of male authority and privilege went largely unchallenged until the nineteenth century. Consider the well-known aphorism "A man's home is his castle."[3] As feminists we ask, who are the vassals and servants at work in these castles? The implication is unavoid-

19

able: a man's life in his home should be as free from domestic drudgery as is a king's.[4] Despite huge changes in the work required to run households, domestic labor remains, for the most part, the province of women just as the injunction to love, honor, and obey remains a part of many marriage ceremonies.

Feminist economists analyze the interaction of patriarchal power and the patterns of resource distribution, domestic labor, and consumption that take place in families. Today, as in the past, many of the economic relationships constituting family life occur outside the market—children do not ordinarily pay parents for the meals they eat, nor do adult family members charge each other for their help and cooperation. For these reasons feminist economists analyze the family without assuming a direct parallel between the family economy and the market economy.

The economy of the market is the familiar public economy of supply and demand, production for exchange, profit, and class conflict. The economy of the household constitutes the "other" economy of domestic relationships in which people are reproduced through expenditures of time, affection, and money.[5] Understanding the development of contemporary Western families is important because the male breadwinner–female caretaker model of family organization is often held up as the ideal. Demonstrating the historical contingency of this view of the family, the gender division of labor it promotes, and the ideology upon which it rests, is essential to a feminist critique of contemporary economic policy. It is not too strong to say that many feminist social policy positions rest on a critical understanding of this family form.

Families Then and Now

While relations of love have undoubtedly played an important role in family life, family relationships have only recently been defined almost exclusively in terms of the emotional ties among family members. Feminist scholars have long recognized that the domestic sphere has significant economic functions.[6] Survival (especially of the very young and the very old) usually depends upon membership in a family group, and the survival of the family is often essential to individual survival. Historically, the daily labor of women and children was as necessary to the economy as was the work of men. Over the long sweep of human social organization, the vast majority of families depended upon everyone participating in household productive activities. All those who worked in the household, including servants and other laborers, were considered family members. And they were all—servants, laborers, wives, and children—subject to the rule and authority of its head.[7]

Prior to the industrial revolution of the late eighteenth and early nineteenth centuries, before mass production and wage labor touched the lives of a majority of people in the West, families grew their own food, made their own clothes, and crafted the items used in daily life. One implication of this type of self-sufficiency is that production and consumption, work and leisure, occurred side by side. These activities were not separated in either time or space. Where a family lived was where that family worked, and what a family consumed was mainly the result of household labor. In agrarian communities of the preindustrial era, economic activity was primarily for use, not for exchange. Thus, throughout much of human history home and economy were one and the same. To our modern eyes, a family living and working together may evoke nostalgic, romantic images of premodern life. But it is very important to remember though that families were patriarchal and the work was unremitting: women and children had little say over their fates, and survival required labor from dawn until dusk.

Households relied primarily on their own labor to spin, weave, and sew cloth; butcher meat and preserve vegetables; make candles and soap. These necessities of life were part of household, not commercial, production. Because households were not perfectly self-sufficient, trade and barter existed. Important items like baskets, barrels, nails, plows, and shoes required specialized labor. Families traded their agricultural products for these handicraft goods. Artisan and peasant households delivered a portion of their output to the civil and religious authorities, who often, in turn, traded these goods for luxuries or the needs of war. But in general households produced what they needed, and most surpluses above household customary needs were accidental. When such surpluses occurred, they would be taken to local markets where they were exchanged for handicrafts.

Although a sexual division of labor existed, men and women often worked side by side in the production of foodstuffs and handicrafts. The self-sufficiency of agricultural villages required that all able-bodied people work at most all of the necessary tasks; thus labor skills were diffused through the population rather than specialized into a few hands. In much of Europe, from roughly the sixth through the sixteenth centuries, the predominant form of economic organization involved this type of relatively self-sufficient agrarian community with large patriarchal families as the primary production units.

During the sixteenth and seventeenth centuries a number of internal and external changes undercut the unity of production and consumption that typified the feudal economy. This process is most clearly illustrated by reference to England. In the English countryside the collective use of the land was slowly displaced as larger farmers began to convert their customary, feudal titles to land into formal, contractual private property rights in land. These new private property rights allowed landowners to make sweeping changes in the organization of agricultural production.[8] Families and even whole villages were swept away as technology revolutionized agricultural production and capital (machinery) was substituted for human labor. Innovations in crop rotation, drainage, plowing patterns, and fencing raised both agricultural yields and the capital needed to run a competitive farming operation.

Many who had worked the land, or who had held rights in use to land, were no longer needed on the farm or were forced through indebtedness to leave their homesteads. Agricultural unemployment soared, as did rural poverty. As more and more families lost their traditional right to work the land, they became dependent on money wages to purchase the goods they needed to survive.[9] At the beginning of the eighteenth century the majority of the British population lived on farms, but by the end of the century this was no longer true. Most people lived in towns and cities. Variations of this process occurred in Western Europe and the United States.

Over the course of the nineteenth century, mass-produced, machine-made goods replaced artisan and home production. More and more people—women, men, and children—became dependent upon money wages for their survival. Household necessities ceased to be items produced by family labor; they became instead commodities to be purchased with money. As this occurred, commodity production and commodity consumption were increasingly separated in time and space. Commodities were produced in workplaces outside the home, while the consumption of commodities occurred outside the workplace.

In many ways economic history is a history of firms producing things that were once made in households—making them better, faster, and more cheaply—and then selling them back to households. The greater efficiency of factory production as compared with home production rendered the home production of textiles, soaps, shoes, candles, tools, and even basic foods redundant. As factories, markets, and the wage labor system eroded traditional economic relationships, the unity of production and consumption came under increasing pressure. These changes had huge ramifications for the economic and affective organization of families. The gradual expansion of capitalist relations of production drove a wedge between aspects of life centered on personal, emotional relationships and aspects of life related to commodity production, employment, and the market.

There is considerable controversy regarding the effects of these changes on women's well-being. Some have argued that these changes made women increasingly dependent upon men and men's wages since it limited their income-earning possibilities, which were traditionally tied to collective access to the commons where they gathered the leftover grains, picked up wood for fuel, and kept small farm animals.[10] Others argued that this freed women from domestic drudgery.[11] One point of agreement is that although women did find avenues for income earning, the general trend during the nineteenth century was that women's productive activities were increasingly relegated to the domestic sphere, and this contributed to the idea that women's work was not work at all.

As industrial production became increasingly important, the household came to be seen as a site where only consumption occurred. Over time the productive activities of the household came to be defined as unproductive.[12] Actually though, important productive economic functions continued to take place in households. The household is to this day the place where the labor force is "produced." Many household activities—shopping, planning, meal preparation, and cleaning—are as much *work* as they are *consumption.* An interesting array of social forces accounts for this transformation and shows how the marginalization of domestic labor contributes to gender inequality.

The Cult of Domesticity

As capitalism displaced feudalism, new social and economic relationships came into existence. In capitalism most people had to exchange labor hours (hours worked) for money wages to purchase their daily bread. This created two new social classes. One class included the industrial, agricultural, and retail workers who depended on wages for their survival. Another new class was the bourgeoisie, who emerged from the ranks of the prosperous farmers, artisans, shopkeepers, and merchants. As the bourgeoisie reinvested their profits, their factories and farms grew. The resulting flood of agricultural and industrial commodities drove down prices, ruining the less efficient, small-scale home producers. As home producers were driven out of business, the class of wage laborers grew. As the bourgeoisie flourished, new ways to mark the power, prestige, and status of this class emerged.

Feudal society had been shaped by the hierarchical economic and political relationships between peasants and landed nobility. The emerging capitalist society was shaped by the hierarchical relationship between wage workers and the bourgeoisie, the owners of the factories, shops, and mines who employed wage laborers. The bourgeoisie accumulated economic resources and came to wield tremendous political power. In the cultural sphere its members sought legitimacy for their privileged status in the new social hierarchy by emulating the behavior of the feudal nobility. During the eighteenth and nineteenth centuries, the families of the bourgeoisie were able to distinguish themselves from workers (and show their similarity to the nobility) by systematically withdrawing the labor of women and children from the industrial workplace. While the entrepreneurial men of this era engaged in the cutthroat competition of early capitalism, women in this class were expected to become housewives, properly occupied with duties that were increasingly seen as natural to their sex—housework and mothering. This arrangement reflected the aspirations of the bourgeoisie to emulate the nobility who had survived for centuries without working.

As these patterns of domestic and industrial life became accepted markers of social status, the ideology of the "cult of domesticity" emerged to justify these household relations.[13] This ideology defined families and households exclusively in terms of nurturing, endearment, and affection. That labor and exertion are needed to maintain households was largely ignored, while relations of economic dependence were cloaked in flowery sentiments regarding women's true nature and calling. This ideology has a number of important effects, not the least is that it reproduces the familiar dualisms of production-consumption, public-private, labor-leisure, and competitive-nurturing.

The cult of domesticity rationalized the belief that unpaid household labor was women's work and that women's work was not work at all. In consequence, the ideal of the Victorian housewife became a norm for all women, and the housewife came to be called the "woman of leisure."[14] But despite appearances and ideology, many women needed (and continue to need today) paid employment. Women need jobs when they are not married, when the earnings of the men on whom they depend are too low to support the family, or when they are the sole support of children due to death, divorce, desertion, or choice.

We should remember too that there is a long *herstory* of women expressing dissatisfaction with their dependent status. Facing tremendous social opprobrium, women sought education, employment, and financial independence. The struggle for women's rights generated intense opposition. An incredible amount of intellectual, cultural, and religious energy was deployed to convince people that a woman's proper place was in the home. Indeed, the fiction authored by women in the eighteenth and nineteenth centuries often details women's oppression and the emotional consequences of their disenfranchisement. Charlotte Perkins Gilman—feminist, economist, and social critic—offers an insightful feminist analysis of this idealized norm in her novella *The Yellow Wallpaper.*

Of course, living in a manner consistent with the Victorian ideal depended upon the success of one's husband or father since women could not spend their time in unpaid activities unless they had access to money income. Only the upper classes were able to realize the ideal of the dependent housewife. For most other women, the industrial economy of the Victorian era was a harsh place. But as the cult of domesticity shaped the social vision of gender, the oppressive economic realities of poor, working women were obscured, and the tightly constrained opportunities for upper-class women were cast in emotional, flowery terms that belied the stifling narrowness of women's appropriate gender role.

Managing a Victorian household required the domestic labor of servants. In the nineteenth and early twentieth century bourgeois households in Europe recruited servants from the lower classes whose distinct patterns of speech and dress marked them as suitable for lives of work and service.[15] In the northeastern United States, well-to-do women hired new immigrants from Eastern Europe and Ireland. In the South, white women hired African-American women who had been enslaved before the Civil War. Although legally free, the system of racial apartheid—Jim Crow—ensured that African-American women would remain miserably paid workers in the worst jobs.[16]

The cult of domesticity was an integral component of the economic and social relations of the period, casting women in the role of full-time homemakers and consumers, while men were cast in the role of full-time wage earners and producers. Proponents of the cult of domesticity sought to root this dichotomized vision of gender in religion, biology, natural law, and psychology. The development of this essentialist view of gender led to a system of laws, conventions, and social customs that ensured the subordinate status of women in the family, the church, and the state.

Women, Property, Employment, and the Law

That women are full human beings with equal rights under the law is a revolutionary concept. Until the middle of the nineteenth century, women—whether or not they were married—had no independent legal existence. In the West where central governments enforced national legal codes, the laws of coverture (or similar doctrines) governed virtually all aspects of women's lives. These laws established man and wife as one, and that one was the man.

It did not matter how women contributed to the livelihood of the family; under no circumstances did she have independent rights to any sort of property or wages. Wives were the property of husbands who were legally entitled to any income they earned or wealth they inherited. Even when women's labor was essential to the success of family farms and family firms, they had no legally enforceable right to allowances, their own wages, or their own property. Similarly, upon the sale of property (and they had no legal right to block such a sale, even when property came to the family as an inheritance from their relatives) they had no right to any of the proceeds of the sale, even if there had been an increase in the property's value. In fact, there were circumstances under which family property could be sold leaving widows and children homeless and destitute. In addition, in many nations where paid employment was common, women could be forced to give up their jobs upon marriage. By the middle of the nineteenth century many women, and some men, began to question the fundamental unfairness of these practices.[17]

Social reformers like Barbara Leigh Smith Bodichon, Elizabeth Barrett Browning, Harriet Martineau, John Stuart Mill, and Harriet Taylor Mill in the United Kingdom worked to change these oppressive laws in the United Kingdom. One of the most significant achievements of these reformers was the passage, in the late 1880s, of the Married Women's Property Act, "which allowed wives to gain control of their personal property and income."[18] The radical idea that a wife had a right to property acquired in marriage, and to wages she earned in the market, was initially received with favor by the revolutionary socialist movements that swept through Europe and the United States in the second half of the nineteenth century.

The view that women should earn wages ran counter to the dominant ideology of the day and was viewed as a threat to worker solidarity. In a political move that still inflames feminists today, the revolutionary socialists Karl Marx and Friedrich Engels repudiated women's demands for full economic equality.[19] Their position does not surprise us—by the last decades of the nineteenth century the notion that women were naturally suited to lives of domesticity was just common sense. When women's roles are defined in relation to home and family, their paid employment seems frivolous. Consequently firms are justified in paying women less than men.

Some economists, like the very influential Alfred Marshall, actually argued that women's wages should remain low to induce them to stay home and tend to their domestic responsibilities. Throughout the mid–nineteenth century the British enacted legislation (the Factory Acts) that expressed Marshall's views since these laws restricted the hours women could work and the wages they could earn. Since 18 to 20 percent of British women were heads of households who depended on their own earnings for survival, restricting women's wages and hours had the direct result of increasing women's poverty.[20]

Similarly, in the United States during the late nineteenth and early twentieth centuries reformers advocated gender-specific protective legislation to restrict the occupations and hours of women's work.[21] Here, protective legislation aimed at women was based on the idea that their wages should not be too high because high wages would jeopardize women's economic dependence. At the same time women's wages should not be too low since extreme poverty could force women into prostitution.[22]

Legislators, clergymen, and newspaper editors argued that the public interest would be best served if policy aimed to preserve the morals and character of the "mothers of the race." As feminist economists Deborah Figart, Ellen Mutari, and Marilyn Power show, femininity, whiteness, and motherhood were linked in public opinion, and laws were enacted to reinforce these links.[23] Legislation protecting Anglo-European women helped to ensure white women's economic survival. In contrast, such protections were not sought for work done by women of color: the few jobs that were open to African-American, Latina, Asian, and Native American women were not covered by the new laws. Racism underscored the view that there was no public interest in preserving their moral character. Women of color were not included in labor legislation as either mothers or workers. Gender and race ideology ensured the invisibility of their lives and experiences.

Liberating Economics

In both Britain and the United States this type of legislation reflected and reproduced the ideology of the male breadwinner–female caretaker family. This ideology had significant negative consequences for the material circumstances of women since it prevented women from becoming economically independent. Indeed, until the 1960s it was legal for firms to pay women less than men for the same jobs.

Today, women are still a long way from economic equality. Women's lower earnings continue to keep them dependent upon and subordinate to men. That men's wages are greater than women's is due, in large part, to the legacy of the family wage system that was the material basis of the ideology of domesticity. Earning a wage sufficient for one adult male to support his family was an important goal of working-class organizations. Sadly, improvement in working-class men's earnings came at the expense of women's economic opportunities regardless of their class.

A Brief History of the Family Wage

Male-dominated working-class organizations sought allies in the upper classes by tapping into the ideology of domesticity. Working-class men sought the exclusion of women from the higher-paying male occupations to protect the family wage in those occupations. Upper-class reformers sought the exclusion of women from paid employment because of their view of women's nature. Indeed, the notion that women are too fragile to be subjected to the rigors of industrial life emerged as an important theme in the labor history of this period. As noted, achieving a family wage was an important goal of unions in Britain, the United States, and the rest of Western Europe. Male unionists actively campaigned for legislation that would bar women from particular industries and specific occupations to limit competition for jobs and raise wages. As a result, by the end of the nineteenth century the top several echelons of workers in key industries, and the managers of the new corporate bureaucracies, had succeeded in winning wages large enough to purchase the food, clothing, and shelter needed by a middle-class family.

A wage of this magnitude was called a family wage since it enabled a worker to support a family largely without a second worker taking a job outside the home. Even today, when more than half of all women work for pay outside the home, many people continue to believe that married women—especially those who are white and middle-class and have young children—should only work outside the home if the family needs the money. The persistence of this collective myth that designates women as the special, almost mystical, source of childcare testifies to the power of ideology. As the ideology of the bread-winning husband and domestic wife became a social truth, the gap between male and female wages was reinforced. Since popular sentiment regarded women as wives, daughters, or mothers, but not workers, their wages were considered "pin money," destined for incidentals rather than necessities.

This perspective ignores the fact that for many women male support is not adequate for the maintenance of the family. In addition, the belief that women's wages were merely "pin money" meshed neatly with the need for a ready supply of low-wage factory, mill, and domestic workers. That is, so long as many people, including women, saw their wages as secondary to the wages of the primary breadwinner, women could be paid less than men. As the family wage system became the expected norm, economic pressure mounted for women to specialize in unpaid household labor. Because women's wages were substantially lower than men's, it was economically rational for women to remain outside the paid labor force. Their wages would be too low to replace the work of childcare, housecleaning, and cooking that they would not be able to do if they were employed outside the home for wages.

It is important to realize that achieving a family wage was always restricted to a small share of the working class. In the United States it was standard practice to exclude particular ethnic groups from good jobs. Native American, African-American, Latino, and Asian-American families, for example, were dependent on the income generated by women and children since racism was used consciously and deliberately to exclude men of color from jobs that paid a family wage. The racist policies of labor unions on this issue not only divided workers but they also helped create different interests for white women and women of color since these women had quite different relationships to the processes of paid employment, fertility, child rearing, and family formation.

As we can see, the household type idealized by the cult of domesticity was erected on racist and sexist foundations. In the United States, racist union membership rules and sexist protectionist legislation restricted access to family wages to the elite "aristocracy of labor." But the exploitation of populations of color within the United States was not the only way that racial exploitation fueled the economic development of the modern family.

Colonial expansion into South America, Asia, and Africa made important contributions to the rising standard of living experienced by many in Europe and North America. The rising wages of the top levels of the working class were made possible, in part, by the profits generated by the massive expansion of trade in colonial products.[24] As the wages of the aristocracy of labor increased, their dependent wives who were not employed for wages could purchase some of the decorative items that marked class status. It was not a coincidence that in this era prestigious luxury goods were the exotic products of imperialist trading relationships. The oriental carpets, mahogany tables, and painted china that were the prized possessions of Victorian housewives gave silent testimony to the exploitation of men, women, and children in the colonies of Africa, Asia, Latin America, and the Caribbean.

Feminist economist Deirdre McCloskey has argued that women unambiguously and uniformly benefitted from the spread of markets and the development of industrial capitalism.[25] This argument rests on the view that the machine production of goods, and the attendant decline in consumer prices, led to a rising standard of living that was widely dispersed. This claim is hotly disputed in economics, sociology, and history. Promarket, mainstream economists endorse this view, while heterodox economists question both the magnitude and distribution of these benefits. This question about the impact of capitalism is analytically parallel to the question posed at the beginning of this chapter: "when a man's home is his castle, who are the vassals and servants?" Can we assume that the benefits of trade and the industrial revolution affected most people's lives for the better? Did specific populations disproportionately bear the costs of these revolutionary changes in economic relationships? Did the women of the bourgeoisie and the women of the working class have the same relationship to these costs and benefits? Did the peoples of the Western imperialist nations experience colonialism in the same way as the peoples of Africa, Asia, and South America? With other feminists and heterodox economists we argue that they did not.

The onerous work and harsh discipline of factories in the nineteenth and early twentieth centuries were principal costs of the industrial revolution. Under these labor conditions, it was a privilege, indeed a benefit, to escape into the home. Protecting women and children became the shared aim of upper-class social reformers and working-class men. Part of this involved removing children from the labor force and making child rearing a major economic activity of the middle-class household. The ideology of domesticity made children's upbringing the exclusive domain of women. This vital economic function has received scant attention. Simultaneously, protective legislation forced women out of many types of paid work, regardless of women's needs for earned income or their desire to hold a job. By casting the male breadwinner–female caretaker model of the family as natural, the cult of domesticity also obscures the divergent interests that shape family life.

Power and Interests in Contemporary Western Families

During the twentieth century, in much of the Western world, families aspired to a form in which husbands and fathers would focus on income-generating activities, while wives and mothers specialized in homemaking and child rearing. Ironically, this is often referred to as the "traditional" family even though it is very modern. Moreover, this mode of organizing domestic life was never a real option for many families. But despite its relatively short history, and the rather narrow cross section of the population to which the definition applies, its impact on society in the spheres of culture, politics, economics, and even psychology has been strong. In fact, the traditional family, which, as we have seen, emerged out of attempts by the bourgeoisie to separate themselves from the lower classes, became the norm or standard by which all other family types were judged.

In traditional families the amount of time spent working, and the type of work done, varies by gender. Men work full-time outside the home to earn income, and women work full-time in the home to sustain the family. There are certainly women and men for whom this family form is worth emulating. For poorer families the prospect of having one person exempt from the harsh conditions of low-wage work undoubtedly has great appeal. For other families, a full-time homemaker is an important status symbol. And for yet other families, assigning the woman to full-time homemaking is a reasonable response to the high cost of quality childcare and the scarcity of jobs with decent pay and benefits.

The structure of traditional households shows how this household gender division of labor reflects men's patriarchal power over women's work, income, reproduction, and general well-being.[26] In traditional households, women have no independent access to income. They are therefore dependent upon the generosity and sense of fairness of the breadwinner, who, as a result, has a great deal of power in important household decisions. Indeed, feminist sociologist Arlie Hochschild's pathbreaking study of the relationship between work and family found that a major factor contributing to the breakup of traditional households involved women seeking additional avenues for achievement and fulfillment and becoming less willing to submit to patriarchal authority.[27]

Another family type, one that is increasingly common, is the "transitional" family. In this family form both partners work for incomes outside the home, but housework and childcare are still largely the responsibility of the female partner. These households are prone to conflict because the work of the household still falls on the woman's shoulders even though she is working for pay outside the home.[28] Childcare, cooking, and cleaning are time-consuming, energy absorbing, and repetitive. Estimates of the time spent on household labor by married women range from eighteen to twenty-three hours per week compared with the seven to twelve hours spent by their husbands.[29] A recent study by Suzanne Bianchi reports that despite the rapid rise in the number of mothers working outside the home there is very little difference between employed and unemployed mothers in terms of the time they spend with their children. She suggests that employed women do less sleeping and volunteering and have fewer free-time pursuits.[30] It is no wonder, therefore, that many employed mothers would like to have paid help with housework.

As feminists, we stress the point that paid household help raises its own set of ethical issues.[31] The people who are hired to help with housework are generally poor women at the bottom of the social hierarchy because of their race, class, or ethnicity. Increasingly, these women are immigrants and refugees who leave their own families to care for families in the rich nations. In the United States domestic work was often the only option for African-American women, and until the 1960s most employed African-American women were domestic workers.[32] Today, the racial and ethnic composition of household employees reflects both the gains that African-American women have made in the workplace and the different face of poverty in the United States. Now, domestic workers in the United States are likely to be poor women from the Philippines, Latin America, or the transition economies of Eastern Europe. The situation in other parts of the world is quite the same. According to feminist geographer Joni Seager, between one million and one and a half million women migrate from Asia to find employment as domestic workers in the oil-rich countries of the Middle East.[33]

Feminists argue over whether it is ethical to hire household workers. Some point out that we have no problem hiring other types of help (e.g., plumbers and gardeners). Others argue that hiring cooks, housecleaners, and nannies is inherently exploitative. Our position is not that it is wrong or immoral to pay for housework, childcare, or cooking. Rather, the problem stems from the conditions of work. These low-status jobs are almost always the province of poor, disadvantaged women who often have families of their own. Bringing these jobs into the formal sector and providing legal protections to all workers regardless of gender, race, or immigration status will improve the status, pay, and security of this work.

Attitudes about female and male gender roles are changing. As women enter the labor force in ever greater numbers, we are seeing the emergence of a new family form, the "egalitarian" family. In this type of family, gender is not the key variable determining who works outside the home for pay and who does the household labor. Both housework and market work are shared. The motto "from each according to their ability, to each according to their need" is operative here.[34]

Many feminists advocate social and economic policies that encourage the formation and reproduction of egalitarian households. Egalitarian households have to reconcile the time demands of paid employment with the time demands of dependent care. Nancy Fraser posits three idealized visions of the family—the universal breadwinner model, the caregiver parity model, and the universal caregiver model—in order to systematically think about which family forms will encourage gender equity and dismantle the gender division of labor.[35]

The universal breadwinner model focuses on equal labor market opportunities for women and men. In this model of gender and paid work the cooking, cleaning, childcare, and eldercare services that are today mostly provided by women in the household would instead be provided by the government or the market. The caregiver parity model aims to enable caregivers (usually women) to care for their families. Such policies would minimize the costs of this traditional gender division of labor by providing generous family allowances and paid employment leaves. Women's lives would be different from but equal to men's lives. On their own Fraser finds both these strategies inadequate for the realization of full gender equity. On the one hand, the universal breadwinner model is androcentric in its exclusive valorization of paid work; on the other, the caregiver parity model fails to promote women's economic independence.

The universal caregiver model is predicated on equal divisions of labor outside and inside the home. In this model both women and men would participate in both paid and unpaid labor. Child and dependent care, along with housework and working for pay, would be shared equally between adult householders. For this division of labor to become a reality, several things need to happen. As in the universal breadwinner model women's earnings need to be equal to men's so there will be no economic advantage to female specialization in childcare and housework. Similarly, as in the caregiver parity model, work for both women and men will have to be restructured so there will be no economic disadvantage to those adults who take responsibility for children and other family members. While these changes may be slow to come, these goals should inform national and international public policies.

Much of the recent attention to family policies by politicians, think tanks, scholars, and activists was prompted by dramatic changes in the composition of families. The number of dual-earner households continues to increase. Worldwide, lone-parent households, the majority of which are headed by women, are becoming increasingly common.[36] And another important change in family structure concerns the rising number of same-sex couples, either with or without children. Many nations in the European Union have progressive social policies regarding the legal status of same-sex marriages. These policies are progressive because sexual orientation is not a legal basis for economic, political, or social discrimination. In many other countries though, the prohibition of same-sex marriage amounts to a form of economic discrimination since there are many benefits that flow from marriage (including favorable tax treatment of joint income, inheritance provisions, and healthcare coverage) and those who can't marry are discriminated against.

In 2004 in the United States, controversy over the status of same-sex couples intensified when the Massachusetts Supreme Court declared "civil unions" unconstitutional. This opened the door for same-sex marriages across the United States. Social conservatives oppose this progress and are working to amend both the U.S. Constitution and state constitutions to prohibit such marriages. Prohibitions like these would prevent gays and lesbians from enjoying the privileges and responsibilities of marriage.

Cooperation and Conflict in Families

Providing for the material well-being of family members by redistributing resources like cash, goods, services, and assets (real and financial) is an important economic function of the family. The social norms that guide the uses to which resources flow vary across and within cultures. Here we provide a feminist analysis of these household decision-making processes.

While disagreements among family members over yogurt or sorbet may not be terribly fractious, there are other spending decisions that may incite intense conflict. For example, when education is not free, will both boys and girls go to school? Other decisions about the division of labor in the household may also be problematic—deciding who will work for pay outside the home, and who will not, is a good example.

The view of the family as a group with common interests is dominant in mainstream economics. In this view, the gender division of labor within the family is nothing more than a particular case of specialization, with advantages for both women and men. The idea that the male breadwinner–female caregiver organization of the family is inherently beneficial is embedded in the "new home economics" via its view of the sexual (and for these economists, the division of labor in households is based on biological sex, not socially constructed gender) division of labor. This approach to the family, originating with the Chicago School's orthodox free-market economists, takes the market as its starting point and places exchange, through relations of supply and demand, at the center of analysis.

In this reading, husbands and wives are coequals, both entering a voluntary exchange that by definition makes them each better off. If there is a member of the household with more decision-making power, this person is seen as the head of the household and is assumed to be altruistic. The altruistic head of household then makes all of the family decisions regarding income, resource allocation, and consumption in the best interests of family members.[37] The sexual (gender) division of labor is thereby transformed into just another consequence of mutually beneficial individual choice, albeit one rooted in biology. As Simone de Beauvoir famously commented, "legislators, priests, philosophers, and scientists, all strive to show that the subordinate position of women is willed in heaven and advantageous on earth."[38]

It is instructive to trace through the logic supporting these conclusions. Couples must decide who will work in the home and who will work outside the home for pay. This is basically a barter system: meals, clean clothes, childcare, and sex can be exchanged for income and wealth. It is no surprise that women will specialize in household services since the new home economics begins with the assumption that they have a natural inclination, following from their biology, for such activities.[39] This natural inclination, coupled with the fact that women's labor market earnings are generally much lower than men's, gives them what economists call a "comparative advantage" in household work. Children are in turn viewed either as a consumption decision, not terribly different from the decision to buy a new car or a house, or as an investment decision, not unlike stocks, bonds, or other assets.

Although this literature, like much feminist literature, takes women and the family as objects of inquiry, it would be a mistake to view the new home economics as feminist. To quote Barbara Bergmann, widely acknowledged as one of the founding mothers of feminist economics, "To say that the 'new home economists' are not feminist in their orientation would be as much of an understatement as to say that Bengal tigers are not vegetarians."[40] First, and in direct contrast to feminist analysis, they fail to question gender differences in autonomy and power. Second, this view is essentialist since it accepts as natural a gender division of labor in which men focus on income earning and women focus on household labor. Bringing feminist theory to bear on economic processes requires us to analyze these ubiquitous assumptions.

Some feminist economists like Notburga Ott and Bina Agarwal find it useful to analyze the family in terms of the relative bargaining power of the spouses.[41] These analyses acknowledge that family relationships have elements of both conflict and cooperation, and they describe family interactions as a type of negotiation. The allocations of resources and responsibilities within the household are the results of these bargains. We are all familiar with this type of bargaining in families—one person agrees to do the dishes if the other will cook, or one picks up the children and the other goes to the grocery store.

These analyses interest us because they explicitly acknowledge the different bargaining power of family members. Not surprisingly, having a good job or some other access to income is a major strength a person brings to the bargaining table. Consequently, a woman's power in her family will be influenced by her labor market earnings, and these earnings are, in turn, influenced by her labor market status: earned income increases as women spend less time in unpaid homemaking activities and as they switch from part-time to full-time paid employment.[42] When the gender division of labor in households assigns women to nonmarket work, women will be less able to influence family decision making. This implication of the gender division of labor in families is conveniently overlooked in the traditional economic view of families.

Feminist economists have also produced interesting analyses of gay and lesbian families. M. V. Lee Badgett points out that bargaining models assume a heterosexual family, and grafting these models onto the families

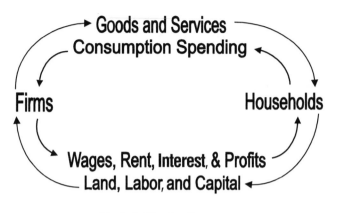

Fig. 2.1. Circular flow

of lesbians and gay men perpetuates heterosexist assumptions about "normal" family forms.[43] She questions the assumption that same-sex and heterosexual couples make decisions in ways that are fundamentally the same. Her research supports the view that the different legal, political, and cultural status of same-sex relationships lead gay and lesbian families to develop alternative family dynamics. Badgett argues that studying same-sex families enriches our understanding of the rich complexity of family life.

It is interesting to note some commonalities between the standard economic view of families and economists' traditional understanding of the relationship between households and firms. Consider a simple circular flow diagram (fig. 2.1) in which households own the raw materials of the economy (in economic terms these are the factors of production: land, labor, and capital). Firms use factors of production to produce the goods and services consumed by households. When households supply factor services to firms, they receive incomes that they can then use to buy the goods and services produced by the firms. When firms succeed in selling goods and services to households, they receive revenues they can use to hire more factor services. Households and firms become perfect complements, each matching the other's needs exactly.

The traditional vision of household and firm has much in common with the traditional view of women and men as complementary opposites. Men are aggressive, competitive, strong, and rational, while women are passive,

Household Activity	Hours required per week	Who does it
Acquiring food		
Preparing food		
Cleaning house		
Caring for young children		
Maintaining and acquiring clothing		
Healthcare of family members		

Fig. 2.2. Household production

nurturing, weak, and emotional. It is not hard to see that these stereotyped characteristics of maleness and femaleness map onto the household (private) and firm (public) dichotomy.

When viewed this way, the economy appears as an unbroken chain of exchanges: land, labor, and capital for wages, rent, interest, and profits, which are in turn spent to consume goods and services. Notice how this chain of exchange renders invisible any activity not part of it. Even though it is perfectly obvious to most of us that maintaining a household requires huge expenditures of work, time, and emotional effort, this work is not compensated with a direct income payment, so it seems to disappear. To render the invisible visible, we ask you to fill out figure 2.2, based on the arrangements in a family you know.

If you filled in your chart the way we filled in ours, a disproportionate amount of household work is performed by females, even when they earn incomes outside the home. This division of labor is naturalized by the new home economics. As a matter of fact, Gary Becker, the founder of the new home economics, won the Nobel Prize for applying standard microeconomic analysis to intrafamily activities, including the household division of labor. He showed that even when there are no explicit cash transactions or market exchanges, supply and demand can still be used to explain family behavior.[44] Many feminist social scientists, inside and outside of economics, object to this approach because it rationalizes the existing gender inequality in families.

Another concern feminists raise when considering the work done in households emerges from the fact that even though families perform many economically vital activities, the value of this work does not show up in any of the statistics that purport to portray the economic health and well-being of a society. Leaving out the value of household production in national income statistics is a matter of serious concern. It results in a distorted picture of the economy and obscures the real impacts of policy decisions on families. For example, eliminating childcare subsidies can appear to be a cost-saving measure. Appearances, however, can be misleading. Such policies merely shift these costs onto the household. When household labor is not explicitly valued, then these costs remain hidden.[45]

Likewise, it obscures the impact of changes in household production on other measures of economic performance. For example, the increase in women's participation in the paid labor force has switched household production into market production. As economist Jeff Madrick argues, the wages and salaries paid to these women show up in the statistics, as do the wages and salaries paid to the people who sell the goods and services formerly provided in the household. Thus, the economy appears to be growing, when in fact the growth is due to a shift in production from the household to the market.[46]

Accounting for the value of unpaid household labor is not difficult, and feminist economists have shown how the system of national income accounting can be changed to reflect this important work. In 1934 feminist economist Margaret Reid suggested using the "third-party criterion": if a third person can be paid to do the work, then an estimate of the value of that work should count as part of the nation's overall output, or gross national product (GNP). The United Nations has established a survey-based methodology for creating these estimates. Surveys of time spent on nonmarket work determine the average amount of time needed for various household tasks. Then, a market wage is imputed to the time needed to complete these tasks. The average time, multiplied by the imputed wage, yields an estimate of the value of the domestic labor. Such an estimate, however, tends to understate the actual value of this work because the imputed wage for doing it reflects society's low valuation of "women's" work.[47]

Even using conservative estimates, the magnitude of this labor is staggering. Kathleen Cloud and Nancy Garrett, specialists in global economic development, estimated the value of unpaid labor in 1990 for 132 different countries. They found that unpaid household labor contributed $8 trillion, or just over one-third of the total official GNP for these countries.[48] The Australian Bureau of Statistics reached a similar conclusion when it estimated that unpaid labor in 1992 (mainly cooking, cleaning, and child-care) was worth almost 40 percent of the gross domestic product (GDP).[49] Clearly, in terms of both time and value unpaid labor is important.

Conclusion

Accounting for unpaid household labor is controversial precisely because feminists and their allies have challenged the patriarchal standards that traditionally defined men's and women's contributions to paid work, housework, family life, and household decision making. Indeed, disagreements about appropriate female and male roles are at the heart of many public policy debates in the world today, including debates within economics. While these questions may seem new, nineteenth-century feminists like Elizabeth Cady Stanton, Lucretia Mott, Sojourner Truth, Ida B. Wells, Charlotte Perkins Gilman, Josephine Butler, and Harriet Martineau, for example, argued that these asymmetries in power and interests were barriers to women's full participation in society.

Although the male breadwinner–female caretaker model of the family has roots deep in our patriarchal past, the ideology justifying these gender roles is an artifact of the industrial revolution. The ideology of feminine domesticity continues to have many negative consequences for women and men, not least of which is that it tends to define out of existence the real diversity of contemporary families. Recognizing diversity is a first step toward a feminist reconstruction of gender roles. But Victorian ideology lives on in approaches to economic and social policy that do not recognize the importance of women's paid work, the real value to society of women's unpaid work, or the negative influence of traditional gender hierarchies. Public policies informed by this atavistic vision of the gender division of labor are unable to see that family members may not share common interests. Feminist perspectives on the family, in contrast, focus on the contradictory pulls of affection and exploitation to show how these contradictions shape gender roles. We turn to these topics in the next chapter.

3. Love's Labors—Care's Costs

How often have we heard the expression "a labor of love" to describe work done for the benefit of family and friends? A moment's reflection reveals that labors of love are most often associated with work done by women in the home. Feminist economists refer to this sort of work as "caring labor." Today, the tasks associated with care are either provided by families, purchased in the market, or provided by socially supported service agencies. For example, the elderly are cared for in both private and public nursing homes; young children are cared for at home, as well as in public and private childcare centers; and the seriously ill are cared for at home by family members, supplemented by paid nurses, or in public or private facilities. In some settings, the work is paid and the caregivers earn incomes. In other settings, care work is unpaid, and no monetized transactions take place. Whether paid or unpaid, caring labor is absolutely essential to economic well-being.

What Is Caring Labor?

The treatment, or should we say nontreatment, of caring labor is one of the most egregious consequences of traditional gender ideology for contemporary economics. Gender ideology led economists to denigrate and ignore all labor that was not paid labor. In addition, they saw no reason to attempt to specify either the content of caring labor or its importance for the overall economy. Feminists seek to reconstruct economics with a fully developed concept of caring labor.

In the history of economic thought attention to household labor arose in two separate areas of scholarship: Marxism and institutionalism. Marxist feminists pointed out that most Marxists were as blind to the importance of unpaid household labor as were mainstream economists. In what came to be known as the domestic labor debates, Marxist feminist economists like

Liberating Economics

Margaret Benston, Nancy Folbre, Heidi Hartmann, Sue Himmelwhite, Jane Humphries, Maxine Molyneux, and Simon Mohun pointed out that unpaid work in households was necessary for social reproduction.[1] Marxist feminists argued that unpaid household labor transformed purchased commodities into cooked meals, laundered clothes, and clean houses for adult workers and provided the childcare that was necessary to reproduce a future generation of workers.[2] The domestic labor debates highlighted the importance of the gender division of labor for the reproduction of capitalism and the economic well-being of families—working-class as well as bourgeois—and showed that even in contemporary, industrialized capitalist societies the household continued to be an important sphere of production. To insist that the home is simply the site of consumption missed this crucial point—hence Marxist feminist economists insisted on the conceptual importance of reproductive labor.[3]

Nineteenth-century institutionalist economists Charlotte Perkins Gilman and Thorstein Veblen were among the first to recognize the importance of the work done in the home. Following their lead, twentieth-century institutionalist economists Hazel Kyrk and Margaret Reid were concerned with the impact of the specialization of labor on the supply of workers available to perform the essential work of the home. Kyrk and Reid spelled out the ramifications of the expansion of paid employment on the supply of unpaid labor.[4] These economists recognized the fundamental importance of unpaid domestic labor. However, in the years after World War II, mainstream economists refused to acknowledge this in their economic theorizing and teaching. Instead, considerations of household labor were relegated to the field of home economics. As a specifically feminist economics emerged, their work was rediscovered, and economists once again began to analyze work done in the home. Feminist economics reframed the discussion of reproductive labor in terms of caring labor to underscore the centrality of love, empathy, compassion, and connection.

The work of economist Nancy Folbre was instrumental in shaping this discussion.[5] Caring labor is constituted by the relationship between those who give care and those who receive care. Consequently, caring labor often takes place between people who are not equals: care receivers are often very dependent upon their caregivers. The care received by infants, young and school-age children, the ill, the disabled, and the elderly depends upon the quality of the relationship connecting the givers and the receivers of care.

In a world where families are under increased pressure to generate market incomes, the demands of paid employment squeeze the supply of caring labor. A "care deficit" emerges as women and men devote increasing numbers of hours to paid employment.

Under the old gender division of labor, the assumption was that women would stay home to do the caring labor needed for social reproduction. But today, women's labor force participation rates are close to those of men, lone-parent families are increasing, and geographic mobility makes extended families the exception rather than the rule. Given these circumstances, we ask, "Who cares?" Feminist economists care.

Feminist economists want to develop social policies that will ensure an adequate supply of caring labor. Here the feminist perspective turns a skeptical eye on an especially revered goal of macroeconomic policy—full employment. If everyone who wants a full-time job has one, and if the work of caring continues to be poorly paid and not unionized, then society's dependents will face high levels of insecurity. This is not an argument for a continuation of the disguised unemployment created when women stay at home to perform unpaid caring labor because their pay outside the home is too low relative to the cost of purchasing caring labor in the market. It is rather an argument for changing the pay and work conditions confronting care workers.

The International Labour Organization was among the first to recognize these problems and has sponsored important research on this and related issues. According to ILO economist Guy Standing, caring labor can be defined as the work of looking after the physical, psychological, emotional, and developmental needs of one or more other people.[6] According to Standing, one way to ensure a sufficient supply of caring labor is to make sure that it is paid well, that there are adequate regulatory guidelines that ensure competence and skill in care delivery, and that regulatory standards are enforced. This suggests that governments have a significant role to play vis-à-vis care work. To ensure that quality care is available to those who need it, the state must also make sure that subsidies and income transfers are available for people who need care but who do not have sufficient income to pay for it. Families also have significant roles to play in care provision. As Standing argues, while formal, paid caregiving provides an important social service, we know that "most of us do not or would not want to rely either wholly or partially on formal care providers if we could avoid it."[7] Care work is a social relationship in which sentiments such as altruism, mutual respect and dignity, and reciprocities play a meaningful role.

Two important points follow from this. First, paying for caring labor does not negate the emotional content of this work. Consider all the work done by nurses, teachers, and social workers. Sometimes these jobs are paid well; other times they are not. The importance of this work is generally acknowledged, as is its stressful, emotionally draining nature, and no one seriously argues that transforming this paid work into voluntary, unpaid work would enhance well-being. Moreover, it does not seem odd to us that nurses, teachers, and social workers are paid for their work. Indeed, the very suggestion of making their work voluntary and unpaid seems odd. Yet when the laborer (caregiver) and the recipient of the labor (care receiver) are family, and the work is performed inside the home, our cultural assumptions about women and altruism in the family lead us to believe that the quality of the work is enhanced precisely because it is not paid.

We pose the following question: why is it that the quality of childcare is thought to be better when it is unpaid, while high pay is thought to ensure quality care for the bedridden elderly or disabled? This paradox follows from the ideological construction of the concept of motherhood. The notion that children need the near-exclusive attention of their mothers is a historically contingent artifact of the industrial revolution. That is, the processes that created mutually exclusive public and private spheres, and assigned women to the private, domestic world, simultaneously defined mothers as the exclusive guardians of their children's well-being. Recognizing that all views of the mother-child relation are socially constructed opens the way for social policies that can produce adequate supplies of quality childcare without enforcing women's full-time domesticity.

Second, caring labor, especially that associated with child rearing, has significant social benefits—what economists call "positive externalities." Although all of society reaps the rewards of children raised to be concerned, productive citizens, the costs of producing people with these attributes fall largely on women.[8] In the eighteenth century Bernard Mandeville's "The Fable of the Bees" discussed private virtues and public vices.[9] He maintained that private virtues like selflessness, generosity, and honesty became problems when used to guide behavior in the public domains of economy and politics. We disagree with Mandeville: these virtues are necessary to ensure adequate supplies of caring labor.

The Economic Costs of Motherhood

There is no better example of caring labor than the work associated with raising children. Politicians, social commentators, educators, and religious leaders wax poetic in support of families and children. Some advocate using tax deductions to help families defray the costs of child rearing; others call for direct subsidies for quality, early childhood education programs; and still others propose policies to encourage work-family balance. Debate over the efficacy of these policies fills volumes, makes headlines, and provides fertile material for the evening news. Participants in these debates often buttress their claims with references to studies examining the impact of a mother's work on children's well-being. Why are we not surprised to find very few studies of the impact of fathers' employment on children's well-being?

The reason is simple: these policy debates reflect the assumption (and what is often the reality) that mothers are primarily responsible for children. Before the industrial revolution, when home life and economic life were contiguous, children worked and played alongside their parents. As jobs moved out of the home and into factories, shops, and offices, a new gender division of labor arose in which housework and childcare became exclusively "women's work." Barbara Bergmann argues that a caste system developed in which women, due to their biology, were designated for one occupation: homemaker.[10] Women, according to the emerging gender ideology, were to stay home providing full-time care for their children. Today, however, this caste system is breaking down as more and more women insist on the right to a fulfilling career and economic independence regardless of marital status. Despite huge increases in women's paid employment, men's unpaid contributions to household labor have not changed very much.

Most children in the United States live in families where all the adults are working. In 1998, 59 percent of women with children less than one year old were employed, while 73 percent of mothers with children over one were working outside the home.[11] Why do all these women work? For the same reasons as do men: jobs, careers, and incomes are as meaningful to mothers as they are to fathers. One legacy of the gender division of labor is that women's demand for workplace equality poses a serious social problem: who will care for the children?

The old arrangement—the male breadwinner model—in which the

male head of household earns a family wage and supports a full-time house-wife simply doesn't work any more. But then it never really did work for everyone.[12] As discussed in chapter 2, in poor families everyone who was able worked. In rural, agricultural communities, the rigors of farm work required the participation of mothers and fathers, grandparents, brothers, and sisters. In families dependent upon money wages, women and children performed industrial labor or were sent into domestic service.

When Mothers Work

Liberals and conservatives, feminists and anti-feminists, recognize that motherhood has pronounced negative consequences for women's labor market earnings. The effect of childbearing on earnings is so significant that journalist Ann Crittenden has dubbed it "the mommy tax."[13] The mommy tax is the income women don't earn because they've become mothers. Economists call this an "opportunity cost." Feminist sociologists Michelle Budig and Paula England argue that there is a 5 percent to 7 per-cent wage penalty for motherhood.[14] After children are born, women often lose job experience, which translates into lower lifetime incomes. In addi-tion, mothers may trade off higher wages for mother friendly jobs, or they may work part-time.

Working mothers who have the primary responsibility for childcare may find part-time work an attractive option, especially when high-qual-ity, affordable childcare is unavailable. Choosing part-time work over full-time work contributes to mothers' lower lifetime earnings because part-time work almost always pays less per hour, it rarely has the benefits that come with full-time employment, and fewer total hours are worked (either weekly, monthly, or annually). Budig and England point out, however, that even after controlling for the differences between full- and part-time work, and other objective measures related to higher pay (experience, seniority, and so forth), they still find that mothers earn less.

The Social Responsibility for Childcare

In the industrialized nations, there are two approaches to childcare. Many nations recognize a social responsibility for childcare and so provide high levels of professional training, well-paying jobs, and substantial public funding supporting parental leaves. In other, socially irresponsible nations—the United States in particular—no such social responsibility has been recognized. The economic burden of children continues to rest on families even as the benefits of well-cared-for children accrue to the larger society.

National policies toward childcare begin with parental leave policies. Table 3.1 displays parental leave policies for seven industrialized countries.

TABLE 3.1.   Maternity/Parental Leave Benefits for Seven Selected OECD Countries

	Length of Leave	Wage Replacement (%)
Australia	1 year	0
Germany	14 weeks	100
Greece	16 weeks	75
Netherlands	16 weeks	100
Sweden	14 weeks[a]	75 for 360 days and 90 days at a flat rate
United Kingdom	14–18 weeks	90 for 6 weeks
United States	12 weeks[b]	0

Source: Data from United Nations Statistics Division, "The World's Women, 2000: Trends and Statistics."
[a]Sweden has a parental leave act.
[b]Parental leave for companies with fifty or more workers.

As the table indicates, the U.S. policy, the Family Medical Leave Act (FMLA), is the least generous. It does require firms to grant unpaid parental leaves of up to twelve weeks; but because the FMLA only applies to firms with fifty or more employees, and most women work in firms with less than fifty employees, there is a large gap in coverage. Also, the FMLA does not replace the parent's income during parental leaves.

Likewise, quality, affordable childcare is in very short supply in the United States. Consequently, many families cannot afford full-time care and education for their children in accredited childcare centers. In many communities, fully certified childcare centers have long waiting lists even though the full-time tuition at these centers often exceeds the cost of a year at the local state university. This leaves families with three options, all of which involve childcare in non-accredited settings. Families with young children can place the children in childcare centers that meet minimal safety and staffing requirements. Even these centers are quite expensive. The other options are home-based childcare or employing a baby-sitter or nanny. All of these options are expensive.

It is important to realize that there are rarely any licensing requirements for these childcare centers. Only a few states and localities require annual safety inspections and set standards for fire safety. State health inspectors

47

are not required to check centers for other hazards. When a home-based center offers an age appropriate curriculum, a high ratio of staff to children, and large and well-equipped play areas, these amenities are purely voluntary. The second option, hiring a baby-sitter or a nanny, offers few safeguards for children's health and well-being since no education or training standards apply.

Financially able women may decide to put off re-entering the workforce until their children enter elementary school. For others, even if they remain in the labor force while their children are young, elementary school seems to hold out the promise of a solution to the cost of childcare. Elementary schools as day-care centers, however, pose another set of problems. One need not be an expert on workplace policies to know that even the most liberated companies do not yet synchronize the working day with school schedules.

Clearly, the lack of coordination between school and work schedules can interfere with parents' employment responsibilities. The traditional view of children as the mother's responsibility limits women's options in ways that are costly and potentially dangerous to children. If equality between women and men means that they face a roughly similar array of choices and constraints, then obviously social policy regarding childcare must be addressed. The situation in much of Western Europe provides important lessons for the United States and the other English-speaking nations as concerns social policy to support parents as they strive to meet their obligations to their employers and to their families.

In the English-speaking nations, parents receive very little in the way of governmental support as they try to figure out how to balance their work and family responsibilities. The Scandinavian welfare states are different because they recognize that all citizens are potentially both workers and caregivers. These nations have pioneered public policy to support both women and men in their roles as paid employees and unpaid caregivers. In other words, state policy actively encourages equality in the workplace and in the home. The social commitment to these policies rests on the recognition that we increasingly live in a world of dual-career households. As a result, we can no longer push domestic labor onto the shoulders of just one adult in the partnership. The costs of such policies are well within our means: annual expenditures for family leaves per employed woman are extremely modest. During the mid-1990s, family leave expenditures in Sweden and Finland were about $900 per employed woman, while in Norway and Denmark they were between $600 and $700.[15] These expenditures represent 0.7 percent to 1 percent of the GDP in these nations.[16] There is absolutely no reason to believe that these generous programs would absorb any greater share of the GDP of any of the other industrialized nations.

Unfortunately, the trend is going in the opposite direction for much of the world. The transition economies of Eastern Europe provide an illustrative example. In the interests of promoting the "free market," these states are severely cutting back on social services. Healthcare, childcare, and education are all suffering. The results are not good. In some of the countries, life expectancy has fallen, enrollment in primary education has contracted, and women's workloads have increased.

Other problems are created when rich nations refuse to provide social supports for childcare. It is often the case that women who work as childcare providers face employment conditions that undermine the economic and emotional security of their families. Childcare work is poorly paid, health and safety conditions are not monitored, and the jobs rarely carry benefits. Historically, in the United States, many women of color (especially African-American women in the South) worked as domestics in the homes of whites. Before World War II, over half of African-American women were employed as domestics. Indeed, an important success of the civil rights and women's movements is the dramatic decline in that number.[17] Today, childcare labor is often provided by immigrants from the developing world and from the formerly communist economies of Eastern Europe, who migrate to the wealthier countries to care for the children of the privileged. But as women migrate in search of better opportunities, many must leave their own children behind.

Arlie Hochschild has dubbed this "the nanny chain," a series of global links based on caring labor.[18] A woman with a professional career in a rich country hires a foreign-born nanny so she can work full-time. The nanny from the poorer nation or region leaves one or more young children at home, where an older daughter or female relative cares for them. These global care chains have many variations. The feature they have in common is that the flow of caring labor is always from the poor to the rich. When migrant women leave their children, this unmasks the hollow promise of the 1959 United Nations Declaration on the Rights of the Child, which says that every child "should grow up in a family environment, in an atmosphere of happiness, love, and understanding" and "not be separated from their parents against their will."[19] The exploitation of migrant women is a contemporary variant of old-fashioned colonialism, wherein rich countries exploit the human and natural resources of the poorer ones.[20]

Working with data from diverse sources, Robert Espinoza identified four transnational flows of women migrating from poor to rich regions to engage in domestic labor. The Gulf states of Kuwait and Saudi Arabia have imported well over a million women from India, Sri Lanka, the Philippines, Indonesia, and Thailand who now work in private homes as domestics.[21] Likewise, many European nations rely on domestic laborers from Sri Lanka and the Philippines. For example, in 1987, 52.5 percent of all domestic workers in Italy were women from the Philippines.[22] The flow of poor women from the African nations of Morocco, Ethiopia, Somalia, and Nigeria to Western Europe is large and growing. And hundreds of thousands of women from Central America, Mexico, and the Philippines migrate to the United States and Canada in search of domestic jobs that will enable them to send money home to their families.[23]

The careful student of U.S. history will see this as a variation on a story as old as racial exploitation. When slavers captured people in West Africa, they deliberately broke up families and villages, forcibly separating parents and children. This continued in the Americas when mothers, fathers, and children were routinely sold to plantations hundreds of miles apart. After emancipation, the strict racial segregation of the South created economic conditions in which the only work African-American women could do involved caring for the children of white women, again often at the expense of their own. Other immigrant women—Irish, Polish, Greek, and central European—who came to the United States in the nineteenth and early twentieth centuries were also under pressure to care for the children of the well-to-do.

Paying poor women to care for the children of the affluent is an old solution that creates as many problems as it solves. First, and most obviously, the children of women who are in domestic service do not have access to their own mothers. Second, these jobs are not well paid, so they perpetuate poverty. Third, these jobs carry few, if any, benefits, and domestic workers have few protections from workplace abuses. Fourth, this organization of domestic work simply carries the gender division of labor forward in time and space. We suggest that the solution requires a sea change in the way we value and compensate caring labor. Making such a change will require challenging the assumption that the care of family dependents, including children, the elderly, or the ill, is a private family matter that is the natural work of women. Today, rich countries continue to exploit the less developed world in part by encouraging the export of caring labor. The women at the end of this chain are in the unenviable and untenable situation of providing emotional support, affection, and care to other people's children, often at the expense of their own.

Maternal love is exchanged for money as poor women provide care, love, and affection to the children of others. In the 1960s the Beatles claimed money can't buy you love. *Au contraire.* The labor of love—caring labor—is in many ways a commodity just like any other. The problem is not, *per se,* in its commodification. Problems arise when commodification rests on exploitation. When caring labor is left to private markets, its value and compensation are low. The reason is that the traditional dualistic views of masculinity and femininity define maternal love as natural. Being natural, this trait does not require training or skill; therefore, it does not deserve a high rate of pay. This, in our opinion, is the root of the problem. If caring labor is recognized as a profession, then the pay will increase, working conditions will improve, and the quality of care will be enhanced.

The traditional assumption that caring labor is unskilled women's work reproduces essentialist views of the gender division of labor. Just as men don't have a monopoly on the ability and skills required for programming computers, managing banks, delivering the mail, performing heart surgery, or enforcing the law, women do not have a monopoly on either the ability or the skills required for caring. Even as women's opportunities in paid labor have changed dramatically in the past three decades, men's relationship to caring labor is only now beginning to change. Full equality requires that men and the cultural construct of masculinity change. It also requires a change in the structure of paid employment so that human requirements of care are on equal footing with employment responsibilities.

Bridging the Work-Family Divide

The assumption that women have primary responsibility for children, coupled with the absence of adequate social support for childcare, creates serious problems for women's careers. Research by law professor Joan Williams found that only "ideal workers" have much chance for career advancement because the best jobs for blue-collar or professional/executive-level workers are organized around the "ideal of a worker who works full time and overtime and takes little or no time off for childbearing or child rearing."[24] Consequently, career advancement depends upon the ability to work in the evening, travel on short notice, or go to the office on weekends. The problem is that children, especially those under age twelve, need adult supervision. It is both unsafe and illegal to leave young children unattended for any length of time (even if they have credit cards and a cell phone). What is a working parent supposed to do if an important meeting is scheduled for 7:00 P.M. and the childcare center closes at 6:00 P.M.? Thus, many women choose what has become known as the "mommy track," a less prestigious and less demanding career path.

Even Aldous Huxley's horrifying vision in *Brave New World* has nurses staffing nurseries where genetically engineered fetuses are hatched in industrial incubators. Given the tremendous importance of raising children, society must consider the costs and benefits attached to the current patterns of reproduction. All of us reap the benefits of adults raised to value culture, education, civic life, and the intrinsic rewards of a job well done. But the costs are considered to be private not social.

An examination of the top tiers of the high-prestige, high-salary positions within law, science, engineering, accounting, medicine, and government service reveals a disturbing pattern: it is almost impossible to combine career advancement with raising children. As Professors Randy Albelda and Chris Tilly famously quip, there are jobs for wives and jobs for people with wives. Their point is that the "normal" expectations for career advancement assume the existence of a caretaker who is available twenty-four/seven in the event of unplanned changes in work schedules. Absent such a caretaker, it is virtually impossible to fill employer demands for mandatory overtime, travel, or weekend work since meeting such demands conflicts directly with parental responsibility. A recent study found that only 49 percent of women who have earned an MBA degree and who are within three tiers of the CEO position have children. In contrast, 84 percent of men with MBA degrees and within three tiers of the CEO position have children.[25] These figures underscore the fact that high-powered jobs are still "jobs for people with wives."

Having a house husband who adopts the role of a traditional, stay-at-home spouse would certainly help the careers of many women as the Betty Good Wife advertisement attests (fig. 3.1).

As feminists, however, we continue to find this problematic. Almost forty years ago Betty Friedan pointed out that "the problem that has no name" is the result of confining women to the home and denying their

Does it seem like there's not enough time in a day
or enough days in the week to get all the little
things done so you can enjoy life?

Call Betty Good Wife at
RENT - A - WIFE

Come Home to a House That's Squeaky Clean
- House Cleaning
- Childcare
- Odd Jobs
- Grocery Shopping
- Ovens, Windows and Blinds
- Cooking
- Laundry
- Run Errand
We Can Take Care of All Your Household Needs!

Fig. 3.1. Betty Good Wife advertisement (flyer posted in North Carolina shop, 1998)

quest for meaningful work and self-fulfillment.[26] We do not believe that turning the tables and creating another caste of wife is an improvement.

Conflicts between work and family obligations have led to the creation of "family friendly" policies such as job sharing, family and medical leaves, and flexible work schedules. The stated goal of these policies is to help working families balance responsibilities to employers that are necessary to generate income and responsibilities to the people in the family. Sweden has been a leader in this movement, and its policies are often seen as a model. Sweden has implemented policies designed to promote the participation of fathers and mothers (regardless of marital status) in child rearing, paid work, and homemaking. Both parents are eligible for extensive, well-paid leaves upon the birth or adoption of a child. Parents are allowed to shorten their daily work hours (their pay is also reduced) while their children are young. Paid medical leave is likewise available to care for sick children. There is, in addition, a professionalized system of early childhood education and care available at very low cost to all workers. Thus, in Sweden, we see an explicit national effort to enable women to combine career advancement with motherhood.

Nevertheless, the Swedish solution is not perfect. Feminist economists Ellen Mutari and Deborah Figart report that despite the gender-neutral wording of the laws concerning parental leave, and efforts to encourage men to take advantage of it, only 6 percent of leave takers are men.[27] One result, according Mutari and Figart, is that the responsibility for "balancing" work and family obligations remains with mothers. Consequently, many Swedish women become part-time workers after their first child is born. Because these policies center on the family, they reinforce the traditional gender division of labor. These findings support Barbara Bergmann's argument that family friendly policies continue to allow women to reap the disadvantages of having primary responsibility for childrearing and housework.[28]

When women's earnings are considerably less than the earnings of men, it makes sense for the woman, not the man, to drop out of the labor force when children enter the picture. Absent strong policies to create wage equity, women will continue to do the lionesses' share of unpaid, largely invisible work. But as women's wages near parity with men's, this advantage evaporates, leaving considerable space for discussions of ways to make parenting a more equally shared venture. Recognizing this, feminists support the deliberate pairing of policies that promote universal caregiver parity with policies that promote pay equity.

Feminists have long advocated pay equity programs. These are relevant with respect to care work because reducing female-male income disparities reduces the rationale for women to drop out of the workforce to take care of their kids. Caregiver parity policies will encourage employers to treat male parents as equal partners with equal responsibility for raising a family. This requires a huge attitudinal shift, a shift as large as that associated with civil rights and universal suffrage. Yet full equality is possible.

Conclusion

Feminists recognize that the best interests of society will be served when all people—fathers and mothers, poor and rich—have the time and economic resources needed for childcare, eldercare, invalid care, and self-care. Creating effective policies to address these issues requires an open discussion about the importance of this work, the obvious inequities of continuing to assume that caring labor is women's work, and the need to make this work well paid and well respected. There is simply no way around the fact that care is time-consuming and labor-intensive. No amount of technical change will alter this. We need social policies to ensure that citizens have access to the resources necessary to create and maintain healthy families. As things stand right now, in most of the world, women do virtually all this work with little assistance from either men or the wider society. The costs remain private in the form of women's lower earnings, the exploitation of poor women as caregivers, and the psychic burdens on families. The benefits, in contrast, are social.

4. Women, Work, and National Policies

All over the world women are participating in paid labor in greater and greater numbers. Today, in many countries throughout the world, women make up approximately half of the paid workforce; however, they do not participate on an equal footing with men. Even the most cursory examination reveals that paid labor is by and large divided into "men's" jobs and "women's" jobs. And men's jobs are better paid. In the United States, before the passage of the 1964 Civil Rights Act, it was commonplace for jobs to be explicitly advertised as "Help Wanted Male" and "Help Wanted Female."

Today, such explicit discrimination is rare, but gendered patterns of employment stubbornly persist. A trip to nearly any dentist's office reveals the same scenario: whether or not the dentist is a man or a woman, the receptionists, hygienists, and assistants are almost always women. Similarly, an examination of jobs in factories in developing countries such as Indonesia, Mexico, or Nigeria reveals that most of the low-wage production workers are women, while the supervisors and managers are men. Such gendered patterns of employment are neither natural nor coincidental. They reflect deeply entrenched social hierarchies based on gender, race, ethnicity, and class.

Social hierarchies are also intrinsic to globalization, a phenomenon that has had a profound impact on the patterns of work over much of the world. Today, transnational corporations are able to move their low-skill, low-wage production operations to countries in the developing world characterized by low wages and business friendly political regimes. This new international division of labor is the subject of chapter 6. In this chapter we are mainly concerned with women's paid employment within the industrialized countries.

Labor Force Participation

One of the most remarkable and persistent changes in the late twentieth century was the feminization of labor, the steady increase in the number of women participating in the paid labor force. Although women have long worked outside the home, and their work has been important in providing themselves and their families with the income to purchase food, clothing, and shelter, their large-scale participation in the paid labor force is a relatively recent phenomenon. During the nineteenth century, with the exception of a few women in the arts and professions, most women in the paid labor force were there because they were poor. Many were women of color or immigrants, and they worked as maids, laundresses, day laborers, and factory workers, all low-wage jobs with deplorable working conditions. Poor women who were fortunate enough to have an education or family connections became governesses or schoolteachers. Other than factory work, much of the work that women did—picking cotton, taking in boarders, selling handicrafts, cooking, and cleaning in the houses of the well to do—lay outside of the official definitions of paid labor and hence was not reported in official statistics. Paid work was generally considered the prerogative of men.[1]

Gradually, however, employment opportunities for women improved. The growth of the modern corporation, and the bureaucracy accompanying it, generated a need for scores of clerical workers to file, type, answer telephones, and keep records. As women's employment opportunities outside the home increased, the type of work in the home changed. More and more of the goods and services necessary for everyday life were being mass-produced and sold in retail stores. Shopping became a central part of women's work and with it the need for income to buy the increasing array of consumer goods. It should be remembered here that these new employment opportunities were generally opportunities for white women. It would take decades of struggle before women of color could avail themselves of these jobs.[2]

World War II, like World War I, had a huge impact on women's social and economic positions. The shortage of men directly exposed the pretense that women could not do male jobs. In the United States the image of "Rosie the Riveter" was the icon for working women. In Europe, and other theaters of action, women's paid labor was even more important. Even in Nazi Germany, where party policy extolled the virtues of the good Aryan wife and mother, the demands of war forced the state to employ women in factories.[3]

Today, the feminization of labor is commonplace. Women's participation in paid labor is measured by the female labor force participation rate. The female labor force participation rate is calculated by the ratio of adult women who are either employed (full-time or part-time) at paid jobs or looking for employment divided by the total population of women. The increase in women's labor force participation rate is illustrated by table 4.1, which shows the rates of women and men in the United States from 1900 to 2002. Women's labor force participation rates have risen steadily over this period, even as men's rates have decreased slightly.

The table also shows the increasing share of women in the labor force. (The labor force is the number of people who are either employed or looking for employment.) Women constituted only about 18 percent of the labor force in 1900. In 2002 they made up a little under half of it.

TABLE 4.1.   U.S. Civilian Labor Force Participation by Sex

| | Participation (%) | | Females as a Percentage of Labor Force |
	Male	Female	
1900	85.7	20.0	18.1
1920	84.6	22.7	20.4
1930	82.1	23.6	21.9
1940	82.5	27.9	25.2
1950	86.4	33.9	29.6
1960	83.3	37.7	33.4
1970	79.7	43.3	38.1
1980	77.4	51.5	42.5
1990	76.4	57.5	45.2
2000	74.8	59.9	46.5
2002	74.1	59.6	46.5

Source: Data from U.S. Department of Commerce, Bureau of the Census, *Historical Statistics of the United States, Colonial Times to 1970,* bicentennial ed., part 1 (1975), 131–32; U.S. Bureau of Labor Statistics data, 1950–2002, annual averages, not seasonally adjusted.

Note: Figures for 1950 and after include persons sixteen years old and over; for prior years, those fourteen years old and over are included.

This phenomenon is not unique to the United States. Consider, as an example, male and female labor force participation rates in ten different industrialized countries (table 4.2). In all ten countries, women's labor force participation has steadily risen. There are, of course, variations among the countries. For example, in 2001, about 36 percent of Italian women were in the labor force compared with 60 percent of Swedish women. These variations can be explained by differences in attitudes toward gender equality and women's paid employment, as well as a government that supports women as both mothers and workers.[4] These issues are explored further in chapter 5. What is important to note here is the overall upward trend.

TABLE 4.2. Civilian Labor Force Participation by Sex for Ten OECD Countries (%)

	1965		1985		2001	
	Male	Female	Male	Female	Male	Female
Australia	85.1	34.8	76.5	47.0	73.1	56.4
Canada	79.9	33.8	77.4	54.7	72.6	59.5
France	79.2	38.2	68.4	46.4	64.2	49.2
Germany	80.9	40.0	70.1	41.1	66.3	48.8
Italy	77.5	27.8	65.3	30.7	61.4	36.3
Japan	81.1	48.8	77.9	47.6	75.5	48.5
Netherlands	—	—	73.8	37.9	75.4	55.7
Sweden	82.2	46.6	72.5	61.5	68.1	59.6
United Kingdom	85.4	41.7	76.1	50.0	70.8	55.2
United States	80.7	39.3	76.3	54.5	74.4	59.8

Note: OECD = Organization for Economic Cooperation and Development

Source: Data from Department of Labor, Bureau of Labor Statistics, "Comparative Civilian Labor Force Statistics, Ten Countries, 1959–2002," April 2003.

An important factor explaining this upward trend is the change in female labor force participation over women's life cycles, particularly the sustained labor force participation of women during their childbearing years. Consider figure 4.1, which charts labor force participation in the United States over the life cycle of women during four different decades.[5]

In the 1950s women's labor force participation exhibited a marked decline for women in the twenty-five to thirty-four age group, indicating that women were leaving the labor force to bear and raise children. By the 1980s this downward dip began to disappear. By 1998 women's labor force participation rose steadily until the beginning of their retirement years, indicating women's sustained labor force attachment throughout their childbearing years. It is becoming more common for women not to drop out of the labor force when their children are born. In 1980 42 percent of women with children under the age of three worked full-time or part-time; by 1998 62 percent did so.[6]

How can we explain the steady and dramatic increase through the decades in women's labor force participation over the course of their lives?

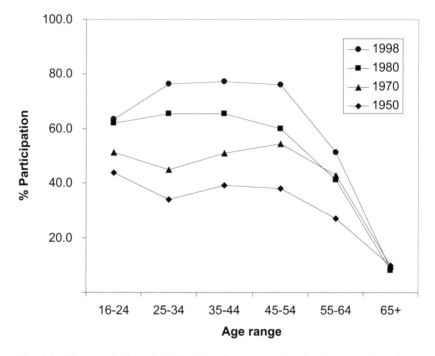

Fig. 4.1. Changes in female U.S. labor force participation by age (data from *Monthly Labor Review* [1996])

Feminist economist Barbara Bergmann notes that although the twentieth century witnessed many upheavals including war and peace, depression and prosperity, women's liberation and its backlash, the rise in women's labor force participation was constant.[7] Wages and salaries were also rising over the same period. She argues that women's retreat from full-time homemaking was a response to changes in the costs and benefits of full-time domesticity. As the benefits from working at a paid job rose, the benefits of staying at home declined since women had fewer children.

Between 1890 and 1984, the real wage quadrupled—increasing the benefits of working outside the home. During the same period women were marrying at later ages and having fewer children. Bergmann argues that one reason for the fall of the birthrate is that raising children has been becoming progressively less economically rewarding. In agrarian societies children's labor was necessary to family enterprises. In modern, industrialized societies, on the other hand, children often remain economic dependents until they are in their early twenties. Another factor leading to declining birthrates is that after the 1960s effective, legal, and relatively inexpensive methods of birth control were widely available. The economist Claudia Goldin has argued that birth control allowed women to respond rationally to economic signals and act in their own self-interest.[8] As women limited the size of their families, this further reduced the benefits of staying at home and reinforced the pull of the market.

The following example illustrates the point. If it takes a woman the better part of a morning to bake a loaf of bread from scratch, let's say three hours, and if she could be earning $10 an hour in the paid labor force, then the real cost of that homemade bread is $30 plus the cost of the ingredients. A very expensive loaf indeed! So as women's real wages increase, the "opportunity cost" of household production does too. Opportunity cost is simply the cost of staying home measured of in terms of the foregone income from a paid job.

In addition to the decrease in fertility, another significant demographic trend that has affected women's labor force participation is the increase in female-headed households. This is due to divorce, to an increase in the number of unmarried women having children, and, in the developing world, to patterns of migration that led to the breakup of families.[9] In other words, women are in the workforce to support their families. Not too much of a mystery here.

Finally we point to an important cultural change in the perception and valuation of full-time domesticity. As documented by Betty Friedan in *The Feminine Mystique,* the life of a housewife can be alienated, isolating, and frustrating.[10] She describes the pervasive dissatisfaction of white, suburban, college-educated women with the life of a housewife as "the problem that has no name." The women's movement was another significant catalyst for married women's entry into the paid labor force.

The Gender Wage Gap

Women, on average, make less money than men. When we quantify this statement, we call it the gender wage gap, and it tells us the value of female wages as a percentage of male wages. The gender wage gap is calculated using the median or average weekly or hourly earnings of workers. If the gender wage gap is 75 percent, that means that on average for every dollar a man makes, a woman makes $0.75.[11] In 2001 the gender wage gap in the United States was 76 percent, up from 62.5 percent in 1979.[12] Worldwide, women's wages range from around 60 to 90 percent of men's. In Australia women earn $0.90 for every dollar a man earns, and in Japan $0.59 (table 4.3).[13] Women's part-time work, combined with their lower wages, is another source of their economic disadvantage relative to men. For example, in the United States 19 percent of women work part-time, and they constitute 70 percent of all part-time workers.[14] In the European Union 83 percent of part-time workers are women.[15]

The gender wage gap in the United States has slowly closed over time. Unfortunately, *slowly* is the operative word. According to feminist economist Deborah Figart, over half the narrowing of the gender wage gap in the 1980s was due to a decline in men's real wages.[16] Figart also points out that many other industrialized countries are doing much better than the United States, and in general the gender wage gap is narrower in countries that have strong commitments to income equality and wider in countries without such commitments. Similarly, countries that emphasize a traditional role for women have a wider wage gap. Thus the wage gap for Ireland is larger than for Denmark or Australia, countries that emphasize gender equality and women's full participation in public life.

The wage gap differs depending on the racial and ethnic characteristics of the groups being compared. In the United States, for example, we find that if we examine African-American women and Latina women as separate

TABLE 4.3.   Gender Wage Gap in
Manufacturing for Ten OECD Countries,
1995–2002

Country	Female/Male Wage Ratio
Australia	0.89
Canada	0.71
France	0.78
Germany	0.74
Italy	0.83[a]
Japan	0.59
Netherlands	0.78
Sweden	0.91
United Kingdom	0.78
United States	0.76

Note: OECD = Organization for Economic Cooperation and Development.

Source: Data from United Nations, Women's Indicators and Statistics Database (Wistat), version 4; U.N. Statistics Division, "The World's Women, 2000: Trends and Statistics"; Statistics Canada.

groups, their wages gaps, with respect to all men, are 67 percent and 62 percent respectively.[17] Moreover, white workers of both sexes earn more than did their African-American or Hispanic counterparts. The wage gap for black women to white women is 87 percent; the gap for Hispanic women to white women is 79 percent.[18] In other words, white women earn, on average, more than black women and Hispanic women. Examining different ethnic groups in other countries yields similar results. Salaries, wages, and working conditions reflect nearly perfectly the social and cultural standing of different ethnic groups.

Age is also relevant to the size of the wage gap. In the United States the wage gap for young women between twenty and twenty-four years is 96 percent, whereas for women between thirty-five and forty-four years, it is 74 percent.[19] A large part of the explanation for this widening of the wage gap is that as women enter their thirties, they are more likely to have responsibility for children than are younger women. As we discuss in chapter 3, gendered childcare responsibilities negatively impact women's labor market earnings.

Occupational Segregation

It is important to realize that when comparing the wages of working women to the wages of working men much of the difference has to do with the different jobs that women and men hold. Women are often clustered into particular types of occupations that are considered appropriate for them. This is called occupational segregation by sex. Nurses, dental hygienists, elementary schoolteachers, clerical workers, secretaries, and receptionists are still most likely to be women. Doctors, judges, police officers, firefighters, and electricians are still most likely to be men. Occupational segregation reflects social stereotypes about women's roles and abilities: women are naturally caring and nurturing, they are followers rather than leaders, they have less physical strength than men, and they are not as good at math and science. Of course, such stereotypes vary according to historical and cultural differences and, hence, differences in occupational segregation. One thing that remains constant, however, is that female-dominated occupations are less prestigious and pay less than those of their male counterparts.

In addition to being detrimental to women, occupational segregation is economically wasteful. Excluding women from a majority of occupations wastes human resources and reduces the ability of economies to adjust to

63

changes.[20] Nonetheless, sex-based occupational segregation is a ubiquitous feature of labor markets all over the world. Table 4.4 reports the percentages of women employed in five different occupational categories: professional and technical workers, including scientists, architects, physicians, and professors; administrative and managerial workers, including government and private sector administrators and managers; clerical workers; sales workers; and service workers, including cooks, caretakers, maids, and hairdressers. We can see from these data that women are disproportionately clustered into particular occupational categories. For example, in Australia women make up 88 percent of the service labor force, and in the United Kingdom they make up 76 percent of the clerical labor force.

TABLE 4.4. Female Percentage in Major Occupation Groups for Ten OECD Countries

		PROF	ADMIN	CLERK	SALES	SERV
1995	Australia	44.9	24.1	78.5	60.2	87.9
1993	Canada	56.0	42.6	80.1	45.6	56.9
1990	France	44.3	9.5	67.9	47.4	67.6
1991	Germany	43.0	24.0	77.0	60.0	89.0
1996	Italy	18.8	54.0	34.5	52.0	47.6
1990	Japan	42.0	7.9	60.1	38.3	54.2
1994	Netherlands	44.8	16.8	59.4	46.6	65.3
1996	Sweden	63.7	59.0	—	48.8	61.2
1993	United Kingdom	43.7	33.0	76.1	64.5	66.1
1996	United States	53.2	43.8	79.0	50.3	59.4

Note: OECD = Organization for Economic Cooperation and Development; PROF = professional; ADMIN = administrative; CLERK = clerical; SALES = sales; SERV = service.

Source: Data from United Nations, Women's Indicators and Statistics Database (Wistat), version 4.

Examining data just from the United States allows us to examine occupational categories, and their monetary compensation, in greater detail.[21] In table 4.5 we see that in 2001 approximately 77 percent of administrative and clerical support workers and 96 percent of household service workers were women. On the other hand, women make up only about 8 percent of precision production, craft, and repair workers and 22 percent of operators, fabricators, and laborers. Where women have made gains is in the executive, administrative, and managerial occupations: the percentage of women has increased from around 34 percent in 1983 to about 47 percent in 2001. The bad news, on the other hand, is that as their share of employment in this category has increased, the wage gap has changed little.

Labor markets are segregated by race and ethnicity as well as by gender, and this segregation reflects the social and cultural status of the groups in question. In the United States, the lower wages and status of work done by poor women of color reflect historical patterns of racism. Until the 1960s the majority of African-American women were employed as domestic workers, a condition that was reinforced by Jim Crow segregation laws in the American South and exclusionary practices of labor unions in the North.[22] In places where people of European descent do not constitute the dominant culture, such differences in wage and status still exist. Women from lower-status ethnic groups experience larger wage gaps than do higher-status women. The feminist economist Mary King has shown that in Great Britain native-born black women are employed mainly in clerical jobs, while black immigrant women are employed in the relatively less prestigious service sector.[23] Similarly, ethnic Malay women in Singapore are concentrated in low-income occupations,[24] while on the Arabian Peninsula poor women from the Philippines or Pakistan find employment as domestic workers.[25]

Things are improving in many parts of the world. We are no longer surprised when doctors, lawyers, or other professionals are women. Full equality is, however, still a long way off when we consider that occupational segregation can be both horizontal and vertical. Horizontal segregation refers to segregation of different occupations. For example, lawyers and doctors

TABLE 4.5.   U.S. Wage Gap for Females by Occupation

	1983		2001	
	Women Employed in Category (%)	Wage Gap	Women Employed in Category (%)	Wage Gap
Managerial and professional specialty	40.9	69.2	49.5	70.5
Executive, administrative, and managerial	34.2	64.0	47.1	66.6
Professional specialty	46.8	72.6	51.8	73.4
Technical, sales, and administrative support	62.5	64.0	61.9	71.0
Technicians and related support	44.5	70.6	50.2	74.1
Sales occupations	39.0	52.7	45.0	62.0
Administrative and clerical support	77.7	68.7	77.0	81.4
Service occupations	49.2	67.8	52.2	76.6
Private household	96.0		95.8	
Protective services	9.5	70.4	17.7	77.4
Other service	57.1	81.0	59.0	88.8
Precision production, craft, and repair	7.9	66.1	8.4	73.8
Operators, fabricators, and laborers	26.2	66.5	22.4	73.5
Forestry, farming, and fishing	11.2	84.2	14.9	84.2

Source: Data from U.S. Department of Labor, Bureau of Labor Statistics, "Highlights of Women's Earnings in 2001," May 2002.

are two different professional occupations. Vertical segregation, on the other hand, refers to segregation within occupations. In law, women are clustered in family and criminal law, while corporate law remains the province of men. We find a similar situation in medicine.

Dr. Frances Conley, a tenured professor of neurosurgery at Stanford Medical School, maintains that medicine is becoming a two-tiered profession. Today, women physicians are found mainly in five major specialties: primary care, pediatrics, psychiatry, internal medicine, and OB-GYN. Many women have become primary care doctors, and patients appreciate a female physician who will take the time to listen to them and be empathetic. As more and more women go into primary care, fewer and fewer will become orthopedic surgeons, cardiologists, neurosurgeons, and so on. If this continues to happen, the fields that opened up to women in the late 1980s are going to close again.[26]

Vertical segregation is so common among the ranks of senior executives and managers that it has a name, the glass ceiling, which refers to the invisible barriers that stop women from reaching the upper echelons of large corporations. This phenomenon has been well studied, and the overwhelming conclusion is that the most pervasive barrier to the women's advancement to the senior ranks is male prejudice.[27] Men stereotype women's abilities, exclude them from informal networks of communication, and fail to mentor them. Women do not reach the top of the corporation because they are not allowed to start up the path.

Vertical segregation is found in nonprofessional occupations as well. For example, if we examine retail sales in the United States, we find that women constitute 77 percent of the sales force in apparel and only 29 percent of the sales force in appliances and electronics. The median weekly earnings of apparel sales clerks is $336, while that of electronics and appliances clerks is $506.[28] So although things are improving and many of the barriers to women's participation as equals in the labor force are falling, the gender wage gap remains.

Although much of the gender wage gap can be explained by occupational segregation, it is not a complete explanation because it persists even when occupations are defined quite narrowly. Even when men and women do the same sort of work, women are still paid less than are men. For example, waitresses earn 87 percent of what waiters earn.[29] This may be due to the fact that women and men may work in different establishments, with men dominating the more expensive ones. For example, the wait staff at upscale restaurants tends to be both male and female, while customers at coffee shops and sandwich shops are usually served by women. Finally it should be noted that the gender wage gap persists within both male- and female-dominated occupations. For example, both female mechanics and female registered nurses earn only about 90 percent of what their male counterparts do.[30]

The fact that much, although not all, of the gender wage gap is explained by occupational segregation raises two related questions. First, why do female-dominated occupations pay less than male-dominated occupations, and second, why are women clustered in these lower-paying occupations?

The Human Capital Approach

For mainstream economists, differences in labor market earnings can be explained by human capital differences. According to this theory, people are paid what they are worth to their employers, and what they are worth is determined by how much they contribute to the firm. Economists refer to this contribution as productivity. Productivity is in part determined by the quality of capital that employees have to work with. In an office environment, for example, productivity is enhanced by state-of-the art computers and telecommunications systems. Similarly, employees' skills, credentials, and experience, what economists call human capital, contribute to their productivity. Human capital refers to the education, skills, training, and experience necessary for particular occupations.

Proponents of human capital theory advance several explanations for why women earn less than men.[31] One explanation is that women acquire less human capital than do men. For example, becoming a dentist requires four years of medical school, while becoming a dental assistant (a lower-paid, female-dominated occupation) requires only two years at the undergraduate level. Another explanation is that women may be more likely to invest in human capital that has a higher non-market return. In other words, women may invest in human capital that is targeted toward non-market activities such as child rearing.

According to human capital proponents women's investments in human capital are the result of rational, cost-benefit calculations. Women, so the theory goes, expect to interrupt paid work to rear children. Since they expect to spend fewer years in the workforce due to time off for child rearing, they have fewer years to reap the rewards from their investment in human capital. While they are out of the labor force, they do not receive on-the-job training. They fail to accumulate work experience, and their human capital depreciates so that when they reenter the workforce they are even further disadvantaged.[32]

Seemingly, women choose occupations that require less investment in training and education and that are compatible with family responsibilities. These occupations pay less because of their lower human capital requirements. At least that's how the story goes. Feminist economists argue with both the presumption of choice and the presumption that the low pay of female-dominated occupations is due to their lower skills. First, differences in human capital may not be the result of individual decisions but rather the result of gender discrimination. For example, human capital may be acquired through on-the-job programs or apprenticeships, both of which depend on the decisions of the employer not the employee.

There are also many instances of male-dominated and female-dominated occupations requiring similar levels of training, education, skill, and responsibility in which we find that male-dominated jobs are better paid. Consider the occupations: receptionist (female dominated) and motor vehicle operator (male dominated). In 2001 median weekly earnings for motor vehicle operators were $575, while median weekly earnings for receptionists were $401.[33]

Economists have done empirical studies to analyze how much of the wage gap is due to human capital differences and how much is due to discrimination. These studies account for years of education, years of experience, interruptions in labor force participation, and differences between full-time and part-time work. In general these studies show that human capital differences explain only 30–50 percent of the wage gap.[34] Such studies underscore the inadequacy of the human capital approach for explaining either the wage gap or occupational segregation.

Human capital theory has likewise been used to explain occupational segregation and wage inequality by race and ethnicity. Feminist economists Rhonda Williams and William Spriggs have argued that explaining present-day racial economic inequality by human capital theory serves to justify such inequality by making it seem both normal and inevitable.[35] Human capital explanations of racial income inequality deny the presence of discrimination, fly in the face of the evidence, and serve to perpetuate labor market inequalities.

Another prominent feminist economist, Jane Humphries, has argued that an even bigger problem with the human capital theory is that it is an exercise in circular reasoning. According to the theory, women invest less in human capital or choose a less demanding job because they anticipate spending less time in the labor force than will their spouses. They anticipate spending less time in the labor force because their potential earnings are lower.[36] In other words, women earn less because they invest in less human capital, and they invest in less human capital because they are paid less.

Occupational Segregation Revisited: A Feminist Perspective

Are there explanations for the wage gap and occupational segregation that are consistent with feminism? One such explanation is the "crowding" hypothesis advanced by Barbara Bergmann. There are fewer female-dominated occupations than male-dominated occupations, and thus women are "crowded" into them. The surplus of workers, relative to the demand for their labor, helps to keep their wages low and male wages high. She argues that, like other systems of dominance and privilege, occupational segregation perpetuates itself through the self-interest of its beneficiaries.[37] Of course, elaborate rationales are constructed to explain why such discrimination and privilege serve the common good. But the bottom line is that occupational segregation based on gender preserves male privilege just as occupational segregation based on race or ethnicity preserves the privilege of the high-status group.

We can also argue that the very definition of human capital is deeply gendered. Work that is performed by women is considered unskilled not because it requires less training and ability but because it is done by women, and like women's work in the home, it is seen as emanating from natural abilities rather than acquired skills. The "nimble fingers" associated with female production workers in the developing world, for example, are considered a natural attribute of women. On the other hand, the "nimble fingers" of dentists and surgeons are conceptualized quite differently. This is not to argue that production workers should perform brain surgery but rather to draw attention to the different ways we represent male and female skills.

Feminists point out the affinities between occupations that are female dominated and gender stereotypes about women's appropriate roles and responsibilities. One feminist approach to wages, pioneered by feminist economists Deobrah Figart, Ellen Mutari, and Marilyn Power, is to consider wage setting as a social practice that reflects, reproduces, and trans-

69

forms social norms concerning gender and race.[38] In this view, stereotypes about the worth of women's work and their identification as housewives rather than as workers keep women's wages low. Consider banking: in the 1940s when most bank tellers were men, it was a path to becoming a bank manager or even president. Now nearly all bank tellers are women with little chance for advancement. Have the requirements for the position changed? Or has the gender composition of the workforce changed?[39]

We also need to take into account the gendered patterns of discrimination that most women face throughout their lives. Richard Anker argues that the patriarchal ordering of society explains why girls are less likely to pursue fields of study that are highly valued in labor markets, such as science or industrial crafts.[40] Expectations about women's appropriate gender roles lead to the perception that girls have a lesser need for such skills. For example, gender norms about appropriate activities for boys and girls discourage girls from acquiring the skills that would enable them to become skilled production and craft workers. In both the United States and Europe, women hold only about 8 percent of all the skilled production and craft jobs, while in the United States women make up only about 2 percent of workers in the construction trades—carpenters, plumbers, electricians, and so forth.[41]

These occupations require fairly small investments in human capital but nevertheless pay relatively well. As the performance of many productive, skilled women has shown, women can and do learn these trades.[42] Nonetheless, when women try to enter male-dominated occupations, they are often subject to subtle and not so subtle hints that their presence is unwelcome. Sexual harassment, lack of mentoring, and inadequate training and resources are common. Acquiring human capital, especially gendered human capital, is not just a matter of personal choice. It is also conditioned by institutional constraints and old-fashioned sexism.

Firefighting is an excellent example of an occupation that is well paid, has very good benefits, and is dominated by white men. It has also been highly resistant to the hiring of women and minorities. Consider the case of Julie Tossey and Kathleen O'Connor, two women who aspired to become professional firefighters in St. Paul, Minnesota. Both of the women were already working as dispatchers in the department and would have entered the force with considerable seniority. The two women went through a yearlong vetting process that included medical and psychological evaluations as well as a grueling physical fitness test. They both passed and became recruits. The story does not, however, have a happy ending.

Tossey and O'Connor tell a story of intimidation, lack of mentoring, and arbitrary rule changes regarding the ongoing physical training for firefighters. In the end, they lost their jobs. Failure to pass later physical fitness tests was the official reason given for their termination. They maintain, however, that they were subject to a concerted effort to wash them out of the academy because their time as dispatchers would count toward seniority and put them ahead of many male firefighters.

A few of the firefighters in the St. Paul Fire Department are women. Probably some of them agree that Tossey and O'Connor were not physically fit. The question must be asked, however, to what extent these physical fitness tests are used to screen out women in order to preserve firefighting as a bastion of white male privilege. (The St. Paul department has also faced discrimination suits on behalf of African-American males.) Being a firefighter does require both strength and endurance. But is that all it requires? No. It requires a variety of technical and mental skills as well. The ability to respond well to others and to keep one's head in dangerous and chaotic situations is also fundamental. As one woman firefighter put it, when you go to a fire you are seeing people on the worst day of their lives. Skills to cope with situations like this are not gender-specific.[43]

National Policies

Most industrialized countries have a variety of national policies explicitly designed to combat discrimination against women and people of color in the labor market. In the United States this began in 1963 with the passage of the Equal Pay Act. That act mandated equal pay for equal work. The notion of equal pay reflects the neoclassical economic notion that wages are the price of labor.[44] When women and men do equal work, they should receive equal rewards. This argument is absolutely correct, as far as it goes. The problem is that it doesn't go far enough in redressing the class and race dimensions of wage inequality among women. As college-educated, mostly white women have moved into professional and managerial careers, equal pay for equal work promotes gender equality while at the same time reifying a divide between professional women in white-collar careers and women in poorly paid, female-dominated occupations.[45]

Opening up better-paid blue-collar occupations to women is another important strategy in combating discrimination in labor markets. Title VII of the 1964 Civil Rights Act was an important step in this direction. Title VII prohibits discrimination on the basis of race, color, sex, religion,

71

or national origin. Prior to its passage women were often kept out of high-paying blue-collar jobs by the protective labor legislation passed around the turn of the century. Title VII effectively eliminated these barriers to women's full and equal participation.

The U.S. Supreme Court case *United Auto Workers v. Johnson Controls* provides a good example of the way that Title VII works to ensure that women have the right to participate in the labor market on an equal footing with men.[46] Johnson Controls, a battery manufacturer, instituted a fetal protection policy in 1982. This policy prevented all women who were capable of bearing children (regardless of whether they were, or ever intended to become, pregnant) from working in its battery-manufacturing division because they would be exposed to relatively high levels of lead, which could harm a developing fetus. The company knew that lead exposure could damage male and female reproductive organs, but nevertheless the ban applied only to women. The company was sued, the charge being that its policy constituted sex discrimination. Among the plaintiffs were two women who suffered economic damages and one man who was denied a leave of absence in order to lower his levels of lead before he became a father.

The Supreme Court agreed with the women, ruling that the policy violated the equal rights guarantee of Title VII. The court held that the policy was discriminatory because it did not apply to the reproductive capacity of male employees in the same way that it applied to the reproductive capacity of female employees. It also held that decisions about the future welfare of children should be left to the child's parents rather than the parents' employers. The court concluded that it is up to women to decide whether their reproductive roles are more important to them and their families than their economic roles. Clearly, this was an important decision in protecting women's rights and combating gender-based occupational segregation.

Affirmative action was another important way that women and people of color were able to make significant inroads into jobs that had previously been the exclusive domain of white males. Barriers to women's employment in traditionally male-dominated occupations have fallen since the 1960s. Nevertheless, it is also the case that men's employment in traditionally female occupations has not risen correspondingly. And more importantly, wages in traditionally female occupations remain relatively low.

To address this problem, feminists advocate policies that are known as pay equity or comparable worth policies. Pay equity relies on comparable worth job evaluation systems designed to ensure that female-dominated jobs equivalent to male-dominated jobs are paid the same. These policies go beyond the equal pay for equal work principle enshrined in current law. Pay equity policies require employers to come up with a way of evaluating and comparing different jobs. These sorts of job evaluations are already done in many large corporations and government offices as a way of setting guidelines for personnel managers. Jobs are assigned points that reflect the jobs' required level of education, skills, effort, working conditions, and responsibility. They are then ranked according to the number of points. What distinguishes pay equity policies from ordinary employee compensation guidelines is their commitment to an explicit comparison of predominantly male jobs and predominantly female jobs. As Barbara Bergmann points out, employee compensation guidelines often avoid this comparison by subdividing jobs into clusters that reflect similar market wages and job duties. So secretaries and maintenance workers will be in different job clusters that reflect both the wage gap and gender discrimination. In contrast, pay equity policies explicitly address gender segregation and the wage gap by ranking all jobs by the same criteria. Implementing pay equity requires that jobs with the same score receive the same pay.[47]

The state of Minnesota legislated pay equity for local government in 1984. They found that maintenance workers (mostly men) and secretaries (mostly women) both received the same job evaluation ratings. But maintenance workers were paid $1,900 per month, while secretaries were paid $1,630. Similarly, a comparison of receptionists and custodians revealed that although receptionists have higher job evaluation ratings, they were paid less.[48] Minnesota's pay equity legislation corrected for these inequalities. It is important to note that in Minnesota pay inequalities must be eliminated by raising the wages of the disadvantaged group, not by lowering the wages of the other.

Although most large companies in the United States use some form of job evaluation programs to set pay for different jobs, very few have adopted explicit pay equity polices. Three states, Minnesota, Washington, and Maine, have mandated pay equity, but only Minnesota and Washington have made the subsequent wage adjustments. Canada is doing somewhat better. Both Quebec and Ontario have passed legislation that mandates pay equity as a principle for both the private and public sectors. The principle of pay equity has been endorsed by the ILO and the European Union as well as Australia and New Zealand. Its implementation, however, remains painfully slow.

The pay equity movement has been eclipsed by living wage campaigns. Living wage movements break completely with the notion of wages as the price of labor, arguing instead that wages should be conceived of in terms of how much money people need to live decent lives. Advocates of the living wage movement are concerned not only with gender equity but also with the failure of the minimum wage to keep pace with inflation, the growing inequality between the rich and poor, the dismantling of welfare, the growth of low-paying service sector jobs, and the weakening of labor unions.[49] The movement explicitly recognizes that both women and men need to support their families and that wages and wage regulations reflect social norms about appropriate living standards. Equality discourse demands that living standards should not differ according to gender, race, or ethnicity.[50]

Conclusion

Gender equality in labor markets is absolutely essential for any economic system that aspires to be fair, to improve the quality of life of its members, to provide economic security, and to use human resources wisely. Gender equality is a necessary, but not sufficient, requirement for fairness. Sufficiency requires that labor markets also be integrated by race and ethnicity. Work, for most of us, is not just a job; meaningful and productive work is an integral part of life. Such work should not be reserved only for those of us who are of the privileged gender and color. If it is, the economic system is not doing its job well. Similarly, economic security, for all women, regardless of their race or ethnicity, requires gender equality in the labor markets. If women are to live their lives as full human beings, they need to be able to earn their own living unhampered by the constraints of gender.

Finally, women's labor market equality is necessary for an economic system to use its human resources to their fullest potential. If women are disadvantaged in their access to acquiring the skills and technological expertise called for in this new century, then the economy is severely underutilizing half of its human resources. Besides being unfair to women, it is a terrible waste of human resources and impairs the ability of the economy to meet human needs. And perhaps most importantly, women's disadvantaged position in the labor market translates into higher poverty throughout their lives. We turn our attention to this subject in the next chapter.

5. Women and Poverty
in the Industrialized Countries

The view that there is an inescapable tension between economic justice and economic growth is an artifact of outmoded economic theories—theories that depend as much upon Victorian notions of gender roles as they do on simplistic notions of aggregate economic behavior.[1] Rejecting regressive views of the economy, like rejecting Victorian views about women's nature, creates a space for reconceptualizing the connections between poverty, gender roles, and ideology.

Diana Pearce coined the term *feminization of poverty* in 1978 to point out that women are far more likely to be poor than are men.[2] The trend continues, and today the poor are increasingly female. Women face a disproportionate risk of poverty because of the interaction of several factors including the gender wage gap, the persistent gender segregation of labor markets, and the scarcity of well-paid jobs with benefit packages. These problems are compounded in the case of lone-mother households because inadequate employment supports—like subsidized childcare—put women's income earning at odds with the health, safety, and education of their children. Because women continue to have major responsibilities for raising children, the failure to eradicate women's poverty means that even in some of the word's richest nations, particularly the United States, the United Kingdom, and Italy, significant numbers of children live in families so lacking in resources that their normal health and growth are at risk.[3] In this chapter we focus on poverty and anti-poverty programs in the industrial nations. We evaluate policies in terms of their impact on women's economic status, the well-being of children and the elderly, and women's economic autonomy.

Poverty is often presented in terms that are simplistic, judgmental, and punitive. Consider the following invective from a leading conservative organization: "To the extent poverty is a social problem, it's moral, not economic poverty we should be talking about. . . . [M]aterial poverty in America—to the extent it exists—is a consequence of the habits of the heart of poor people, and poor communities."[4] Feminist economists are concerned to counter these widespread misrepresentations about the causes of poverty and the poor that root economic circumstances in individual pathology or individual effort. In contrast, feminists stress the ways in which economic processes reinforce institutional structures that restrict women's ability to form autonomous households that are not poor.

Contemporary media characterizations of poverty and the poor are misleading and often play to racist and xenophobic prejudices.[5] Media representations of the racial, ethnic, and geographic characteristics of the poor have contributed to a demonizing discourse that roots poverty in the antisocial, pathological behavior of poor people.[6] The situation in the Untied States is illustrative. Since the middle of the 1960s the print and broadcast media have depicted poverty as mainly afflicting people of color living dysfunctional lives in the inner cities. Feminist political scientist Susan Thomas shows how contemporary arguments about the "culture of single motherhood" replicate earlier discussions of the "culture of poverty."[7] In both approaches allegations about individuals' pathological characteristics, such as laziness, promiscuity, and illiteracy, are seen as the most important causes of poverty.[8]

If the behaviors of the poor are the cause of poverty, then there is no social responsibility for reducing poverty. As feminist economists, we reject such arguments and instead insist that the causes of poverty can be found in the structure of the economy, especially in the conditions of employment, including employment supports. To explain high rates of poverty among women, lone mothers, and children, we have to examine how policies designed to promote economic growth have affected labor markets and the distribution of income. Since the 1980s, the view that unregulated "free" markets are the best way to promote economic growth has gained credence. Many people—male and female, young and old— have been negatively affected by economic policies enacted in the name of economic growth as the conditions of employment have deteriorated.[9] Evidence of this can be seen in the relative decline of the wage share of national income, the stagnation of wages and other employee compensation relative to profits and executive pay, and in the secular trend toward higher rates of unemployment.

The economic policies of privatization, deregulation, flexibilization, and trade liberalization unleash competitive pressures that exacerbate the tension between corporate profitability on the one hand, and employee compensation, working conditions, and benefits, on the other.[10] In response to these conditions many firms have expanded their use of contingent part-time workers and reduced the number of full-time unionized workers. Consequently, jobs with decent wage and benefits packages have become increasingly scarce, while low-skill, dead-end jobs in the service sector have proliferated. Gender and race are key determinants of who gets the relatively scarce good jobs. Absent well-paid employment in tandem with significant socially provided work supports like low-cost or no cost childcare, public transportation, subsidized housing, and universal healthcare, it is all but impossible to escape poverty.[11]

The persistence of poverty can not, for example, be attributed to overly generous assistance programs. The nations with the highest levels of assistance (those in Scandinavia and Norway) have the least poverty, while the nations with the stingiest programs (the United States, Canada, and the United Kingdom) have the most poverty. The persistent poverty among children is not due to the high cost of antipoverty programs since the total amount needed to eliminate child poverty ranges from a low of .07 percent of national income (in Sweden) to a high of .66 percent of national income (in the United States).[12] Nor can we blame rapid social and economic changes for persistent child poverty since the post-Communist nations of the Czech Republic, Hungary, and Poland (where national income has fallen dramatically in the past decade) have managed to enact policies that effectively reduce child poverty, while nations that have not experienced economic change on anything like that scale have significantly less effective antipoverty policies.[13]

The antipoverty policies implemented in the Scandinavian countries can be easily replicated, and when adequately funded, they work very well. The unfortunate trend in many rich nations, however, is to ignore these successes and instead put in place punitive programs that shore up patriarchal control of economic resources by reinforcing women's economic dependence on individual men.

International Comparisons

In all of the Western industrial nations, except the United States, poverty is defined in relative rather than absolute terms. Absolute poverty refers to a level of income (or other resources) that separates poor from nonpoor households. The level at which such thresholds are set is subject to debate. Some observers believe that poverty thresholds should be just adequate to meet bare, biologically defined subsistence, while others believe that the poverty threshold should be set at a high level, reflecting the society's criteria for what is necessary for full participation in the community. Some argue that the absolute deprivation of the world's poorest people is an accurate benchmark for assessing poverty in the industrialized countries. We, however, do not believe that it is appropriate to compare the poverty experienced by women who live a few blocks from the Paris metro with the poverty experienced by women who have to walk miles for a bucket of water. Using biological subsistence to define poverty obscures the substantial hardships of poor women in the industrialized countries and trivializes the daily struggle for survival that confronts poor women in the global South.

In contrast to absolute poverty, relative poverty measures stress the relationship between poverty and income inequality. Measures of relative poverty look at the distance separating the poor from the economic mainstream. Under the industrial world's relative poverty measure, households with incomes less than half of the median national income are defined as poor. In other words, if the median income is $50,000, then those households with incomes less than $25,000 are considered poor.

It is instructive to compare poverty rates among the Western nations that are at similar levels of economic development. The disparities are startling. The United States has the highest incidence of poverty of any industrialized nation, despite its great riches and its role as a world superpower. During the 1990s 16.9 percent of the U.S. population lived in poverty. Poverty in the European nations was far lower: 8.1 percent for the Netherlands and France, 7.5 percent for Germany, 6.6 percent for Sweden, and 5.1 percent for Finland.[14] These large variations can be explained by the different national policies for reducing poverty. Income maintenance, employment support, labor market, and tax policies all have large effects on national poverty rates.

After World War II, with the specter of the Great Depression still fresh in collective memory, many shared the view that all citizens were entitled to protection from poverty, unemployment, and hardship. This led Western nations to expand their social welfare programs. Different national attitudes about inequality, and social justice, meant that there were significant differences in the ways in which these programs were designed and implemented.

Gøsta Esping-Andersen classifies the different welfare state regimes as liberal, corporatist, or universalist.[15] His classification sorts nations by how well their citizens are able to achieve a decent standard of living, independent of their labor force status. Regimes premised on the notion that free markets are the best mechanism for determining the distribution of income are called liberal in this classificatory scheme (although in the United States such a premise is associated with conservative policies and ideology). Liberal welfare states, which include the United States, the United Kingdom, Australia, and Canada, do little to alter the distribution of income to make it more equal, their programs are characterized by meager assistance levels, eligibility for these programs is means-tested, and the recipients of public assistance are highly stigmatized.

Corporatist regimes, in the Esping-Andersen schema, are premised on the notion that the state has a significant responsibility to alleviate the inequities resulting from markets. Although corporatist state policies are relatively more generous, class status and gender hierarchies are reinforced because benefits are differentiated according to occupation and status. Germany and France are good examples of corporatist welfare state regimes.

Universalist regimes are premised on the notion that all citizens are entitled to a decent standard of living. These regimes provide widely available, generous income subsidies, universal access to healthcare, early childhood education and care, eldercare, inexpensive public transportation, and significant housing subsidies. The Scandinavian countries and the Netherlands have adopted this approach with the positive result that in these countries poverty rates, including those for women and children, are the lowest in the world.

Esping-Andersen's typology, however, gives us only part of the picture. We want to analyze the gender dimensions of poverty to illuminate those causes of poverty that are most important for women. We can expect households headed by women to have lower earned incomes than male-headed households for several reasons. First, women work in female-dominated jobs that pay less than do traditionally male jobs. Second, many women have full responsibility for childcare or care of other relatives, and this requires them to work fewer hours of paid work. As noted earlier, part-time work pays less and carries fewer benefits than does full-time work, and this is an important cause of women's lower income vis-à-vis men's. In many countries, and especially in United States, these conditions interact with very low levels of income support and the lack of subsidized childcare to ensure that lone mothers will remain poor. To better understand the interconnected causes of women's poverty, feminist scholars consider the ways in which welfare state regimes either transform or reproduce gender relations.[16]

To this end Diane Sainsbury proposes a typology that classifies welfare regimes based on how well they help women form autonomous, nonpoor households absent marriage to a male or living with other related adults.[17] The male breadwinner regime is premised on traditional gender ideology. It assumes that men should participate in the paid labor force and women should remain economically dependent in the home, responsible for housework and child rearing but not income earning. Here marriage is a privileged institution, supported and encouraged by the structures of tax and benefit policies. Women's benefits are tied to their marital status, and married women's labor force participation is discouraged. Since traditional marriage is the preferred norm, single women and divorced women are at a relative disadvantage. As shown here, the U.S. welfare-state regime falls squarely in this category.

The individual earner-carer regime posited by Sainsbury is based on an ideology of equal rights for women and men based on their shared roles and obligations. Both women and men are entitled to benefits. Policies are structured to encourage men to become caregivers as well as workers and likewise for women to become workers as well as caregivers. Social rights and tax obligations accrue to individuals rather than to families. Shared parenting, female labor force participation, and gender equality are all features of these sorts of regimes. Moreover, the costs of children and other dependents are shared through the public provision of services and childcare allowances.

Sainsbury's work helps us understand the persistent and disproportionate poverty of lone mothers, especially in the English-speaking world. Despite much recent conservative rhetoric to the contrary, this poverty is not the result of the pathological behavior of single mothers; it is instead the result of the gendered structures of the economy. Effectively fighting poverty among lone mothers requires a combination of income supports, childcare subsidies, and generous parent leave policies. Janet Gornick has constructed an index of such supports, and according to her calculations, the United States, the United Kingdom, and Australia have programs that give relatively little support to single mothers and their children, while Finland, Sweden, and France have programs that give extensive support to lone-mother families. Hence it is no surprise that in the English-speaking nations single-mother families are quite poor, while in these latter nations social policies mitigate many of the negative consequences of low market incomes.[18]

Extending the work of Sainsbury, Gornick, and others, Karen Christopher examines the effectiveness of welfare state regimes in helping lone-mother families to form autonomous, nonpoor households. Some of her research findings are presented in table 5.1.[19]

This table rank orders nations by their single-mother poverty rates. Simple inspection shows that the United States has the highest rate of single-mother poverty, Germany has the next highest rate, and Sweden has the lowest rate. Although the correlation is not perfect, countries that do not offer a strong package of employment supports for lone mothers tend to have a higher incidence of single-mother poverty. In the Netherlands the package of employment supports is ranked at 34. This policy mix reduces single-mother poverty by 73.2 percent, leaving only 20.4 percent of lone mothers in poverty. The French government provides a package of employment supports that earns an index ranking of 53, reducing lone-mother poverty by 63.7 percent, leaving 12.9 percent of lone mothers in poverty. This table shows us that as a nation's policies supporting employment are enhanced, the percentage of single mothers in poverty generally declines.

As the preceding data illustrate, tax policies, transfer payments, and the provision of generous public services including childcare dramatically reduce the poverty of female-headed households. Thus, if the object of social and economic policy is to improve the well-being of families, then policymakers can and should enact welfare state regimes that couple

TABLE 5.1.   Effectiveness of Welfare State Regimes

	Poverty Rate	Index of Employment Supports	Reduction in Poverty Due to State Policies (%)
United States	45.4	14	14
Germany	40.9	36	28
Canada	38.3	35	31.4
Australia	31.8	21	44.2
United Kingdom	31.6	22	56.9
Netherlands	20.4	34	73.2
France	12.9	53	63.7
Finland	5.1	66	86.3
Sweden	4.4	62	89.1

Source: Karen Christopher, "Welfare State Regimes and Mothers' Poverty," *Social Politics: International Studies in Gender, State, and Society* 9 (spring 2002): 60–86.

employment supports with generous subsidies. If, in contrast, the object of social and economic policy is to punish the poor by making lone-mother families scapegoats for social problems, then policymakers will enact welfare state regimes that compel low-skill workers to choose between caring for their children or working at jobs that do not pay living wages. In this latter case, lone mothers and their dependents suffer even greater deprivation as material poverty interacts with increasing social isolation, demeaning regulations, and public humiliation. Unfortunately, recent changes in U.S. economic and social policy seem far more concerned with scapegoating the poor, especially poor mothers, than with actually alleviating economic hardships.

Gender and Poverty in the United States

When the United States began to officially measure poverty in 1961, government analysts calculated the dollar cost of a survival level of caloric intake using the U.S. Department of Agriculture's least expensive plan for emergency nutrition, the economy food plan. To get the cash minimum needed for subsistence, analysts simply multiplied the amount of money it cost to purchase the economy food plan by three because, in 1961, the average family spent one-third of its income on food. To take into account the fact that different size families have different nutritional, housing, and clothing needs, this amount (the minimum cash needed for nutritional subsistence times three) was adjusted for the number and age of people in the family to produce a poverty threshold based on family size.

Because the price of food, like the price of most other goods, has increased over time, U.S. poverty thresholds have been adjusted upward, based on the consumer price index. These adjusted cut-off amounts form the basis of the official definition of poverty in the United States today. Both conservatives and progressives find fault with the forty-plus-year-old measure used in the United States. Analysts with divergent views about the causes and consequences of poverty believe that when measuring income it is important to take into account the many noncash transfers (like food stamps, the money value of health insurance, and housing subsidies) that are received by low-income households.

In 1963 the poverty threshold for a family of four was $3,100; it was $17,960 in 2001.[20] Conservatives look at the income figure of $17,960, add in the value of noncash transfers, and conclude that poverty thresholds are way too high and overstate the extent of poverty in the United States.

Robert Rector, a researcher from the right-wing American Enterprise Institute, has this to say:

In reality the typical "poor" person in the U.S. has a standard of living far higher than our normal images and expectations for poverty. According to the government's own data, the typical American, defined as poor by the government, has a refrigerator, a stove, a clothes washer, a car, air conditioning, a VCR, a microwave, a stereo and a color TV. . . . By his own report, the typical poor individual is able to obtain medical care for himself and his family; he lives in a home that is in good repair and is not over-crowded. By his own report, his family is not hungry and in the last year he had sufficient funds to meet his essential needs.[21]

This view is troublesome for several reasons. First, we must comment on Rector's repeated use of the masculine pronoun despite the fact that most of the poor are women. We also point out that refrigerators and stoves are hardly luxuries. Neither are washing machines or air conditioners (further, we know nothing about the age or working condition of these appliances). Moreover, Rector's assertions regarding the extent to which poor families can access decent housing and adequate food are contradicted by easily verified facts.[22]

For example, research conducted in 2001 for the U.S. Conference of Mayors paints a grim picture of many Americans unable to meet their essential needs.[23] In twenty-five of the twenty-seven cities surveyed, the requests for emergency food assistance had increased an average of 23 percent, while resources to support emergency food assistance increased by only 12 percent. As a result, two-thirds of cities reported that they were unable to provide adequate quantities of food to hungry people with nowhere else to turn. The need for emergency shelter, like the need for emergency food assistance, also increased sharply. Comparing 2001 with 1999, the mayor's report found an average 13 percent increase in the demand for emergency shelter in 73 percent of the cities surveyed. Even more distressing is the fact that requests for emergency shelter by homeless families with children increased an average of 22 percent, and slightly more than half of the cities reported that the length of time that people stayed in shelters had increased to an average of six months.[24]

In the face of this staggering chronicle of need, it is difficult to accept the sanguine portrait of poverty painted by American Enterprise Institute researchers. But the even more basic point is this: poverty thresholds are based on annual incomes, and as a society we need to know if earnings at the threshold level are sufficient to permit a family to live a decent life. This question motivated feminist economists Barbara Bergmann and Trudi Renwick to develop the basic needs approach to poverty.[25]

Bergmann and Renwick pioneered this approach to poverty measurement both to counter conservative arguments and remedy defects in standard methods of calculating poverty. They point out that the official methodology for measuring poverty in the United States is flawed. First, relative prices have changed so that food and housing expenses no longer count for one-third each of a household budget. As a matter of fact, for many families, not just the poor, housing expenses now absorb over half of household income. Second, the official U.S. measures ignore nonincome transfers like food stamps, Medicare, housing subsidies, and so forth. Third, standard measures only consider before-tax income and hence ignore the need to pay taxes as well as tax adjustments such as the earned income tax credit.[26]

Bergmann and Renwick began by identifying the actual expenses a household must pay for necessities such as housing, utilities, food, transportation, childcare, healthcare insurance, and taxes. Household costs for these items will vary by household size, the age of household members, their labor force status, and their location. Basic needs budgets are sensitive to these variations, whereas other measures of absolute poverty are not. The fundamental advantage of the basic needs approach to measuring poverty is that it establishes the income a household needs to live at a level that is widely accepted as "decent." There is, of course, room for debate over the meaning of decent, but surely we would agree that in the richest nations even low-income households should have safe housing with functioning utilities, healthy food, reliable transportation to and from work, basic medical care, and quality childcare.[27] Basic needs budgets cover these costs while accounting for the value of noncash benefits received by households as well as the taxes they need to pay. For all these reasons, basic needs budgets present a far more accurate picture of poverty, as well as the cash assistance and subsidized services needed to relieve it, than do traditional measures built on simple multiples of emergency food costs.[28]

The Economic Policy Institute (EPI) has done extensive research on constructing basic needs budgets (*basic family budgets* in the EPI terminology). They are geographically specific budgets that account for every major budget item, including housing, childcare, healthcare, food, transportation, and taxes. Its research shows that the official poverty thresholds are much lower than that established by basic needs budgets. Consider the following evidence: in 2001 the official poverty threshold for a family of three, one adult and two children, was $14,269. Table 5.2 shows the basic family budget for this family in several diverse locations and what percentage of the poverty threshold it is.[29]

In New York City, the basic needs budget is more than three times the poverty threshold. In other large urban areas it is two and one-half times the poverty threshold, while in suburban areas of the Midwest it is a little more than twice the poverty threshold. Likewise, estimates of people living in poverty using the basic family budget threshold are more than twice as much for all the states considered. It must be remembered that the EPI budget figures are minimums—they do not allow for any savings. Moreover, in calculating the number of people in poverty, taxes and in-kind subsidies such as food stamps and Medicaid have been taken into account. Clearly, it seems that the official poverty statistics seriously undercount poverty in the United States.

A Brief History of U.S. Antipoverty Policies

Like all the other industrial democracies, the people of the United States suffered enormous deprivations during the Great Depression. In the 1930s

TABLE 5.2.   Basic Family Budgets

	New York, NY	Atlanta, GA	Chicago, IL	Los Angeles, CA	South Bend, IN	Akron, OH
Family budget ($)	43,602	33,748	35,307	34,839	29,246	29,380
Official poverty threshold (%)	305	236	247	244	204	205
People in state below family budget line (%)	37.5	29.0	25.5	33.1	17.8	21.9
People in state below official poverty threshold (%)	14.0	12.5	10.4	12.6	8.5	10.3

Source: Data from Economic Policy Institute, "EPI Issue Guide: Poverty and Family Budgets," http://www.epinet .org/content.cfm/issueguides_poverty_poverty (May 22, 2004).

almost one-quarter of the workforce was unemployed, the nation's output fell by a third, severe drought combined with falling agricultural prices led to massive waves of farm foreclosures, and hundreds of thousands of family businesses, banks, and large corporations went bankrupt. This was the economic environment in which Franklin D. Roosevelt was able to muster support for the sweeping social legislation of the New Deal.

The programs of unemployment compensation, publicly funded retirement pensions, and workers' compensation were either started in the New Deal or were massively expanded as the federal government stepped up its role in providing some measure of economic security for white male workers and their dependents. Of the many alphabet soup policies and agencies comprising the New Deal, the most important for our discussion is the 1935 Social Security Act. The Social Security Act created a system of benefits including Supplemental Security Income, social security pensions, widow's pensions, and income for the handicapped that were seen as rights, not as welfare. To this day, everyone is eligible for these benefits, receipt of these benefits is not means-tested, and there are no government social workers monitoring the behavior of beneficiaries. But access to these programs was not, at the outset, available to all citizens.

Pressure on Roosevelt's progressive Democratic alliance from conservatives, especially those in the segregated Jim Crow South, led to policy guidelines that excluded agricultural and domestic workers. As a result, African-Americans, and other ethnic minorities, were not covered by these programs because in the 1930s they were still largely employed on farms and as household servants. In addition, eligibility standards were not enacted at the federal level, leaving state and local authorities (especially in segregated rural areas) free to discriminate against ethnic minorities. Even more important for our understanding of the feminization of poverty, the programs of social security and unemployment compensation were premised on a traditional male breadwinner–female caretaker model of the family.

There are two points worth noting about this. First, African-American women have a long history of working for pay, so the construction of policies based on the male-female division of labor effectively excluded them from benefits. Second, defining need in terms of this model of the family casts women not attached to male income earners in a negative light. Since women were supposed to be economically dependent upon men, those women who were not dependent—because they had never been married, they had been deserted, or they were divorced—were seen as morally deficient.

A moral code informed by patriarchal values (one that is still with us today) separated the deserving from the undeserving poor. The distinction between the deserving and undeserving poor informed the development and implementation of all the programs of the Social Security Act: unemployment compensation, publicly funded retirement pensions, and income supports for women with dependent children were all deeply affected by the view that women should be dependent upon men.[30] White male breadwinners and their dependents were seen as deserving because the hardships they faced—loss of income due to retirement, disability, or unemployment for men, or widowhood for women—were due to circumstances beyond their individual control.[31] Thus, programs that benefited white men and their traditional families were considered entitlements and were relatively secure. Such was not the case for programs aimed at women with children who were not connected by marriage to a male earner.

The one program designed specifically to help poor mothers who were neither married nor widowed was Aid to Dependent Children (ADC), which later became Aid to Families with Dependent Children, (AFDC). ADC was not an entitlement but rather a publicly funded charity.[32] It provided low levels of means-tested support for mothers who were divorced, abandoned, or never married. In addition, program provisions required that persons receiving these benefits have their lives closely scrutinized by caseworkers who had enormous power to increase or decrease benefits levels, to provide or withhold access to noncash benefits, and even to break up families by declaring a woman "unfit" for motherhood.

In the early 1960s President Lyndon Baines Johnson's war on poverty programs expanded U.S. welfare state policies. Civil rights groups, women's groups, welfare rights organizations, and other activists worked with the Johnson administration to create a host of new programs and policies. In this period there was an increase in the minimum wage, Medicaid and Medicare were enacted, food stamp programs were expanded, and many new public-housing projects were constructed. In addition, other subsidies and services to expand opportunities for low-income Americans were enacted. Civil rights activists were able to get obstacles to African-American participation in many entitlement programs removed so that African-Americans too could receive benefits for which they were eligible. Other notable gains for African-Americans were won in Congress and at the state level, and for the first time an African-American served on a president's cabinet. These policy changes were an important positive step toward the expansion of opportunity, greater economic equality—especially for Americans of color—and the reduction of poverty. But despite their progressive intent, these Great Society programs were, like the New Deal policies of the 1930s, built on a male breadwinner–female caretaker model of the family. Thus this policy mix actually contributed to the feminization of poverty.

An irony worth pointing out is that the poverty of lone mothers increased as a share of the U.S. poverty population in part because the antipoverty programs aimed at other populations were so successful. As poverty among the elderly, widows and their dependents, the handicapped, and the unemployed decreased due to the expansion of social welfare programs, those who remained in poverty were disproportionately lone mothers and their children who were not eligible for those programs. At the same time, AFDC, the primary program for poor women, was premised on the idea that mothers with young children ought not be in the labor force. As a result this program contained many strong disincentives for mothers' participation in the paid labor force. AFDC recipients, for example, faced an effective tax of 100 percent on all earned income since for every dollar they earned they lost a dollar of benefits. Another disincentive included the treatment of assets. Even when a woman's only asset was her house, the value of the asset could be used to disqualify her from receiving benefits despite her level of need. A third disincentive was the lack of affordable childcare.

In the United States, stringent regulations concerning assets and earnings combined with the near total absence of subsidized childcare, no guaranteed paid parental leave, limited public housing, and expensive private transportation left single mothers with no real choices about how to organize their lives. Consider the options facing a lone mother with limited job skills. Lacking access to the income of a man, either she could try to take care of her family by stretching the miserly benefits paid by state welfare agencies or she could take a low-wage job that did not offer benefits (medical, paid vacations, or contributions to her retirement account) and pay for childcare out of pocket. This policy combination did indeed create a trap for lone mothers.

In addition, as Linda Gordon points out, the AFDC program was stigmatized from the very beginning. Under the prevailing gender ideology, women and children were seen as male dependents.[33] Needing government support due to the absence of a male head of household has long been seen as evidence of deep moral failure. Today, this attitude has allowed conservatives to cast income transfers to lone mothers as undeserved handouts that lead to dependency, promiscuity, and other social pathologies. Even though many other income support programs are analytically indistinguishable from what Americans have come to call "welfare," the beneficiaries of those programs—veteran's benefits, social security, Medicaid, and unemployment compensation—are rarely demonized as lazy slackers feeding at the public trough.

In the 1980s, the rhetoric in the media and in political speech about poverty became even more racialized. The race coding of America's poverty problem helped conservative politicians mobilize support for the dismantling of the progressive policies of the 1960s. President Ronald Reagan is infamous for his racist remarks about welfare queens and their Cadillacs. During this decade conservatives promulgated a number of myths about welfare recipients, including the idea that mothers on welfare have additional children to qualify for greater benefits as well as the idea that welfare spending has skyrocketed and is a burden on the taxpayers. In fact, no reputable research has ever shown a positive correlation between benefit levels and the number of children of welfare recipients, nor was AFDC (as a share of federal spending) particularly large.[34] Nevertheless, this inflammatory rhetoric shaped a political climate favorable to the virtual elimination of any federal guarantee to a decent standard of living for lone mothers and their children.

During President Bill Clinton's first term, AFDC—welfare as we know it—was eliminated. The Personal Responsibility and Work Opportunity Reconciliation Act created a block grant titled Temporary Assistance to Needy Families (TANF). Under TANF the states have considerable leeway in determining benefits levels, most all states require recipients to work to qualify for benefits, and most states exclude education and training from what counts as work. Perhaps most onerous is that TANF establishes a lifetime eligibility limit of five years for federal assistance. Not surprisingly, in the boom conditions of the mid- to late 1990s, these new rules did lead to a dramatic reduction in the number of people receiving welfare. Some states have the dubious distinction of having cut their welfare caseloads nearly in half with no simultaneous decline in poverty. We should not be surprised. The jobs of former TANF recipients were almost all low-paid, service sector jobs with low benefits and little chance for advancement. Over three-fourths of former TANF recipients are concentrated in four low-wage occupations: service, clerical, laborers, and sales.[35] Of course, draconian cuts in cash assistance to poor families reduced the welfare rolls. But because the increase in social spending for childcare, housing, public transportation, education, and skills development was minimal, these policies failed to reduce poverty among lone mothers and their families.

The sad fact remains: in the United States, many low-income lone mothers have been forced into what Randy Albelda calls a match made in hell.[36] The combination of low pay and no benefits with scheduling inflexibility and minimal provisions for time off interferes with parents' ability to meet the regular health and educational needs of their children. According to the U.S. Department of Health and Human Services, employment among low-income single mothers with young children grew from 44 percent in 1996 to 59 percent in 2000. Recently released statistics show the magnitude of the childcare crisis: in California there are two hundred thousand families waiting for childcare subsidies, in Florida there are more than forty-six thousand, and in Texas there are more than thirty-six thousand. Without subsidies these families must pay half their income for childcare, and only one in seven eligible children actually gets these subsidies.[37] The link between women's poverty and the well-being of children could hardly be clearer.

Poverty among the Very Young and the Very Old in Rich Nations

An important indicator of a society's support for the diffusion of opportunities is the extent to which children and the elderly escape poverty. Most people believe that children should not suffer when their parents are too poor to secure adequate nutrition, housing, supervised care, medical attention, education, and recreation. Another widely shared value is that the elderly should be able to retire comfortably after a lifetime of productive employment. Thus, a focus on the poverty of children and the elderly, rather than on the poverty of able-bodied adults (male or female), allows us to avoid acrimonious debate over the deserving versus the undeserving poor.

The idea that a decent society should provide opportunities that enable all children to fully develop their human capacities and potentials allows us to see how important it is to eradicate child poverty. The Canadian Council for Social Development (CCSD) provides a well-reasoned approach to the importance of reducing child poverty. This approach takes the attributes of healthy, productive adults as a starting point and then identifies the resources and environments that enable children to grow into adults who possess these socially desirable traits. By the standards of the CCSD, healthy, productive adults have good social skills, know how to learn in different environments, and are able to pursue meaningful work. To reach maturity with these attributes, children need economic resources, shelter, healthcare, attentive parenting, attentive childcare, schooling, recreation, physical safety, and concerned, nurturing communities.[38] It is important for any society to make sure that children have access to the things they need to become healthy adults. In other words, fighting child poverty means more than just choosing a poverty line or providing basic food and shelter.

These sentiments are echoed in a recent report calling for common welfare policies across the European Union. Gøsta Esping-Andersen, Duncan Gallie, Anton Memerijck, and John Myles argue that the foundations of people's live are established in childhood.[39] Therefore they argue for a comprehensive social investment strategy that explicitly focuses resources on children and families with children. They claim that investing in children will reduce much childhood disadvantage and as a result fewer children will drop out of school, use drugs, live on the streets, or experience violence.[40]

Poverty is, of course, directly related to how much you have to spend, but it is also reflected by the deprivation and disadvantage you face in your daily life. As a report from the New Policy Institute in Great Britain points out, those who face persistent poverty live in marginal neighborhoods; use schools, clinics, and hospitals that are strapped for resources; and have only limited access to public transportation or childcare. They face a higher risk of crime and drug-related attack. Poverty is not only about income and consumption, or even only about aspiring to social and economic advancement.[41] It is about whether people are able to live decent lives and fully participate in their societies.

Even if it were possible or desirable to put aside ethical, compassionate considerations (which we don't), there are still compelling, pragmatic reasons for alleviating the poverty of children. In all the industrial nations, the rapid aging of the population means that there will be fewer and fewer workers to support each retiree. The viability of pension schemes like social security is dependent upon widespread participation in the labor force and the growing productivity of labor. The poverty of children undermines both of these because children from poor families have weaker labor force attachment and lower educational attainment than do children from families that are well-off. Mean-spirited and stingy responses to poverty are neither sound nor ethical economic policy.

It is also worth pointing out that absent publicly funded pensions like social security, poverty among the elderly would increase dramatically. In fact, the reduction of poverty among society's elders is one of the great achievements of twentieth-century social policy. Table 5.3 compares the incidence of poverty among children and the elderly in nine selected countries.

These data illustrate the stark difference between child and elder poverty in English-speaking countries and in Western European countries. In Sweden and Finland, policies have been set in place to drive down the incidence of poverty among children so that children are less likely to be poor than Swedish or Finnish adults. In contrast Germany, Canada, the United Kingdom, Australia, and the United States all have child poverty rates substantially greater than the poverty rate of the total population. And the United States once again takes the prize for having the highest rate of child poverty in the industrial world, while Australia has the distinction of having the most elder poverty among the rich nations.

Although publicly supported pension schemes for older adults have done a remarkable job of reducing elder poverty, it remains the case that in many countries elderly women are disproportionately poor. Women who are divorced, separated, widowed, or never married are at the greatest risk of poverty.

Comparing female elder poverty in six industrialized nations, Jürg Siegenthaler finds that the Netherlands and Sweden have the best record of preventing poverty among older single women, while France ranks a close second.[42] As usual, the United States ranks last: seven out of ten of the poor elderly are women, and the poverty rate for women over sixty-five is 13.1 percent, nearly twice that of men (7 percent).[43] The poverty rates for

TABLE 5.3. Population in Poverty in Nine Selected Countries

	Poverty in Population as a Whole (%)	Children in Poverty (%)	Elderly in Poverty (%)
Finland (1994)	5.1	4.5	6.7
Sweden (1995)	6.6	2.6	2.7
Germany (1994)	7.5	10.6	7
France (1994)	8	7.9	9.8
Netherlands (1994)	8.1	8.1	6.4
Canada (1997)	11.9	15.7	5.3
United Kingdom (1995)	13.4	19.8	13.7
Australia (1994)	14.3	15.8	29.4
United States (1997)	16.9	22.3	20.7

Source: David Jesuit and Timothy Smeeding, "Poverty Levels in the Developed World," Luxembourg Income Study Working Paper 321, July 2002.

African-American and Hispanic women are even higher. In 1998, almost one-third of black elderly women and one-quarter of Hispanic elderly women were poor.[44] This underscores the salience of race and ethnicity in determining economic status.

Eliminating poverty among single, older women requires national commitments to old-age security systems that are available to all and that are high enough to prevent poverty among the recipients. Absent a strong commitment to ending poverty among elder women, the future looks bleak. The European welfare states show us that elder poverty is not an inevitable feature of contemporary economic life. It can and should be alleviated.

Conclusion

Contemporary poverty research recognizes the personal and social costs of poverty. Poverty is more than just a lack of income or inadequate consumption. Poverty creates multidimensional hardships when people and communities confront unemployment, low income, family breakdown, inadequate housing, bad schools, high crime environments, and poor health. Since poverty is multidimensional, solutions to it require multidimensional responses. Unfortunately, however, power has accrued to politicians who advance the view that the private costs of market intervention are greater than the social benefits of reduced poverty, deprivation, and misery. Conservatives argue that in market economies hard work and effort allow people to lift themselves out of poverty. For them, unregulated capitalism with minimal state intervention is the best way to fight poverty because competition creates both incentives and opportunities. One must work very hard to find empirical evidence supporting this claim. Indeed, the historical record shows quite the contrary: as government intervention in the economy expands and income redistribution programs are extended, poverty falls.

Despite nearly fifty years of evidence to the contrary, conservatives continue to insist that markets create an environment rich with opportunity and anyone who can't achieve success in that environment is deeply flawed. For conservatives, poverty reflects individual pathology not the structural defects of the economic system. There is a huge and unbridgeable gulf between an explanation of poverty that rests upon a negative characterization of the poor and an explanation of poverty that roots poverty in the structure of the economy.

As feminists and economists, we cast a skeptical eye on such individual-istic arguments. This is not to argue that certain people are inevitably doomed to poverty. Many remarkable stories document the escape from poverty through hard work and effort. One person's escape from hardship does not, however, forestall another person's slide into poverty. Individual upward economic mobility should not be confused with the elimination of poverty. As long as a society refuses to recognize the inextricable link between gender and racial equality and economic opportunity, poverty will continue to be the fate of too many women and children. As we have stressed, well-paying jobs with security and benefits are the route out of poverty. As these jobs become increasingly scarce, inadequate incomes for some are the necessary result. In this analysis it is not difficult to under-stand the roles played by hierarchies of race, gender, and ethnicity: these are precisely the social mechanisms for allocating poverty. The economic and social changes attending globalization make these problems even more acute.

6. Globalization Is a Feminist Issue

The Barbie dolls, soccer balls, and stuffed animals that fill toy store shelves in the United States and Europe were probably manufactured in other, less prosperous countries. In fact, many of the clothes, shoes, appliances, and housewares sold in the United States and Europe are produced by workers in the global South—Asia, Africa, the Caribbean, and Latin America— specifically for export to the rich industrialized countries. This is one of the most visible manifestations of economic globalization. Workers on this global assembly line,[1] the majority of whom are women, are subject to hazardous working conditions, poor pay, and long hours. Understanding the link between globalization and gender requires a vision of the process that is multifaceted and goes far beyond export production to its effects on cultures, identities, and politics. Even so, these aspects of change are rooted in the growing integration of national economies as people, goods, machines, and financial capital flow across national borders.

Relations of trade and exchange have long had significant international dimensions. Venetian merchants, for example, facilitated trade between Europe and the Middle East during the Crusades. Marco Polo's travels led to trade with China, and Dutch merchants plied their wares between northern Europe, Indonesia, and Africa. In 1600 Queen Elizabeth granted a monopoly charter to the English East India Company to secure the rights of English merchants to exploit India. These examples highlight the long global history of commerce.

But international trade today differs in both qualitative and quantitative ways from the global trading of earlier eras. Electronic technologies make global communications instantaneous, and new methods of handling cargo (containerization) have drastically reduced transportation costs. As a result, transnational corporations are now able to relocate their manufacturing operations to parts of the world characterized by low wages and business-friendly political regimes. The geographic mobility of capital limits the ability of national governments to protect their citizens and undermines the power of workers to organize for better working conditions. At the same time, an increasingly conservative political rhetoric has emerged that champions free markets and rationalizes the dismantling of progressive labor legislation, health and safety standards, environmental protections, and social welfare programs.

Globalization creates winners and losers, exacerbating relations of dependency and exploitation. Critics of globalization argue that unfettered global trade causes greater inequality within and between nations. Income, wealth, health, and education are concentrated into fewer hands, while an ever larger share of the world's population is consigned to poverty, disease, and illiteracy. The proponents of free trade argue that narrowly circumscribed government regulation, combined with the free mobility of capital, will, in the long run, benefit everyone everywhere. In this view, free markets have the potential to bring prosperity, via Western-style economic growth, to the impoverished peoples of the world. As feminist economists we are suspicious of the claim that national and transnational markets will meet everyone's social needs. As demonstrated in earlier chapters, markets often fail to value caring labor, they do not eliminate discrimination, and they do not, on their own, reduce poverty or unemployment. Globalization is a feminist issue precisely because it plays a central role shaping labor markets by reinforcing the *status quo* gender division of labor and undermining the ability of states to enact progressive social policies.

What's in a Name?

The terminology used in any taxonomy of the world's peoples and economies reveals quite a bit about the various ways of understanding global hierarchy and privilege.[2] The term the Third World has its origins in the Cold War. In this taxonomy, the capitalist economies of the industrialized world were designated the First World, while the centrally planned economies of the Soviet Union and its satellites were designated the Second World. To assert their independence from the superpowers, leaders of countries in Asia, Africa, the Middle East, the Caribbean, and Latin America formed an alliance they named the Third World. Initially this alliance reflected their common interests stemming in a shared agenda for economic development. But by the end of the 1980s the Third World nations were more different than alike so that today the name no longer designates a cohesive geographical group.[3]

The terms center and periphery are similar to the terms First World and Third World. This classification was created by Marxist development economists to highlight the relationships of power and dependency between the rich, industrialized countries of Europe and North America and the poor, primarily agricultural exporting countries of Latin America, South America, Asia, and Africa. In this view, the colonizing center had tremendous economic power, while the colonized periphery depended on the center for education, capital, and technology.

Taxonomies do not correspond exactly to geography. There are pockets of the Third World within the First World. Some of these communities are created as poor people migrate, legally or illegally, to the wealthy industrialized countries seeking work as domestic servants or migrant farm laborers or other poorly paid, unpleasant jobs. Others are created when deindustrialization—the export of manufacturing to low-wage regions—destroys the economic base of cities. In many rural areas in the United States, the increasing concentration and centralization of food production by transnational agri-business has driven thousands of small family farms into bankruptcy, undermining regional prosperity.[4] In sharp contrast, privileged elites in both the North and the global South live lives of luxury and ease in walled compounds and gated communities.

Scholars still use the category Third World but call attention to the fact that it is a contested term, expressing a relationship to centers of privilege and power. It does not refer to an essential attribute of people so designated, nor does it necessarily refer to a particular geographical location.[5] Nevertheless, it can still be said that the poor countries of the Third World, or the periphery, retain certain characteristics that set them apart from the rich, industrial nations. Many Third World countries suffer from severe economic deprivation, the people and the environment are harshly exploited, and the processes of globalization have created more misery, violence, and political unrest.[6] For this reason, the terms North and global South, with their geographical specificity, are often useful. The North refers to the rich, industrialized countries of North America, Europe, Japan, and Australia, while the global South refers to the countries of Latin America, South America, Asia, Africa, the Caribbean, and the Pacific Islands.

Some international organizations classify nations by income or their degree of development: as high, middle, or low income or as industrialized, developing, or least developed. These classifications require us to specify exactly what we mean by the term economic development. Is economic development a synonym for market-driven economic growth? Or is it a process that is directed at creating greater income equality, less poverty, cleaner and safer environments, better maternal health, reduced infant mortality, improved mass literacy, and greater longevity? The United Nations tacitly adopts the latter view of economic development when it promulgates the Human Development Index (HDI), a way of ranking nations that goes beyond the simple metric of per capita income to address the degree of human development, as measured by factors such as life expectancy, literacy, and education as well as income. The HDI yields important information because it reflects a much more robust vision of economic well-being than the usual per capita income rankings.

Global Privilege and Global Misery

The dehumanizing brutality of poverty and deprivation that haunts much of the world's population does not go away with our choice of global taxonomy or development metric. Almost half of the world's population, 2.8 billion people, live on less than $2 a day, and 1.2 billion of them live in even more extreme poverty, surviving—barely—on less than $1 per day. In South Asia, for example, 44 percent of the population lives at this level.[7] Today, the average income in the richest twenty countries is now thirty-seven times that of the poorest. There are, moreover, enormous disparities of income and wealth within the industrialized countries. Recent international estimates find that one person in eight in the rich countries will experience some aspect of poverty like long-term unemployment, income less than the national poverty line, or a literacy level below that which is needed to function in society.[8]

Women and girls experience far more than their share of this deprivation. According to the United Nations Development Programme (UNDP), three-fifths of the world's billion poorest people are women and girls. Two-thirds of the one billion adults who cannot read are female, and women also represent a growing proportion of the people living with HIV/AIDS. More than half the world's migrants are women, and women and children comprise more than 80 percent of the world's fifty million refugees.[9]

Today's global inequalities are a continuation of the West's colonial excesses. The former colonies of England, France, Holland, Spain, Portugal, Germany, and Russia provided the raw minerals, precious metals, and cash crops like coffee, tea, tobacco, cotton, and sugar that were essential to the emergence of capitalism and consumer society.[10] The colonies were also important markets for manufactured goods. As Eric Hobsbawm's *Industry and Empire* makes clear, Western economic progress depended upon colonial exploitation.[11]

From the seventeenth through the twentieth centuries, the imperialist nations of Europe relied upon a combination of bribery, force, and persuasion to impose political, cultural, and economic systems upon the institutions and customs of indigenous peoples. When indigenous kinship structures, economic relations, or patterns of land use interfered with colonial interests, they were undermined or destroyed. Consider the transformation of indigenous family life. European colonizers brought with them a model of the Western, patriarchal family, with all its rigidities regarding the sexual division of labor and appropriate spheres for women and men. When Victorian gender ideology was grafted onto existing traditional, patriarchal social norms, gender inequalities in colonial societies were exacerbated, worsening women's social and economic status. An example illustrates this point.

In many African and Asian countries, women, not men, had primary responsibility for agricultural work. The land was held and farmed communally. When the Europeans changed the laws of land ownership and the patterns of land use to mirror those of the West, women lost their customary rights to farm the land. Women thus lost the food security provided by subsistence agriculture.[12] In Asia and in Africa, as in much of the rest of the world, feeding families is a woman's responsibility. As women were squeezed out of agriculture and pushed into economic dependency in the household, their social status declined. Under colonial rule, this process occurred around the world, systematically undermining women's ability to carry out the work of social reproduction.

The period of colonial expansion came to an end in the decades following World War II as the European colonial empires in Asia, Africa, and Latin America were overthrown and newly independent nation-states were formed. These new nations, which came into existence in the context of the international order shaped by the Cold War between the United States and the Soviet Union, faced serious challenges in creating cohesive national identities and sovereign political institutions.[13] They were extremely poor. Their industrial infrastructure—roads, factories, and communication networks—had been built to meet the needs of the colonial powers rather than their own. Moreover, their economic, social, and political structures and institutions had been severely disrupted. These problems were exacerbated by the Cold War because these new countries became the terrain upon which the ideological battles between the United States and the Soviet

Union were played out. This created a fertile ground for an international economic order that overwhelmingly favored the interests of the industrialized North while pushing the new nation-states of the Third World deeper and deeper into poverty and militarism.[14]

The institutions for regulating international economic relations—the International Monetary Fund (IMF), the International Bank for Reconstruction and Development (now called the World Bank), and the General Agreement on Tariffs and Trade (GATT)—also came into being at the end of World War II. Regulating international finance was the job of the IMF, providing long-term development loans was the function of the World Bank, and setting the rules for international trade was the province of the GATT (which is no longer in existence, having evolved into the World Trade Organization, or WTO). All of these institutions were dominated by policymakers and academics trained in Western Europe and the United States. They believed that the solution to the extreme poverty and immiseration of the Third World was Western-style economic development. Economists and policymakers endorsed a simple recipe: Third World development required rural, subsistence-agricultural economies to transform themselves in the image of the West and become modern, industrialized, high-consumption market systems. The stages through which economies passed in their development from traditional to modern could be speeded up through large-scale, government-directed investments in infrastructure like dams, factories, roads, and energy generation.[15]

Women and Development

From its inception, economic development affected women and men differently. Systematic attention to the issues around women and development began in 1970s as a result of the convergence of interests of two different groups of women, the United Nations Commission on the Status of Women and the global women's movement.[16] The United Nations group was primarily interested in legal and educational equality for women, while feminists in the U.S. women's movement were primarily interested in equal pay and equal employment. As their interests converged, the United Nations declared 1975 the Year of the Woman and marked this with a world conference in Mexico City. Subsequently, 1976 to 1985 was designated by the United Nations as the Decade for Women, with two more conferences, one in Copenhagen (1980) and one in Nairobi (1985).

Although a variety of interests and agendas regarding women's status and gender equality were advanced, by 1980 the emphasis on women and development was firmly established. "'Women in Development' became the Decade's overnight catchphrase, a seductive one, which for a time at least, could evade the question of what kind of development women were to be drawn into."[17]

The work of the feminist economist Ester Boserup played a crucial role in turning attention to the impact of development on women. Boserup's monumental 1970 work *Women's Role in Economic Development* set the stage for a long-running, extremely influential debate. Boserup accepted the dominant view that development involves the gradual change from subsistence family production to specialized production and commodification.[18] Her important insight was that as development takes place, the socioeconomic functions of the family change, and these changes lead to changes in women's roles and status. Boserup questioned the prevailing gender ideology that saw men as farmers and women as housewives. She argued that although women the world over did seem to have a monopoly on food preparation and other household tasks, this did not mean that men were the ones who did the farming. On the contrary, in much of the developing world food was produced primarily by women, with little help from men. In these female farming systems women's agricultural work was essential to familial and hence national well-being. Nowhere was this better exemplified than sub-Saharan Africa, which Boserup deemed the "region of female farming *par excellence.*"[19]

Boserup showed how women's status in agricultural societies was determined by their contributions to food production. Thus the change from female to male farming systems entailed the loss of both status and freedom for women. As farming became more Europeanized, men monopolized the ownership of animals and machines. This process was exacerbated by European colonial administrators who, blinded by their Victorian gender ideology, ignored female farmers and reorganized agricultural production in ways that forced men to cultivate commercial crops for export. Although they saw that it was the women, not the men, who were chiefly responsible for farming, the Europeans believed that farmwork was far more appropriate for men than it was for women. The fact that indigenous men didn't actually do agricultural work was attributed to laziness and not to the patterns of work and reproduction that had prevailed in the precolonial era. So great was the distaste of the Europeans for female farming systems that in many cases women's customary land use rights were taken

American River College Library

away and given to their husbands. Boserup forcefully demonstrated how women's loss of status and freedom in African societies followed directly from the colonial policies of European imperialists.

The emergence of small family business in villages and towns also plays an important role in the transition from a subsistence agricultural economy to a commodity exchange economy. Here, too, Boserup saw women's disadvantage. In the transition from an agrarian precapitalist economy to an industrial capitalist economy, men's customary right to dispense of women's labor often is transformed into a right to a woman's wages (if she works for pay) or a right to any profits women may earn as a result of their handicraft activities or the sales of foodstuffs. It is also important to consider the differential importance of human reproduction and fertility in agrarian versus industrial/urban society. As an economic system becomes more commercialized, the physical labor of children becomes less necessary to familial well-being, so children are no longer economic assets to the family. Pregnancy and breast feeding become obstacles to women's economic independence since, according to Boserup, they interfered with women's ability to fully participate in a modern industrial economy. Boserup, always mindful of similarities between developed and developing societies, reminds us that the power structure within large institutions continues to mirror the gender and age hierarchies of subsistence economies: the old men hold the highest positions, young men vie with each other to step into the shoes of the male leaders, women serve men, and the only space for very young women is at the bottom. Indeed, one fundamental difference between women and men that is relatively constant across cultures, economies, and continents is that few women are permitted to rise in the social hierarchy as they age.

Boserup's work has been subject to feminist criticism. Lourdes Benería and Gita Sen argue that Boserup ignored the exploitation of women in global capitalism.[20] In other words, Boserup saw the spread of capitalism as a basically liberating force for women since she believed that the expansion of wage labor, and the commodification of food, clothing, health, and education, would free women from drudgery and domestic subordination. Benería and Sen point out the flaws in this view, arguing that even as capitalism spreads, women continue to be economically marginalized, not because they are less productive but because their subordinate gender status is reinforced as they are drawn into female occupations. Moreover, Benería and Sen point out that Boserup overlooks the social significance of the unpaid labor performed in households and communities that is necessary to maintain and reproduce the labor force. Reproductive labor includes childcare, cooking, and cleaning. (This concept is very close to the concept of caring labor discussed in chapter 3, the main difference being it includes tasks necessary to sustain life that do not necessarily involve caring: e.g., doing the laundry.) Since women are responsible for the overwhelming majority of reproductive work, one cannot understand women's economic roles without considering how the tendency of market systems to under-value reproductive labor determines the relationship between reproductive and productive labor.

Boserup had, of course, noticed that in the societies she studied women did the cooking and cleaning. She also wrote about the adverse impact of this division of labor on women's status and freedom. Ultimately, however, it was her conception of modernization and development that prevented her from treating reproductive work as analytically separate from produc-tive labor. As economic development proceeds, fewer and fewer goods and services are produced within the family, and more and more are produced by specialized private firms, the government, or other public institutions. The question is how far should this process of specialization and com-modification go?

Although Boserup did not answer this question directly, she did argue that all contemporary societies are in a process of transition whereby sub-sistence production within the home will be (eventually) supplanted by specialized production for exchange. In her view, reproductive labor is not and should not be looked at as analytically distinct because work is work. This is not a trivial issue, and in many ways Boserup anticipated the con-temporary debates about welfare-state policies, especially as they relate to the provision of childcare and eldercare.

It is also important to note that Boserup's conception of development mirrors the processes and transitions that occurred in Europe and North America. In this she is not alone. Most development economists (this was an interesting point of tangency between mainstream and Marxist econo-mists) agreed that the development of the Third World would mimic that of the First. In other words, the processes of industrialization and modern-ization that characterized the West embodied inevitable and universal stages that the rest of the world had to pass through to develop. The path from nomadic farming, to peasant landholding, to small artisan enter-prises, to industrial capitalism was inevitable. Nations and peoples could be helped through these stages by experts from the World Bank, the United Nations, and other international development agencies.

Gender, Debt, and Development

In the decades of the 1960s and 1970s development agencies like the World Bank financed massive, large-scale industrial projects encouraging nations to build high-technology factories and huge hydroelectric systems to provide energy to growing urban centers. Development agencies also encouraged the introduction of large-scale mechanized farming to increase agricultural productivity. As yields per acre rose, this increased crop supplies and drove down market prices. Falling output prices pushed subsistence farmers off the land, while export-oriented plantation monoculture expanded.

This process was typical of the Green Revolution, which championed the widespread use of new hybrid seeds to increase farming yields. The new seed types, unlike traditional crops, required massive amounts of fertilizer and water. Subsistence farmers could rarely afford the fertilization and irrigation needed to cultivate these crops, but large plantations could. The Green Revolution promised more rapid growth and prosperity for all, but these did not materialize. Instead in many instances the Green Revolution sparked a decline in the production of food for domestic consumption, widespread migrations of men from the countryside to the cities in search of employment, and a significant rise in the number of poor, female-headed households.[21] By the early 1980s these problems were compounded by what came to be known as the Third World debt crisis.

The conditions for the Third World debt crisis of the 1980s were put in place during the 1970s. The steep rise in the price of oil that took place in 1973 and 1979 fattened the bank accounts of the oil-exporting nations. The accumulation of these proceeds, called petrodollars, in international banks allowed the bankers to go on a lending spree, ignoring virtually all known principles of sound lending policy.[22] Simply put, in the 1970s the world's financial markets were flush with cash, demand for loans in the Western economies was weak, and real interest rates were extremely low. Governments and entrepreneurs in the Third World countries sought financing for extravagant development projects, and the international financial community was happy to oblige.[23] The net result was that by the 1980s the poor and middle-income countries were deeply mired in international debt.

In the 1980s the economic climate changed with serious repercussions for the international balance sheets of the export-dependent Third World nations. In the 1980s the industrialized economies were in recession, the prices of basic commodities (grains, coffee, sugar, and the like) were falling, and interest rates were rising. The interest on Third World nations' debts rose at the same time that their foreign export earnings fell. As if these problems were not serious enough, double-digit inflation and badly managed, often corrupt, public sectors further undermined economic recovery. In this situation many Third World countries were simply unable to meet the payments on their international loans. The crisis came to a head in 1982 when Mexico announced that it was close to defaulting on its $800 million foreign debt. Other countries soon followed suit. These nations faced a difficult choice. If they defied the international financial community and defaulted on their debts, they would lose the opportunity to borrow in the future. Or they could accept the stringent conditions imposed by the lending agencies—structural adjustments—for debt rescheduling and payment.[24]

Structural adjustment policies (SAPs) are austerity programs implemented in indebted countries as a condition of receiving the additional loans necessary to meet debt obligations and avoid default. SAPs were designed and implemented just as economists and politicians rejected the belief that government planning (with help from development experts) was good for economic development. In the old view, tradition was seen as the principle impediment to economic development. In the new view, government intervention in markets—including public works projects, public support for health and education systems, and income redistribution—is the main problem. This shift in thinking reflects the influence of neoliberalism. Proponents of neoliberalism advocate a restricted role for national governments and promote market-oriented policies such as free trade, deregulation, and the privation of social services.

Reflecting this thinking, SAPs were premised on the notion that countries could return to economic health and repair their economies if and only if they reduced the size and influence of government on economic activity and opened all their markets to international economic forces. SAPs called for the reorganization of the economy: nations were to increase their exports and decrease their imports. As their foreign exchange balances rose, they would be able to meet debt repayment schedules, and as their debt was reduced, economic growth would accelerate. To these ends countries were required to devalue their currencies to encourage exports, make substantial cuts in public sector spending to reduce the size of the government sector, remove subsidies and price supports to eliminate interference in markets, and shift resources toward the production of goods for export rather than domestic consumption.

It is certainly true that policy changes were needed in Third World countries. Borrowed funds were often wasted by politically powerful and corrupt elites. Some development projects were ill-conceived. Third World rulers were encouraged to spend billions on weapons, and billions more ended up in the Swiss bank accounts of arms merchants, politicians, and drug dealers.[25] Moreover, most Third World countries are characterized by extreme inequalities of income, wealth, and status. This results in what the economists Juan Antonio Morales and Jeffrey Sachs have called fiscal indiscipline.[26] When powerful, high-income groups refuse to bear their share of the tax burden needed to maintain basic public sector activities, the government is forced to borrow (deficit finance) to keep roads passable, electricity flowing, hospitals open, schools operating, and the militaries armed.

Borrowing is the easy way out in this situation. But when debt service becomes unsustainable, and the IMF steps in, the poor are left to pay for the ruinous policies of the well-to-do elites, and the public programs upon which they depended are eliminated. The poverty, hardship, and deprivations caused by SAPs fall disproportionately on the shoulders of women and children because women comprise a disproportionate share of the poor. Under the conditions imposed by SAPs, women's work burdens increase: they have to work longer hours to earn the same income, they have to do more household labor because public supports are gone, and they have to work harder to get food since more food is directed to export markets.[27]

Feminist economists recognize the gendered effects of the debt crisis and structural adjustment. Many believe that the women in development (WID) framework, informed by Boserup's work, is not adequate for theorizing these new problems. The question for WID practitioners and scholars was how to integrate women into existing development processes. They did not question the underlying view that equated development with Western-style modernization or the Anglo-European gender division of labor. Women's subordination was seen as the result of conflicts between individual women and men, not the result of the impact of globalization on the complex intersections of gender, race, class, and nationality. Gender and development (GAD) emerged as a new framework for addressing the economic bases of the structural problems facing poor women in the global South.

The GAD framework, which emerged during the 1980s, takes the social construction of gender and its interconnections with class, race, ethnicity, and nationality as its starting point. In this view, gender is a relational term, referring to the differing roles, rights, and opportunities assigned to women and men. Women's subordination can be understood as a consequence of a gender division of labor that assigns them to reproductive tasks. (As discussed in chapter 3, the gender division of labor has significant consequences for families and for the economy as a whole.) The GAD approach illuminates unequal power relations between women and men and facilitates an examination of all social, political, cultural, and economic structures from a gender perspective. The implication is that all economic policies and programs are likely to have asymmetric impact on women and men since they occupy different social locations. Gender analyses highlight asymmetric effects of economic and social policies that are hidden by conventional theorizing.

For example, GAD theorists Diane Elson and Lourdes Benería demonstrate that macroeconomic models that treat labor like non-produced inputs such as land are misleading. Diane Elson argues that the implicit assumption in such models is that the work necessary to maintain and reproduce the labor force, what has come to be known as caring labor, will be forthcoming independent of its valuation and compensation. When feminist analysis is applied to SAPs, this assumption is revealed and demonstrates that the full economic costs of structural adjustment were seriously underestimated. The bulk of these costs fall mainly on women and girls as they increase their paid and unpaid working hours.

Structural adjustment required government spending cutbacks on health, education, and other social services. As public provisioning was reduced, families had to provide these services for themselves or go without them altogether. Costs were shifted from the monetized public sector to the nonmonetized household sector. Policymakers assumed that there was an unlimited supply of women's labor available to compensate for the reduction in public sector social services. Since the value of household labor is not officially counted, these costs were hidden.[28]

Although the costs were hidden, the facts are not. The unavoidable conclusion is that SAPs have failed to help poor countries. Today, the majority of middle- and low-income countries are still weighed down by international debt obligations. That this debt can never be repaid is also coming to be recognized. At this count there are forty-one heavily indebted poor countries (HIPCs), most of which are in Africa. In 1999, the leaders of the G8 (Canada, France, Germany, Italy, Japan, Russia, the United Kingdom, and the United States) endorsed the HIPC Initiative. The initiative built on the Jubilee 2000 movement that was an international campaign to pressure the leaders of the leading industrial nations (the G8) to cancel the unpayable debts of the poorest countries by the year 2000. Research by Oxfam found that the HIPC Initiative will not resolve the debt crisis of the world's poorest countries since it is too little too late.[29] The entire initiative remains tied to IMF structural adjustment conditions, and like other debt relief efforts it is designed to bail out the creditors, not the region's poor.

Although SAPs are a failure, a few of the middle-income countries have had some success emerging from poverty and debt. These countries, mainly but not exclusively, in Southeast Asia are known as the newly industrializing countries (NICs). South Korea, Singapore, Hong Kong, Taiwan, Mexico, and Brazil all pursued what are known as export-led development strategies. Following the advice of the World Bank and the IMF, these countries opened themselves to world trade to generate export earnings. Simultaneously they opened their financial markets to international investors to attract large inflows of private capital. This capital was used to finance export-led development strategies, the most significant form of which involves subcontracting in export-processing/free-trade zones.

Factories without Borders

Free trade is not a new idea. Indeed, it's been at the heart of mainstream economics for a long time. The idea is that different countries have different natural resources, labor force talents and skills, and industrial capacities. Due to these differences, some countries can produce certain goods at relatively lower costs than others. Every country will benefit if it specializes in the production of those goods and services where it has the largest relative cost advantage (i.e., faces the lowest relative production costs) and trades for the others.[30] This is the principle of comparative advantage, and it provides a theoretical and rhetorical justification for free trade.

Free trade is, however, somewhat of a misnomer. In practice the statutes and regulations that govern international trade fill countless volumes and vast libraries. Trade agreements—the formal, negotiated rule and regulations guiding how and what nations can trade with each other—can be multilateral (like the WTO), regional (like the North American Free Trade Agreement, or NAFTA), or bilateral (between two countries) agreements. These agreements have made it easier for transnational corporations to move their relatively labor-intensive production processes to poor, low-wage countries in the Global South. These poorer countries, so the story goes, have a comparative advantage in assembly line production. Since wages are low in poor countries (since water is falling from the sky when it rains), internationalizing production benefits poor nations because employment and export production will rise, increasing national income and economic growth. This sanguine state of affairs also benefits transnational stockholders since the company can now produce at lower costs. Not to be left out are First World consumers who gratefully purchase the goods at their lower prices. Even a cursory examination of the facts, however, casts doubt on this Panglossian conclusion.

One of the ways that countries attract foreign capital is through the development of special geographic areas called free trade zones (FTZs) or export-processing zones (EPZs). The *maquiladoras* on the U.S.-Mexican border are well-known examples. Foreign factories import components for assembly and then export the finished, or nearly finished, products. The owners of the firms that do the product assembly are not required to pay tariffs on the unassembled goods when they are imported or the assembled goods when they are exported. In addition to offering tax-free imports and exports, governments attract foreign investors to their EPZs by subsidizing infrastructure support services such as water and electricity and exempting employers from labor laws and other regulations. In the words of the government of Bangladesh, "the primary objective of an EPZ is to provide special areas where potential investors would find a congenial investment climate, free from *cumbersome procedures*."[31] Similarly, the Zimbabwe government tells us "[the EPZ's] highly streamlined investment facilitation framework allows an investor to set up operations without *unnecessary delays*. Its business is to help Zimbabwe develop into a value-added, technology driven, export-oriented economy."[32]

Transnational corporations can internationalize their production in two ways. The first involves actually opening new factories in developing countries like Mexico or Indonesia. This is called foreign direct investment (FDI), and research shows that most, around 80 percent, takes place between rich countries.[33] Thus FDI is relatively rare in the developing countries. A far more common way for transnational corporations to carry out international production limits their involvement to the beginning and end of the product chain. That is, the transnational carries out the research needed to design the products and also the distribution and marketing needed to get them into consumers' homes. The actual manufacturing, which is the relatively labor-intensive part, is contracted out to factories in countries where wages are low, unions are either weak or nonexistent, and environmental regulations are lax. Often these small to medium size factories are not owned and managed by the transnational corporation but rather by local entrepreneurs.

The feasibility of export-led industrialization is based on the availability of cheap labor to produce goods for export. In practice this means that export-led industrialization strategies require significant pools of women willing to work for low wages at monotonous, often hazardous, tasks.[34] All over the world, most of the workers on the factory floor are female, while the supervisors and managers are male. This occupational segregation leads to a significant wage gap between women and men in the newly industrializing countries. As Table 6.1 illustrates, women make up anywhere from 31 percent to 47 percent of the nonagricultural labor force, and the gender wage gap ranges from 52 percent to 80 percent.

It's important to point out that cheap labor means more than extremely low wages. Cheap labor also refers to the absence of health and safety protections, employee benefits, and social insurance to cover retirement, unemployment, or worker disability.[35] Cheap labor is also flexible labor: the work requires minimal training, the labor contracts are short-term, and there is no employment security. Around the world—in rich nations and poor—irregular labor force participation and a willingness to work for low

TABLE 6.1.   Female Share of Labor Force and Gender Wage Gap for Ten Selected Countries (%)[a]

	Female Share (%)[b]	Gender Wage Gap (%)
Botswana	47	52
Brazil	45	61
Eritrea	31	66
Hong Kong (China)	45	66
Korea (Republic)	38	59
Malaysia	36	63
Mexico	37	70
Philippines	41	80
Singapore	45	59
Thailand	47	68

Source: Data from UN Statistics Division, "The World's Women, 2000: Trends and Statistics"; Development Fund for Women (UNIFEM), "Progress of the World's Women, 2002."
[a]Latest availability data, 1995–2001.
[b]Nonagricultural employment.

wages at jobs that do not require extensive training and carry little opportunity for advancement are characteristics associated with women workers.[36] The perception is that women in the developing world are docile, passive, and highly union resistant and hence easily subject to the discipline required by factory work.[37] Thus, women's attractiveness to transnational capital stems from their subordinate gender status. Yet poor working women all over the world challenge this perception. At great personal cost, often risking their lives, they fight to unionize and to force employers to provide more humane working conditions. The perception that women in the global South are docile reflects their extremely limited options for earning income rather than any intrinsic gender traits.

Some argue that globalization entails a conversion of all labor to the conditions of female labor. They see a future where the global economy promises jobs that are more insecure, more flexible, and even more poorly paid. As Guy Standing notes, the proportion of jobs requiring craft skills acquired through apprenticeship has declined, labor market regulations have been eroded, and unionized, full-time, stable jobs are disappearing. These jobs were traditionally the preserve of men who belonged to the aristocracy of labor. Standing refers to them as market insiders.[38] Whatever we call them, they are becoming an endangered species as more men, as well as women, are pushed into insecure forms of labor. In Mexico, for example, large numbers of men are now doing what was once considered women's work: they are low-wage employees doing work that requires little training in factories producing textiles and electronics.[39] The contemporary situation of workers in the global South reminds us just how easy it is to exploit labor when there are few options for earning a livelihood, when there is an unlimited supply of people willing to work for subsistence wages, and when the power of the state to quash labor organizations is virtually unchecked by national or international institutions.

Globalization, and the technological change that fuels it, has created a situation in which only a minority of workers need specialist skills that require training and investment in human capital.[40] The majority of people are consigned to jobs that require only rote learning and for which docility and malleability are the most important worker attributes.[41] As early as the 1840s critics of capitalism talked about the division between manual and mental labor and decried the spread of mind-numbing work. Today, the global division of labor along these lines is becoming more not less pronounced. Sadly, after nearly one hundred years of progress we are seeing the reemergence of these labor conditions in the developed world as well. Here, sweatshops, low-paid domestic labor, and menial, dead-end service sector jobs are now very likely to be the fate of many in the world's largest, most cosmopolitan centers.

The Marketization of Governance

One of the important results of the liberalization of trade and finance is that developing countries now compete with each other to attract foreign capital to finance export-led development. Beginning in the mid-1980s, and continuing till the present, the IMF, the World Bank, and the WTO urged countries all over the world to open their economies to the free flows of goods, services, and international financial capital. Only one commodity can't follow the whims of the market: people. People, unlike goods, services, and money, are constrained by border police and immigration officials. The asymmetry of free-flowing commodities and capital, combined with the legal barriers to legal migration, further increases the power of transnational corporations to seek profits and disregard human costs. Nonetheless, free trade, capital mobility, privatization, and decreased government regulation of transnational corporate activities were the panacea held out by elite policymakers as the solution to poverty and underdevelopment. Because this view reflects the disproportionate influence of the United States on international institutions, this conceptual framework is called the Washington consensus.[42]

The SAPs that were imposed in the 1980s were one manifestation of this framework. The ways that multilateral and regional trade agreements are constructed and enforced is another. These agreements, like SAPs, ignore gender equity and other social concerns and implicitly assume that women will continue to provide the caring labor necessary for social reproduction, regardless of the additional burdens placed on them.

The scope of contemporary trade agreements far exceeds the movement of goods and capital. Indeed they are replacing democratically enacted laws and regulations on the national level with international edicts. This has been referred to as marketization of governance.[43] The rights of citizens to enact laws protecting public health, workers' rights, or the environment are secondary to the "rights" of corporations to expand their markets and earn profits. The WTO, for example, has no minimum standards regarding health, safety, workers' rights, or the environment but does have the judicial power to dismantle national standards regarding these things.

This power stems from the fact that trade agreements do more than just eliminate tariffs on imported goods and services. They also require nations to eliminate what are called nontariff trade barriers. Nontariff trade barriers are national regulations that prohibit imports that do not meet certain content standards, licensing requirements, or safety and environmental regulations. These regulations may be deemed barriers to trade under the rules of the WTO. For example, the WTO has required Europe to allow the importation of hormone-treated beef despite well-founded concerns about its health effects, and the United States has been forced to abandon its efforts to outlaw the sale of tuna caught with nets that endanger turtles and other fish.[44] When national standards about content, safety, and the environment are replaced by international standards (set by supranational organizations and negotiated in secret), trade "harmonization" is said to take place. George Orwell was prescient: under the rules of globalization, war is peace, and harmony is dissonance on a world scale.

Trade rules, which also apply to investment, prohibit national governments from giving preferential treatment to domestic industries and can even require that governments compensate corporations for any loss of profits caused by changes in public policies. NAFTA provides a case in point. It explicitly allows Canadian, U.S., or Mexican investors to sue the host government if their companies' assets, including the intangible property rights of expected profits, are damaged by laws or regulations. The case of *Methanex v. United States* is an excellent example. In this case the California legislature voted to ban methyl tertiary-butyl ether (MTBE), a carcinogenic fuel additive. Methanex, the Canadian company that manufactures MTBE, sued the U.S. government for $970 million in compensation for the damage California was inflicting on its future profits.[45] Cases such as these do not go to court but rather are heard by secret arbitration panels. This case was no different. It was eventually settled, and California has dropped its opposition to MTBE. A similar situation occurred when the Canadian government proposed requiring all cigarettes to be sold in plain black-and-white packages with vivid warnings about the health effects of smoking. Cigarette companies in the United States threatened to sue, and although the suit was dropped, the Canadian government dropped its plan to regulate cigarette packaging.[46]

These examples are all from wealthy, industrialized countries with the legal, financial, and political resources to resist corporate abuses. Consider then how much more dire the situation is for developing countries without such resources and with the urgent need to create jobs. The environmental degradation of the global South is well-known: severe air pollution in major metropolitan areas, water pollution from the runoff of pesticides and fertilizer in the countryside, deforestation and soil erosion, and the loss of animal and plant habitats. The marketization of governance and unchecked power of transnational corporations only exacerbate these problems.

Privatization, in particular the privatization of services, is another key component of the marketization of governance. Health, education, and water services are all targets of transnational corporations who view them as profit-making opportunities rather than as services that states are obligated to provide for their citizens. Privatization is a key component of SAPs, and so as a condition for debt relief, many poor countries were forced to abandon public spending on water, health, and education. This has created opportunities for private, for-profit companies to come in and sell these services as commodities. As a result, many people who lack the income to purchase these basic services must make do without them.

The trend in water service is particularly troubling. Water, which is an absolute necessity for human life, and access to it should be a human right, is becoming increasingly scarce. According to United Nations estimates over one billion people do not have access to clean water and two and half billion do not have adequate sanitation and sewage. In the face of this scarcity, water is becoming just another commodity to enhance corporate profitability. The World Bank provides financing for water privatization. The WTO allows national laws protecting public water systems to be challenged as trade barriers, and the IMF has required countries to adopt water privatization as a condition for loan renewal.[47]

The consequences of privatization, combined with the protections offered to transnational corporate profits, raise particularly troubling problems for all citizens concerned with gender equity and progressive public policies. As has been shown time and time again, women are generally responsible for providing healthcare, education, safe food, and clean water for their families, tasks that are made far more difficult by the privatization of social services. Feminist economist Marjorie Griffin Cohen points out that national governments are increasingly reluctant to subsidize national services providing childcare, healthcare, and so forth because some of these services are provided by private, for-profit companies who may charge that government-subsidized services constitute nontariff trade barriers and threaten their profits.[48] Likewise, Farah Fosse, of the International Gender and Trade Network, points out that women make up the majority of service workers. Many of these jobs are in the public sector, which provides relatively better job security and benefits. When public sector employment is reduced, women lose good jobs. In addition, affirmative action programs and other preferences for marginalized workers may be considered trade restrictions further limiting women's opportunities.[49] And, of course, when education is privatized, particularly in the poorest countries, girls are pulled out of school first.

The liberalization of international finance is another aspect of the marketization of governance. Countries were persuaded to open their financial markets—their markets for stocks, bonds, and currency—to foreign speculators working for large institutional investment firms. Money managers send speculative balances around the world seeking the highest returns. This is called portfolio investment. Managers of mutual funds, hedge funds, and pension funds can buy and sell at a whim the financial assets—stocks, bonds, and currency—of other countries, including developing countries.[50] This has drastically changed the structure of debt in the developing countries. In 1981, before the Third World debt crisis erupted, 77 percent of the foreign investment in developing countries was financed by stable, long-term, bank loans. By 1993, 74 percent of the foreign investment in developing countries was portfolio investment.

Portfolio investment can induce widespread economic instability because capital is as free to leave as it was to arrive. Moreover, the investment decisions by money managers are not made on the basis of sound calculations about the profitability of particular ventures like new factories, infrastructure, or housing. They are instead gambles, pure financial speculation. The current term for this phenomena is casino capitalism.[51] As early as 1936 the economist John Maynard Keynes was critical of casino capitalism. Students of economic history may remember his famous quote, "when the capital development of the country becomes a by-product of the activities of a casino, the job is likely to be ill-done."[52]

Casino capitalism fuels speculative bubbles that always burst. When they do, the people who borrowed the money and enjoyed its benefits are rarely the same people who are left to pick up the tab. The Asian financial crisis is a good example. It began in Thailand during the late 1990s. Large amounts of unregulated and unrestricted capital flowed into the country in the form of short-term loans. These loans financed the construction of shopping malls, office buildings, and apartments, fueling a speculative bubble that pushed real estate prices above their sustainable values. When the bubble burst, and speculative capital fled, the results were predictable. The *baht* (Thailand's currency) fell radically in value, the Thai economy

115

went into recession, and unemployment skyrocketed. Again the IMF bailed out the international financiers and left the Thai citizens saddled with more international debt and a deeply devalued currency. Once again, the consequences of financial speculation were gendered: the poor suffered the most—women make up the largest proportion of the poor, and women's work burdens increased even as male unemployment increased.[53]

Conclusion

This chapter has covered a wide terrain both chronologically and conceptually from the origins of development, to gender and development, to the marketization of governance. We have been quite critical overall of the effects of globalization on the lives and material well-being of the majority of the world's population, and we have stressed that women and girls are the ones who suffer the most from neoliberal policies. The rights of corporations to cross borders and earn profits are enshrined in law, while the rights of citizens to protect their health, their environment, and their economic futures are swept aside. Our critique does not, however, make us protectionists or isolationists. What we are arguing against is the marketization of governance, the dismantling of publicly provided social services, and the unchecked power of elites to use people and natural resources without regard for the real social costs of their actions.

One significant social cost of globalization has been its pernicious effect on caring labor. To the extent that globalization encourages the expansion of markets, it has penalized the providers of care. Countries are able to stimulate economic growth by shifting production from unpaid care services to the production of market commodities. This is precisely what has happened as developing countries have pursued industrialization policies that rely on the labor supply of poor women willing to work for low wages and few benefits.

Women's increased labor force participation means that the care services they traditionally provided must now be purchased in the market or provided by the state.[54] As discussed in previous chapters, relatively affluent women are able to purchase care services from the market. Women in poor households, on the other hand, have to shoulder the burdens themselves. The poorer the household, the greater the burden. In parts of Asia and Africa where male migration from rural areas to towns and cities is prevalent, women are left to take care of the children and elderly. Absent support from either husbands or the state, these women face triple burdens of caring labor, farming, and wage employment.[55]

One of the ways that women are coping with greater demands on their labor time is to participate in the informal sector of the economy. There they work as domestics, as home-based pieceworkers, as street vendors, and as sex workers. This sort of work is flexible and allows women to combine earning a living with caring for their families. It is also insecure and poorly paid. We turn to this topic in our next chapter.

7. Dickens Redux

Globalization and the
Informal Economy

All over the world poor women, children, and men eke out an existence as street vendors, home-based pieceworkers, domestic servants, gardeners, and sex workers. When you step off a tourist bus in the global South, street vendors selling their wares eagerly meet you. Street musicians serenade travelers waiting for the metro in Paris, Berlin, London, and Amsterdam. In the early morning suburban joggers in Southern California run past Latina women and men hustling to their jobs as maids, nannies, and gardeners. And an evening stroll through the red light district finds sex workers advertising their trade. All this work takes place in what economists call the informal sector. But not all work in the informal sector is so visible. Hidden in homes and sweatshops around the world, poorly paid workers sew clothes, weave rugs, stitch soccer balls, and assemble electronics.

The informal sector is the unorganized and unregulated sector of the economy. Workers and businesses in the informal sector generally operate outside the official rules and regulations of the state. According to the International Labour Organization (ILO), the overwhelming majority, from 60 to 66 percent, of informal sector workers are women.[1] Women often work in the informal sector because it is characterized by extremely small levels of start-up capital and minimal skill requirements and does not require access to organized markets or channels of distribution. Workers in the informal sector work in unsafe, crowded conditions and earn very low wages. Because the informal sector is so large and diverse, huge variations exist among and within countries. Still the ILO concludes that the informal sector is expanding: it is already large in developing countries, it is growing rapidly in the transition economies, and it is (re)emerging in all the industrialized countries.[2]

The size of the informal economy is quite large. According to the World Bank, the informal economy in Africa is estimated at 42 percent of GDP in 1999–2000, and in Latin America it is 41 percent of GDP. It comprises between 19 and 67 percent in the transition economies and 20 percent in the Western industrialized nations.[3] These are, of course, rough estimates. It is particularly difficult to measure the informal economy since some of it is illegal, most of it is unlicensed and unregulated, and many of the people who participate in it are clandestine immigrants who are not allowed to work in the official economy.

The emergence of the informal sector in industrialized countries is particularly interesting. Feminist geographer Saskia Sassen argues that this phenomenon is best understood in the context of the structural changes in the economy that accompany globalization: increased income inequality and the restructuring of consumption in both high-income and very low-income groups.[4] An expansion of demand for cheap goods and services is fueled by growth in the low-income population, and the expansion of the informal sector helps meet that demand. The many gypsy cabs, unlicensed group day-care providers, and street food vendors in any large city are examples of the ways that the informal sector works for low-income people. At the same time consumption patterns among high-income groups are characterized by custom-produced designer clothing, luxury homes, gourmet food, and many personal services. High-income households hire limousine services, live-in nannies, and private cooks. These examples illustrate how the needs and wants of the high-income people are coterminous with the expansion of the informal sector.

Not for Love or Pleasure: Sex Work in the Global Economy

Consumption patterns vary by both income status and by gender. The sex industry is a paradigmatic example of gendered consumption: the needs and wants of men create the demand for sexual services from women, men, and sometimes children.

Prostitution has been the subject of heated debates among feminists. Some see it as inherently sexist, degrading, and humiliating. In this view, prostitution rationalizes male dominance and encourages violence against women, and it should be abolished. Others have seen it as a liberating choice. In this view women should be able to use their bodies as they wish, including selling their sexual services. As feminist economists, we take a different view, one that regards the sale of sexual services as a type of work.

Our interest is in understanding the working conditions of the industry and its place in the global economy. To emphasize this point of view, we use the term sex worker rather than prostitute.[5]

Like other forms of feminized labor, sex work has been affected by the forces of globalization. The economic hardships and dislocations that have accompanied globalization have created conditions where sex work is an increasingly viable option. For many young women, sex work is likely to be better paid, more flexible, and less time-consuming than factory work. Feminist sociologist Wendy Chapkis cautions us to remember that prostitution is often chosen from a desperately limited range of options.[6] Likewise, feminist economist Jean Pyle argues that deciding whether or not to engage in sex work is not made in isolation from broader economic conditions.[7] The sex industry is flourishing because the global liberalization of trade and finance has eased international travel for sex workers and sex customers. Moreover, structural adjustment policies (SAPs) require countries to generate foreign exchange earnings, and sex tourism, by catering to men from the rich nations, is one way to do this. Sex tourism is a growing industry.

One of the particularly troubling aspects of this trade is child prostitution, a growing worldwide problem. In virtually every country, children are engaged in commercial sexual activity. The United Nations Children's Fund (UNICEF) finds that over one hundred million children worldwide are sexually exploited.[8] The root causes of child prostitution are poverty, lack of economic opportunities, and failures of national and international policies to protect children. Moreover, there are no international agreements that prevent governments from generating foreign exchange earnings through the sale of sexual services.

A recent report by the ILO examined the sex industries in Indonesia, Malaysia, the Philippines, and Thailand, where commercial sex has become increasingly important following the economic hardships caused by the Asian financial crisis.[9] In addition to the sex workers themselves, the industry supports a wide variety of other workers including managers, procurers, cleaners, waitresses, cashiers, and security guards. Despite the difficulty in obtaining precise statistics, the ILO estimates that several million people earn a living either directly or indirectly through the sex industry. The industry accounts for anywhere from 2 to 14 percent of national income in these four countries, and these revenues are crucially important to the economic well-being of many outside the industry. In Thailand, for example, close to $300 million is transferred annually to rural families by women working in the sex industry in urban areas.

The report also shows that financial hard times affect women and men differently. Widespread layoffs in manufacturing and services are likely to drive women into the sex industry as opportunities for paid employment decline. The net effect is an increase in the supply of sex workers. On the other hand, the demand for sexual services by men is not much affected by unemployment or the decline in national income. Consequently, the total demand for sexual services may increase in the aftermath of economic crises if hard-hit nations devalue their currencies and make sex tourism even cheaper.[10]

Whether or not sex work is a good or bad job depends on working conditions that vary widely along the lines of class, race, ethnicity, and nationality. The feminist sociologist Kamala Kempadoo points out that in general white sex workers have safer, more comfortable, higher-paid work, while persons of mixed ancestry, Asians, and Latinas form a middle class, and black women are disproportionately the poorest sex workers in the most dangerous street environments.[11] This can be partly explained by the colonial ideology that eroticized women of color. One of the ways that the colonial system produced a racialized gender ideology was to link inferiority to heightened sexuality. Thus the inferiority of indigenous women was constructed, in part, by seeing them as more sexual than white European women. As "primitives," sex was "natural" to them.[12] As we have demonstrated repeatedly, that which is deemed natural does not require the same compensation and prestige as that which is not.

This dynamic presents an important challenge to feminists interested in improving the working conditions in the sex industry and protecting the rights of sex workers. It goes back to the perennial problem in feminism, which is how to reconcile the often conflicting interests of women who are in different social and economic locations in a way that will create a collective agenda for change. Today, many women are forced out of economic hardship to migrate. As we have seen in earlier chapters, many of them end up as domestic workers. Many also end up as sex workers, and they are not always well received by their more fortunate colleagues who enjoy the status of citizenship. For example, in the Netherlands, where sex work is legal, Asian, African, and Eastern European women are prohibited from working in licensed brothels and are consigned to working in illegal establishments or streetwalking. Moreover, the Dutch sex workers do not allow illegal migrants to join their lobbying organization, Red Thread. They see the migrants as a threat to the wages and benefits of Dutch workers.[13] Of course, the issues raised here in the context of the sex industry are much the same as debates about the influx of migrants on any other sort of labor market.

The Dutch case is also interesting because it sheds light on the debates between legalizing prostitution and decriminalizing it. Legalization generally entails regulating and taxing the industry. Such laws are often made to protect the health of the prostitutes' customers and increase state revenues. State regulation of prostitution is an old story. Wherever armies are sent, prostitution is tolerated, if not encouraged. Indeed, this is the origin of the term hookers, which refers to General Hooker's policy during the U.S. Civil War (1861–65) of bringing prostitutes along with the troops. Regulations that required sex workers to undergo regular medical exams were supposed to safeguard the soldiers' health. These regulations put the responsibility for safe sex on the sex workers rather than on the customers. The regulations were often intrusive and humiliating, so feminists concerned with the rights of prostitutes argued for decriminalization rather than legalization. Feminists emphasize the importance of protecting the health of sex workers as well as their customers and point out that sex workers, like all workers, need protection from violence and coercion. From this perspective it is clear that the issues facing sex workers are not terribly different from the issues facing other workers in the informal economy.

Decriminalization is, in our view, a better way to protect sex workers, their customers, and the general public. The critical questions are how to understand the gender-specific needs of women (especially around childcare, pregnancy, STDs, sexual harassment, and violence), and how to create labor organizations that are not based on hierarchies of race, gender, class, ethnicity, or nationality. One might argue that given the dire problem with HIV/AIDS transmission it makes sense to regulate prostitution to stop the spread of disease. This only makes sense if it works. The problem is that mandatory medical examinations that make it illegal for women with sexually transmitted diseases to sell sex will not stop the spread of sexual diseases. Slowing or stopping the spread of STDs will happen when more people use condoms.[14] Oftentimes poverty, customers' demands, or workplace prohibitions prevent sex workers from using prophylactics. When sex worker rights are protected, they will be able to require their customers to practice safe sex.

Protecting the rights of all sex workers, including both legal and illegal immigrants, is also an important strategy in combating global trafficking in women. Here we define trafficking as the illegal transport or sale of human beings to exploit their labor. According to Human Rights Watch, the trafficking of women and children into bonded sweatshop labor, forced marriage, forced prostitution, domestic servitude, and other kinds of work is a global phenomenon.[15] Victims are coerced through deception, fraud, intimidation, physical force, and debt bondage. Women are placed in abusive conditions of employment and forced to pay off their "debts" before they receive their wages or gain their freedom. Human Rights Watch advocates treat this problem as a human rights violation and pursue legal sanctions against the traffickers. The trafficking problem points to the need to regard sex work as a legitimate kind of work and therefore create a climate wherein sex workers know they can seek legal redress without fear of legal sanctions or deportation. Here the issues are not so different than in other parts of the informal economy, and particularly in the case of domestic workers.

Maids, Mothers, and Workers

One of the ways that affluent women reconcile the often conflicting demands of work and family is by hiring domestic help. Rising global inequality has made this easier as women from poor countries migrate to richer ones in search of the incomes necessary to support themselves and their families. Data suggest that women constitute half the world's immigrants, and in some countries they account for as much as 80 to 90 percent of the total.[16] A woman's decision to migrate is motivated by financial and economic conditions. Lack of local employment opportunities combined with the prospect of much higher wages in wealthier countries makes migration an attractive option to many.

Domestic work is difficult work. Domestics work, and often live, in private households. They are isolated, their work is unregulated, and they are subject to abuse by their employers. Long workdays, low wages, and poor living conditions, along with verbal, physical, and sexual abuse are often their lot. According to a study by Human Rights Watch the median hourly wage for domestic workers in the United States was $2.14 after deductions for room and board. The median workday was fourteen hours, and many workers were not free to leave their employers' homes without permission.[17] Domestic workers are vulnerable to such abuses because they lack the protection and information that would allow them to defend themselves. Fear of deportation and unemployment keep many of them locked into abusive situations.[18] In addition, loneliness and worry may be their constant companions because they have often left their own children behind.

Domestic work is low-status work, and immigrant domestic workers are unlikely to be invited to participate in economic policy discussions with world leaders. Perhaps they should be. Governments have a significant interest in the economics of migrant domestics since for some nations migration reduces unemployment and increases the remittance of foreign exchange.[19] Migrants typically send a portion of their earnings home to their families. These remittances are important for two reasons. First, they allow governments to reduce public spending for social services that benefit poor families. Second, these remittances are an important source of foreign exchange that can be used to service foreign debts. The host governments also benefit since immigrant women's low-wage labor allows them to avoid providing public support for childcare and eldercare.[20]

Of course, childcare and eldercare are needed by both the rich and the poor. The demand for domestic services is not only from upscale professionals but also from single mothers who need affordable childcare, elderly people on pension incomes, and two-earner working-class families.[21] These last three groups can afford a quite different pay scale than can upscale professionals and so will have different standards for their employees. Since this is an informal, unregulated market, those who can afford to pay the most are free to discriminate on the basis of race, ethnicity, age, sexual orientation, good looks, or any other feature they wish. It would be very surprising therefore, if hiring practices did not mirror societal prejudices and stereotypes. Young, attractive, light-skinned women will be found in the top tiers of the market, while women whose skins are darker, who are older, or who do not fit European beauty standards will be found toward the bottom.[22]

Microcredit, Small Enterprises, and Homework

Despite hazardous conditions and low pay, national governments and international organizations encourage women's work in the informal sector by promoting microcredit. Microcredit (sometimes referred to as microfinance) refers to extremely small loans made to poor women to enable them to start small-scale enterprises in the informal sector. The

Grameen Bank, located in Bangladesh, is the progenitor of microcredit. Small loans are made to women organized into groups called loan circles. If one woman in the circle does not repay her loan, the others in the circle are ineligible for future loans. In this way the collective liability of the group serves as collateral. The interest rate on the loans is 16 percent. The Grameen Bank boasts its successes: loan repayment rates are nearly 95 percent, and they are empowering the "poorest of the poor."[23] The microcredit phenomenon has captured the imagination of many organizations who see it as a way to transform the poor into small-scale capitalist entrepreneurs. It is promoted as an effective tool to fight poverty since it is an investment not a "handout."

Despite its rosy aura, the reality is less appealing, and the situation is more complex. It is certainly true that microcredit has been a success for many of the banks that have adopted it. The loan repayment rates are extraordinarily high. We must remember, however, that lending to the poor has long been a lucrative enterprise. Pawnshops, finance companies, and loan sharks profit handsomely when poor people find themselves desperate for cash and unable to secure regular credit. In these conditions they are forced to pay high interest rates. One would be shortsighted, indeed, to think that profitable lending to the poor was a new innovation. The real questions about microcredit are these: Does it reduce women's poverty, or does it exploit the poor? Does it empower women, or does it make them dependent upon lenders?

The evidence is mixed. Proponents of microcredit usually offer stories of individual success—women whose lives were transformed after they purchased a market stall or some simple inputs that allowed them to start handicraft production. There is no doubt that many individual poor women and their families have been helped through microcredit. There is also no question that when women take out loans, the whole family is likely to benefit and the impact on child welfare will be greater than when men take out loans.[24] At the same time, there is little evidence that microcredit has had any impact on poverty rates in the developing countries. A study commissioned by the Canadian International Development Agency (CIDA) concluded that only a small percentage of borrowers realized sustained income increases, most only realized very small gains, and the poorest benefitted the least.[25] The study also concluded that there was little relationship between loan repayment and business success.

The evidence concerning the impact of microcredit on women's empowerment is also ambiguous. According to the World Bank, microfinance empowers women by allowing them more control over household assets, more autonomy and decision-making power, greater access to participation in public life, and more control over household resources.[26] Other findings suggest that microcredit increases women's dual work burdens of market and household labor.[27] Microcredit can also increase household conflict when men rather than women control the loans. Men sometimes use women to get loans and make women responsible for paying the loans back.[28] Conflict among women can also be exacerbated because of group repayment pressures. In the repayment rules imposed by the Grameen Bank, for example, monthly payments must be made regardless of extenuating circumstances. When a woman cannot make her payments, the other members of her loan circle can force her to sell her belongings to meet her loan obligations.

Feminist economist Naila Kabeer argues that empowerment should be understood as an expansion in the range of potential choices available to women. Women's potential choices are shared by specific relationships of dependency, interdependence, and autonomy that characterize gender relations and structure the risks, incentives, and opportunities in different cultures.[29] Conceived in this way, it is possible to understand the specific circumstances under which microcredit can be empowering to women.

Although microcredit provides some benefits for individual women and their families, it does nothing to change the structural conditions that drive women into the informal sector in the first place. As an antipoverty program, microcredit fits nicely with the prevailing neoliberal ideology that defines poverty as a problem of individual failing. To solve poverty, the poor must work harder, get educated, have fewer children, and act more responsibly. Markets reward those who help themselves, and women are no exception. This rhetoric shifts poverty solutions away from collective, social efforts and onto the backs of the poor women. It should come as no surprise that microcredit solutions are gaining currency in the United States as the solution for poverty there.

Feminists need to ask if, and to what extent, does microcredit help people in the informal sector by improving their working conditions. As one commentator has noted, encouraging the growth of the informal sector sounds like advice from one of Dickens's more objectionable characters.[30] Microcredit encourages the movement of production from the factory back into the home via piecework. Indeed, one of the ways that women reconcile their responsibilities for family duties and the need to earn a wage income is by engaging in homework, and the vast majority of homeworkers are women working in their homes or in small workshops.[31] Homeworkers are generally paid by the piece not the hour. They sew garments, weave rugs, make toys, and assemble electronic components. Homeworkers, mainly women and children, face particular challenges because this work is often beyond the reach of either national or international regulations. Consequently, they often work long hours for very poor pay in unsafe, hazardous conditions.

Many firms seek to boost their profits by setting up shop in the informal economy, where they have reduced labor costs and no regulations on employment. This often takes the form of subcontracting, whereby large transnational corporations put out bids for smaller, local entrepreneurs to set up production or assembly facilities where piecework is carried out. The intermediary agents who connect local and global assembly lines are rarely held accountable for the conditions of work. They are not required to provide safe work spaces, and wages are so low that those at the end of the production chain receive pennies for every $100 of final sales. The informal economy is no oasis of equality: microentrepreneurs and small enterprises have the greatest status, prestige, and income, while homeworkers have the least. Not only are women the majority of workers in the informal economy, they are heavily represented at the bottom of it.[32]

Conclusion

The expansion of the informal sector provides many benefits to the globalized economy, which is dominated by the profit-seeking strategies of transnational corporations. But the informal sector is unlikely to solve the problems of global poverty, women's subordination, and economic insecurity. To the contrary, the growth of the informal sector actually exacerbates the feminization of poverty in part because it weakens the power of nation-states to enforce labor standards that ensure decent conditions of work. The growth of the informal economy highlights the failures of globalization. There is no way that unregulated markets will ever provide gender equity and economic security to the most vulnerable. The individualistic solutions of microcredit and entrepreneurship are not answers. While national and international policies are needed, care must be taken to craft them in ways that do not simply create bureaucracies and red tape that force more poor women, men, and children into the unprotected, unregulated informal economy.

8. The Liberated Economy

Mainstream economists claim that their conceptual building blocks are objective, value-free, and scientific. We disagree; the fundamental categories of economic analysis are not neutral with respect to existing patterns of social subordination and power.[1] The concepts of, for example, rationality and scarcity, maximization and equilibrium, commodities and exploitation, embody historically specific visions of normative masculinity, femininity, whiteness, and heterosexual orientation that are particular to the West. Indeed, the establishment of Anglo-European world dominance depended upon the creation of new patterns of social hierarchy and the intensification of old patterns of domination.

Feminist economists begin with this observation, a starting point that would not raise an eyebrow in philosophy, sociology, or the history of science. But those who practice mainstream economics deny the historical specificity of the discipline's basic concepts. Instead, mainstream economists believe that the central organizing categories of economics are a mirror of nature. Dare we point out that the commodities of everyday life do not roll off assembly lines with equilibrium prices stamped on their foreheads? Nor does a nation's income split itself in two, with wages on the one side and profits on the other, with the ebb and flow of the tides. And sunspots do not cause business cycles.[2] If economic concepts do not mirror the natural world, then these concepts must be socially constructed—in which case gender and sexuality, like race and class, matter.

Throughout this book we have stressed the connections between social constructs that assign people to particular types of work and women's subordinate economic status. We certainly hope that no readers have interpreted our advocacy for women as a call for turning the tables on men. To the contrary, our commitment is to a freer, more just world, one in which women and men regardless of social or geographic location can shape their

128

destinies by sharing power and responsibility in the workplace, the home, and the government.[3] But as discrimination and gender bias prevent women from exercising their fair share of power and responsibility, they continue to suffer disproportionately. The persistence of this economic disadvantage underscores the need for continued feminist activism and scholarship.

Even as women's participation in paid labor has increased, the feminization of labor on a global scale means that work continues to be segregated by gender, race, ethnicity, and nationality. Simultaneous with the expansion of women's participation in paid labor, we've seen a dramatic increase in income inequality in both developed and developing nations. The women and men who hold good jobs—whether as knowledge workers (workers in information technologies) in the "new" economy, or as executives and managers in traditional industries, or as professionals in the service sector—are well compensated for their labor, while other, poorly paid workers—male as well as female—assemble products or provide services necessary for the daily functioning of highly paid workers.[4] Yes, women do the majority of this supportive work. Why? Precisely because this work is feminized: it is flexible, poorly paid, monotonous, and low status. How ironic is it when social conservatives blame feminism for the erosion of masculinity when it is actually the very economic forces they celebrate—free markets, free trade, and globalization—that undermine the conditions of work and threaten all workers with the specter of feminization.

Toward an Inclusive, Egalitarian Division of Labor

The confluence of representations defines some work as women's and other work as men's. Such coding is largely, but not wholly, an effect of culture, discourse, and ideology. Generally speaking, the types of work associated with reproduction are precisely those viewed as natural, unskilled, and less than. At the same time, positions in the division of labor largely, but not completely, determine incomes. Those fortunate enough to match the characteristics needed to claim masculinity, whiteness, heterosexuality, and other markers of class privilege are assigned the most privileged positions in the division of labor, and consequently they receive high incomes, status, and power (although being a white male does not guarantee economic success). It is neither whiteness nor maleness per se that is rewarded; it is rather that positionality *vis-à-vis* the social division of labor determines how much of society's assets a person can acquire. Yet as we have argued, social location is itself an effect of representation. In this way cultural norms determine how people with various characteristics are assigned to positions in the division of labor.

Feminist economics shows how material processes of production/reproduction and cultural processes of representation shape the division of labor. This analysis reveals the need for new systems of representation in which the many identities that were defined as less than, pathological, or deviant are revalued. Recall the historical origins of the received system of representation: culturally dominant groups claimed their superiority by casting difference in terms of naturally given, hierarchical binaries. Positive traits were associated with elites, and negative traits were associated with the "other."

Because feminist economics illuminates both the cultural and material dimensions of the division of labor, it is able to link sociocultural processes of representation with political-economic processes of valorization. Divisions of labor, in all their various manifestations—manual and mental, rural and urban, agricultural and manufacturing, productive and reproductive—always mark, and thereby value and devalue, human work.

We can imagine different systems of representation, ones that acknowledge the inherent value of all human beings regardless of social location. Likewise, we can imagine an egalitarian division of labor that respects all forms of social labor and does not privilege productive over reproductive labor, creative over repetitive work, or mental over manual effort. Given the limitations of technology, there are always likely to be distasteful, monotonous, backbreaking jobs that need doing. We need to envision democratic ways of accomplishing this work that do not assign the people who do it to a life sentence of drudgery reflecting their positions in the cultural system of representation. An inclusive, egalitarian division of labor will ensure that everyone—independent of their performance of manual or mental, creative or repetitive labor—will have the opportunity to participate in the full range of productive and reproductive activities, and everyone can give as well as receive care. The conditions of work need to change to eliminate the pressures on reproduction/caring that stem from the overvaluation of production, and the status of reproduction needs to change to reduce tensions between caring and earning.

Our vision of inclusion begins from the idea that we all belong to communities and have a range of reciprocal rights, obligations, and responsibilities.[5] Institutions, and the cultural norms which support them, are the mechanisms that integrate people and groups into the social whole. In many societies today, institutions like the family, the church, and the state serve to control access to resources by privileging certain groups of people and excluding others.[6] In this way, the rules, norms, and practices of exclusion simultaneously produce difference. As we have argued throughout this book, it is precisely the enactment of such rules, norms, and practices that produce and reproduce social hierarchies. The division of labor, including being exempt from labor, is a key element in every social hierarchy. A society structured by principles of inclusion must, therefore, strive for an egalitarian division of labor. It is not enough to simply redistribute the fruits of labor. It is just as important to call into question the social institutions, practices, and political-economic structures that produce exclusion and difference in the first place.

Envisioning a society with an inclusive, egalitarian division of labor requires an approach to social analysis in which group disadvantage is not simply the result of obstacles to individual achievement. Some believe that group disadvantage, the outcome that women or people of color, for example, tend to be less well off than elite males, occurs because individuals (whether female, black, or migrant) have not been able to compete on the same terms as elite men. For them, the goal of economic and social policy is the removal of impediments to individual competitive advancement. In this view the economic system is fair if it provides equal opportunities. If, in other words, policies were enacted and enforced such that women and people of color occupied the same locations in the division of labor as elite males, then the problem of inequality would be eliminated.

But if everyone fit into the division of labor in the way that elite males do, then who would do the caring labor, the physically demanding work, and the poorly paid, monotonous tasks? Given the way that systems of representation (over)determine economic winners and losers, we can predict exactly who will end up with these jobs: women, people of color, and other culturally devalued groups. The equal opportunity approach described above dodges questions of social structure and class by reifying individual traits as the cause of social hierarchies. When, in contrast, income, occupation, wealth, and opportunity are analyzed in terms of structures of inclusion and exclusion, then the need for fundamental change is obvious.

The principle of inclusion directs our attention to all the structural causes of exclusion, including those that emanate from the spheres of discourse, representation, and culture. Exclusion and devaluation occur when those who contribute to the socially necessary work of production and reproduction, whether this labor is manual or mental, creative or repetitive, do not receive shares of society's resources that permit them to live decent lives, with access to the food, clothing, shelter, education, healthcare, and recreation that are the mark of full enjoyment of human rights. In societies structured by exclusion there are more people than there are social spaces that provide economic well-being. Indeed, the purpose of exclusionary practices is to block access to the activities, occupations, and symbols that are the mark of economic success.

In contrast, feminist, egalitarian principles of inclusion call for the restructuring of society's political-economic system to create conditions in which everyone can participate in the production of the goods and services we need for our daily lives, as well as fully participate in the many activities associated with reproduction. In this view, paid and unpaid work, productive and reproductive work, are of equal social importance. The full development of our potential as human beings means that all of us must have the access to the material and cultural resources necessary to engage in both types of labor.

Our feminist goal of inclusive representation accompanied by an egalitarian division of labor is neither more nor less utopian (or dystopian, depending upon one's values and politics) than are the prevailing neoliberal principles of free trade and free markets, on the one hand, or the traditional Marxist principles of class solidarity and the dictatorship of the proletariat, on the other. Every school of social analysis—feminist, Marxist, or neoliberal—has utopian underpinnings. Indeed, implicit and explicit values that inform social policy are always rooted in a utopian vision.

International Interventions

A central theme that has emerged in these pages is that gender equity and social justice require public policies that supercede or modify market-based outcomes. Unregulated markets never have and never will meet all social needs, especially for services like childcare, eldercare, and household labor. Moreover, to the extent that these services are purchased in markets, the work will be poorly paid, low status, and feminized. Likewise, markets alone can not solve the structural effects of discrimination, poverty, and other forms of social exclusion. Thus, states and communities must play an active role in creating the conditions for inclusive economic systems.

As we note in chapter 6, however, the power of the state to enact socially progressive policies to protect the rights of workers, ensure the supply of caring labor, and create a more equal distribution of income has been seriously eroded by the combination of neoliberal policies and economic globalization. National governments today are far more accountable to corporate interests than they are to the needs of their citizens. Making this situation even more problematic is the fact that, in this age of globalization and migration, more and more of the residents of any particular country are denied the privileges of citizenship. Once again, poorer, underprivileged women are disproportionately represented in these immigrant populations.

Many feminists have responded to this dilemma by participating in international and transnational organizations, including the United Nations, which in 1995 sponsored the Fourth World Conference on Women in Beijing, China. A parallel, nongovernmental organization (NGO) forum was held in Huairou, and over thirty thousand women from around the world attended, including, we are proud to report, representatives from the International Association for Feminist Economics (IAFFE). The NGO forum provided a space where groups could raise awareness of issues particular to their region or area of concern, brainstorm and share strategies, and lobby government delegations. Both the NGO participants and the official delegates worked through a daunting array of obstacles to collectively put forward a strategy for removing all impediments to women's active participation in public and private life. In the end, the United Nations adopted the Platform for Action, a document that affirmed a new international commitment to the goals of equality, development, and peace for women everywhere.

The Platform for Action identified twelve critical areas of concern and called on governments, the international community, and NGOs to take strategic actions to redress them.[7] These twelve critical areas are

- The persistent and increasing burden of poverty on women
- Inequalities and inadequacies in and unequal access to education and training
- Inequalities and inadequacies in and unequal access to healthcare and related services
- Violence against women
- The effects of armed or other kinds of conflict on women, including those living under foreign occupation
- Inequality in economic structures and policies, in all forms of productive activities, and in access to resources

133

- Inequality between men and women in the sharing of power and decision making at all levels
- Insufficient mechanisms at all levels to promote the advancement of women
- Lack of respect for and inadequate promotion and protection of the human rights of women
- Stereotyping of women and inequality in women's access to and participation in all communication systems, especially in the media
- Gender inequalities in the management of natural resources and in the safeguarding of the environment
- Persistent discrimination against and violation of the rights of the girl-child

Not surprisingly, every item on the Platform for Action is related to the economy. Women's poverty, education, and health are obvious examples. Concerns about women in the media, women and the environment, and violence against women may seem to be at some remove from economic processes and institutions. Television, radio, movies, print journalism, and popular music, however, tend to represent women as dependent and passive, existing not for themselves but for the sexual pleasure of men. One does not need an advanced degree in cultural criticism to recognize the importance of such ubiquitous images for the perpetuation of women's economic subordination. Consider too the connections between environmental degradation and women's social status. Feminist research has documented the relationship between environmental stress and violence against women, forces that limit women's freedom and their economic independence.[8]

The Platform for Action also reflects the commitment of the United Nations to the notion that achieving equality between women and men is a matter of human rights and a condition for social justice. The Platform reaffirms the principles articulated in the Convention on the Elimination of All Forms of Discrimination against Women (CEDAW), adopted by the United Nations General Assembly in 1979. CEDAW calls for nations to incorporate the principle of equality between men and women in their legal systems and to enact laws that prohibit discrimination against women.[9] Importantly, the Platform recognizes that without strong governmental commitments to women's rights there will be a significant distance between the existence of these rights and women's effective enjoyment of them. In reaffirming the importance of CEDAW, the Platform recognizes that gender equality is a necessary but not sufficient condition for building a sustainable, just, and developed society. The phrase "women's rights are human rights" expresses the close connection between gender equity, women's empowerment, and economic development.

The Platform for Action is not, however, an international treaty, so national governments are not legally obligated to support its strategies or recommendations. The Platform does, however, provide a document that women's groups and other NGOs can use to pressure national governments. It also facilitates the creation of international, national, and regional institutions to monitor efforts to promote women's equality in all spheres of life, public as well as private. As our colleagues at the Beijing Plus 5 conference held in 2000 noted, ratifying treaties and signing conventions are not enough. Each nation must evaluate the progress it is making toward women's "full enjoyment of human rights and the fundamental freedoms of all women throughout their life cycle."[10]

Like all international declarations the Platform reflects bargaining and compromise. Under pressure from social conservatives, in the Vatican and in some Islamic states, the language around issues of sexuality and human reproduction is ambiguous. Moreover, the document does not specifically address the structural problems associated with the neoliberal policies of supranational organizations like the World Bank, the WTO, and the IMF that increase poverty, undermine the welfare state, and reinforce patriarchy. By failing to challenge the underlying causes of global inequality, subordination, and powerlessness, the Platform for Action is an attempt at reform, not a call for radical economic change. In the feminist analysis that we support, the existing institutional framework is the problem. Ours is a radical vision that calls for rethinking the very terms of economic performance.

What Is to Be Done?

The evaluation of economic performance and economic well-being is central to all economists, including feminists. Feminist analysis places the values of inclusion and equity at the center. In mainstream economic analyses, economic performance and economic well-being have been cast in terms that refuse the validity of the categories of gender, race, and class. Instead, these questions are assumed to be gender, race, and class neutral. This move allows mainstream economists and policy analysts to conveniently overlook the fact that people have different structural relationships to the processes of production, reproduction, and consumption and that these different structural positions mean that economic policies affect different people in different ways. One size fits all is as poor a guide to economic policy formation as it is to shoes, socks, and pantyhose.

Feminist economic analysis insists on the centrality of the many different social divisions of labor including those by gender, race, ethnicity, class, sexuality, and nationality to show that income, status, and power follow not from one's economic contribution to society but rather from one's relationship to valued or devalued identities. More specifically, work that is socially coded as feminine is devalued, and the people who do this type of work, regardless of the sector within which they work (public or private, manufacturing or service, domestic or international), are similarly devalued.

Conceptualizing economic performance in ways that resist such devaluing practices requires us to consider the relationship between modes of representation and the social division of labor on the one hand and economic well-being and social inclusion on the other. Interestingly, these connections are rendered irrelevant in the dominant view of economic success where wealth creation through the engine of free trade is seen as the solution to every economic problem. In the neoliberal worldview, problems like poverty and women's subordination are problems of insufficient economic growth. Since, according to the neoliberal view, free markets and free trade cause the economic pie to grow more rapidly than under any other conceivable economic regime, the rising tide of wealth and prosperity that inevitably follow marketization will improve everyone's standard of living. In earlier chapters we present a range of arguments, both theoretical and empirical, that debunk these claims.

As feminist economists, we pose five evaluative criteria that allow us to explicitly address the social values that should lie at the heart of every assessment of economic activity.

1. **Is the economic system fair?** What is a fair share of society's output? Under what conditions are some people entitled to more than enough for the enjoyment of life, liberty, and the pursuit of happiness? When is it acceptable for others to suffer lifelong malnutrition or live without basic medical care, education, and shelter? These questions lie at the heart of our religious, ethical, and philosophical traditions. Of interest here is the fact that, far more often than not, religious leaders, ethicists, and philosophers have sided with the less fortunate, arguing that as a community we share a responsibility for the health and well-being of our sisters and brothers,

daughters and sons, mothers and fathers, coworkers and neighbors. No less ink has been spilt reminding the well to do that their social responsibilities are commensurate with their individual privilege. The world's major religions all have significant teachings focused on the importance of economic equality and social justice. Feminist economists contribute to this discussion.

We argue against the view that extremes of wealth and poverty are necessary, the inevitable reflections of an innate, unchangeable human nature. Instead, we insist that the institutions within which people produce, reproduce, and distribute the articles of daily life can be brought into line with human aspirations for fairness, justice, and gender equality. Compare, for example, the records of Sweden and the United States as regards income distribution and women's poverty. In the United States, the richest 10 percent of households earns nearly six times the income of the poorest 10 percent of households. In Sweden, on the other hand, the richest 10 percent of households earns less than three times as much as the poorest 10 percent of households.[11] Similarly, in the United States, nearly 50 percent of all lone mothers live below the poverty line, yet in Sweden less than 5 percent of lone mothers are poor.[12]

At least two points are worth making in this context. First, if extremes of wealth and poverty are both necessary to a well-functioning economy and reflections of natural human proclivities toward greed and selfishness, then it is impossible to explain the very large variations in poverty and income inequality in otherwise similar economies. A nation's economic policies produce income inequality just as directly as they produce income equality. For example, during the past two decades the United States has seen a significant increase in income inequality. Much of this is due to the decline in well-paid manufacturing jobs and an increase in low-wage, service sector jobs.[13]

While this may seem an inevitable consequence of market forces, one must also remember that this trend is accompanied by a decline in the proportion of unionized workers and a decrease in the real value of the minimum wage, both of which are directly related to government policies that increasingly favor the interests of corporations over the rights of citizens. In addition, with increasing income inequality the rich capture more political power. They use this power to avoid paying their fair share of the taxes needed to finance necessary public expenditures for roads, public safety, health, and education. As the tax system becomes more regressive, the quality of life declines for everyone, except the very rich.

Poverty and inequality are not the unavoidable but unfortunate results of otherwise well-functioning economies. They are the results of conscious policy decisions, they can be markedly reduced, and the means to do so are at hand. As progressives have argued for years, all nations need to enact social welfare spending programs to provide subsidies for housing and transportation, a national system of free or low-cost early childhood education and care, and, of course, universal healthcare. There are plenty of examples of how to achieve these important social goals. The obstacles we face in the industrial world are ideological and political, not technological and financial. Problems in the global South are similarly amenable to policy interventions. Indeed, if our vision of fairness is to have a meaningful international dimension, then certainly the rich nations of the world must accept some responsibility for the immiseration of the global South.

Many close to the situation agree that the North should provide debt relief, practice fair trade, and insist on high labor standards. Demilitarization, environmentally sound development policies, and shifting resources to domestic consumption are a few of the policies that the South should pursue. Together these can be part of a renewed international movement for economic justice that will go a long way toward relieving human suffering in the developing world. The content of these strategies must be determined locally and reflect the experiences and perspectives of the people whose lives will be affected. Process is crucial to a feminist egalitarian inclusive economy, and who has a seat at the table is a key determinant of fairness.

2. Does the economic system provide an enhanced quality of life over time? What is an enhanced quality of life? Clearly it is more than just growth in per capita goods and services. There are several reasons why economic growth is an inadequate indicator of enhanced quality of life. From a gender perspective the most obvious problem is that it only counts that which has an explicit monetary price tag. Attempting to correct this deficiency by imputing market values to nonmarket work is not really helpful because nonmarket work is usually undervalued. Another problem with using growth as an indicator of an enhanced quality of life is that there is no debit side.[14] Every market transaction—good, bad, indifferent—is counted as adding to our pile of consumables even when the market transaction is for cancer treatments, incarceration, or cleaning up oil spills. When activities highly valued by the market—building shopping centers, malls, and luxury condos—harm wetlands, forests, and rivers, the loss of these irreplaceable natural resources does not show up as a cost to anyone because they are public rather than private property.

Despite the fundamental assumption of mainstream economics that more is always preferred to less, many have questioned the necessary connection between owning more things and having a better quality of life. Indeed, recent studies in the United States show an opposite correlation: as people's incomes and consumption have grown, and their material possessions have increased, many report less, not more, happiness.[15] To envision an enhanced quality of life in a multidimensional way, a number of different groups have developed alternatives to simple quantitative measures like gross domestic product (GDP). For example, a progressive San Francisco Bay area organization developed the genuine progress indicator (GPI) to try to net out the negative effects of consumerism, environmental degradation, overwork, and disease.

What to include in quality of life? One measure crucial to well-being is the extent to which reproductive labor is shared between women and men. The environment—clean air, clean water, safe streets, and green space—is another important aspect of the quality of life. We should also include access to housing, adequate nutrition, medical care, education, and leisure. Our critique of traditional measures of growth does not make us Luddites. We understand the economic importance of growth and capital accumulation. The problem is that current measures of growth do not give us good information on how the expansion of output influences human well-being.

3. **Does the economic system provide enough economic security?**
What is economic security? Clearly economic security means something about the ability to care for one's self, family, and community. To what extent can people count on the economic system to allow them to realize their plans for the future economic well-being of their families and their communities? That is, if you are a person who shows up for work and does a diligent job, are you likely to find yourself out of work for reasons having nothing to do with your job performance?

This is a question of macroeconomic stability since individual workers are not responsible for the unemployment caused by downturns in the business cycle, technological innovation, or changes in the pattern of international trade. It is also the case that environmental issues, like access to clean water and breathable air, play a significant role in affecting people's ability to work, which in turn affects their economic security. When policymakers are concerned about promoting equity and social justice, and protecting the environment, they will enact a range of economic policies that will minimize the vicissitudes of markets, afford generous unemployment compensation, provide education and retraining programs, and carefully assess the environmental consequences of private market activity.

People who do not have full-time commitments to paid work also deserve economic security. In chapters 3 and 5 we discuss the tension between earning and caring. Here we reframe this tension in terms of the traditional macroeconomic policy goal of full employment: when economic security is reduced to a commitment to full employment, then policy is bound to ignore the range of familial and community responsibilities that run counter to paid employment. In a feminist, egalitarian, inclusive vision of the economy, all people are entitled to economic security regardless of their position in labor markets, the largess of their partners, or the generosity of their families. To actualize this dimension of economic security, everyone must have access to basic income supports, paid parental leave, high-quality, low-cost early childhood education, and significant paid vacation time.

4. **Does the economic system waste human and nonhuman resources?** What does it mean to waste human and nonhuman resources? Clearly if there are millions of people who want to work, but who are unable to find jobs, human resources are being wasted. Similarly, if a factory can produce one hundred widgets per day, but is only producing fifty, then the productive capacity of machines is wasted. And if while producing widgets, firms pour toxic wastes into rivers and spew gasses that cause acid rain into the air, then natural resources are wasted.

Since its inception, industrialization has gone hand in hand with the exploitation of the natural environment: mining, logging, and quarrying scar the earth. The sulphurous skies hanging over industrial cities in the former Soviet Union, poisoned rivers running through the northeastern United States, and deforestation in the Amazon River basin are just three examples of how the production of goods for human use can waste nonhuman resources. Changing this pattern of ecological destruction requires a change in policies.

It is not a matter of state versus private industry. Instead it is a matter of making those responsible for production decisions accountable to the community. Decisions regarding what to produce, how to produce, and where to produce all have environmental consequences. We need laws and regulations to ensure that production decisions fully incorporate all environmental costs. When natural resources are undervalued, environmental destruction is the result. It is, however, crucially important to carefully consider the reasoning behind the valuation of natural resources.

Consider the following example. In 1991 Lawrence Summers, then the chief economist for the World Bank (now president of Harvard University) wrote an internal memo calling for more pollution in poor countries: "I think the economic logic behind dumping a load of toxic waste in the lowest wage country is impeccable and we should face up to that. . . . I've always thought that under-populated countries in Africa are vastly under-polluted; their air quality is vastly inefficiently low compared to Los Angeles or Mexico City."[16] His reasoning reflects standard neoliberal economic logic. The costs of pollution are measured either in terms of the output lost due to sickness from pollution or the willingness and ability to pay to clean up pollution. In poor countries wages are lower, hence the value of the lost output is less, and because income is lower, people's ability to pay for a healthy environment is likewise less.

The ethical bankruptcy of this reasoning is obvious. We know that the poor suffer the most from environmental degradation. The condition of the environment also has important economic security aspects since well over half the people in the global South rely directly on natural resources like arable land, forests, rivers, and fisheries for their daily sustenance. Women in particular are vulnerable to the negative effects of resource depletion, the degradation of natural systems, and the dangers of toxic pollutants since they are the ones who provide for their families and communities. In addition, women are at higher risk for environmentally based illness since they have different susceptibilities to the toxic effects of various chemicals. These risks are particularly pronounced in low-income urban areas where the concentration of polluting industrial facilities is highest.[17]

Discrimination is another significant source of economic waste for two reasons. First, individuals face circumscribed opportunities that limit their ability to contribute to society. Second, sorting people into occupations by social identities rather than by their individual skills, talents, and potentials stifles economic growth. Indeed, a recent *International Labor Review* study found that occupational segregation by sex wastes human resources, prevents change, disadvantages women, and perpetuates gender inequalities.[18] Another aspect of the negative economic impact of discrimination can be illustrated via the racialized consequences of segregation in the United States. Variations in educational resources, access to credit markets, and limited employment opportunities are especially problematic for young African-American men. Their economic prospects are bleak. To date, the policy response of the U.S. government has been mass incarceration that justifies their social exclusion. In a feminist, egalitarian, inclusive economy a commitment to economic stabilization, more equal access to good jobs, and more good jobs will reduce the waste associated with all forms of discrimination.

5. **Does the economic system provide sufficient opportunities for meaningful work?** What is meaningful work? What distinguishes a job from a career, profession, vocation, or calling? This distinction does not necessarily depend on the specific type of work done. The conditions in which people work are just as important. At a minimum, the conditions of work must meet basic standards for health and safety. But meaningful work goes beyond this minimum to include opportunities for advancement, some degree of autonomy, the chance to exercise judgment, interactions with coworkers, and an environment that is free from harassment and intimidation.

We can see from this that good jobs are not defined exclusively by monetary compensation. The social relations of production matter a great deal. As we observe the world of work, however, we notice that high pay, prestige, and job satisfaction often go together. This may seem to contradict the standard economic view of work in which labor breeds disutility and people can only be induced to give up leisure by the promise of money.

By this reasoning, less pleasant jobs offer compensating pay. This, however, flies in the face of experience. Engineers and doctors obviously earn more than janitors and assembly workers. Why? One answer is that poorly paid jobs require few skills. Many people can do the work, so even though the work is unpleasant and repetitive, employers don't need to pay a lot to get the labor that they need. But the association of low pay, low skills, and a lack of intrinsic meaning is misleading. Much poorly paid work is not low skill, nor is it boring, repetitive, or meaningless: teachers, nurses, social workers, childcare workers, and eldercare workers do demanding, highly skilled work, yet they are poorly paid. Once again we see that it is the way the work is coded—as feminine not masculine, as caring not productive—that determines its pay and prestige, which in turn shapes the social perception of its inherent worth.

A final consideration is that work should not violate the ethical, political, or aesthetic values of the people who do it. For example, scientists should not have to depend on military contracts to pursue their research. Nor should people in poor communities have to accept prison expansion and hazardous waste disposal sites to provide jobs.

Lola Weikal, in *The Life and Times of Rosie the Riveter,* quotes the Yiddish proverb "work makes life sweet."[19] This reflects our view that labor can be a creative part of the human experience. In a feminist, egalitarian, inclusive economy, meaningful work promotes human dignity and demonstrates society's commitment to genuine human equality.

Concluding Remarks

Gender equity and social justice are central to economic theory and policy. This book offers an understanding of the economy that promotes these goals. We go beyond the demonstration and measurement of the disadvantages associated with social location to develop an analysis that connects modes of representation and modes of production. This is especially important because dominant ideologies, like those associated with the male breadwinner–female caregiver model of the family, work to the advantage of the elite. To counter these ideologies, we have shown how cultural representations valorize some activities and devalue others. It is clear that gender ideologies play fundamental roles in structuring economic systems. A central contribution of feminist economics is that it names and demystifies the relationship between ideology, theory, and policy.

Notes

1. For a brief summary of the current economic status of women, see the International Labour Organization, "Facts on Women at Work," http://www.ilo.org/public/english/bureau/inf/download/women/pdf/factssheet .pdf (accessed June 2, 2004).

2. Julie A. Nelson, *Feminism, Objectivity, and Economics* (New York: Routledge, 1996).

3. A manageable excerpt from this work is contained in Robert C. Tucker's edited volume *The Marx-Engels Reader* (New York: Norton, 1978), 734–59.

4. See Nils Gilman, "Thorstein Veblen's Neglected Feminism," *Journal of Economic Issues* 33, no. 3 (fall 1999): 689–712.

5. Susan M. Shaw and Janet Lee, "Learning Gender in a Diverse Society," in *Women's Voices, Feminist Visions: Classic and Contemporary Readings,* 2d ed. (New York: McGraw-Hill, 2004), 107–44.

6. For a moving fictional account of this process see Virginia Woolf's story of the imaginary figure of Shakespeare's sister in *A Room of One's Own* (1929; reprint, New York: Cambridge University Press, 1996).

7. The upward gaze in a cinematic sex scene refers to shooting the scene from the woman's perspective. Since in movie sex scenes women are generally under men, the camera was looking upward. Depicting women as active participants rather than passive objects of the male gaze was a significant change.

8. Lourdes Benería, "Towards a Greater Integration of Gender in Economics," *World Development* 23 (1995): 1839–50.

9. The work of feminist historian Carroll Rosenberg-Smith, *Disorderly Conduct: Visions of Gender in Victorian America* (Oxford: Oxford University Press, 1986), remains the classic work on these topics.

10. Rhonda Williams forcefully argues this point in her essay "Race, Deconstruction, and the Emergent Agenda of Feminist Economic Theory," in *Beyond Economic Man: Feminist Theory and Economics,* edited by Marianne A. Ferber and Julie A. Nelson (Chicago: University of Chicago Press, 1993), 144–52.

11. As Patricia Hill Collins argues, "By presenting race as being fixed and immutable—something rooted in nature—these approaches mask the historical construction of racial categories, the shifting meaning of race, and the crucial role of politics and ideology in shaping conceptions of race." Patricia Hill Collins, "Defining Black Feminist Thought," in *Black Feminist Thought: Knowledge, Consciousness, and the Politics of Empowerment* (New York: Routledge, 1990), 19–40. In this essay she is critiquing a particular strand of black feminist scholarship that accepts these categories as stable. Available at http://www.hsph.harvard.edu/grhf/WoC/fesminisms/collins2.html (accessed November 23, 2003).

12. See Michèle A. Pujol, *Feminism and Anti-Feminism in Early Economic Thought* (Aldershot: Edward Elgar, 1992); Ulla Grapard, "Robinson Crusoe: The Quintessential Economic Man," *Feminist Economics* 1 (spring 1995): 33–52; and Williams, "Race, Deconstruction, and the Emergent Agenda of Feminist Economic Theory."

13. Sandra Harding, "Can Feminist Thought Make Economics More Objective?" *Feminist Economics* 1 (spring 1995): 7–32; Helen Longino, *Science as Social Knowledge: Values and Objectivity in Scientific Inquiry* (Princeton: Princeton University Press, 1990); and Lynn Hankison-Nelson, *Who Knows: From Quine to a Feminist Empiricism* (Philadelphia: Temple University Press, 1994).

14. Marianne A. Ferber and Julie A. Nelson, "Introduction: The Social Construction of Economics and the Social Construction of Gender," in *Beyond Economic Man: Feminist Theory and Economics,* edited by Marianne A. Ferber and Julie A. Nelson (Chicago: University of Chicago Press, 1993), 1–22.

15. The work of Diana Strassman was highly influential in demonstrating the relationship between the demographics of the economics profession and the persuasiveness of mainstream economics. See, for example, "Not a Free Market: The Rhetoric of Disciplinary Authority in Economics," in *Beyond Economic Man: Feminist Theory and Economics,* 54–68. See also Arjo Klamer, *Conversations with Economists: New Classical Economists and Opponents Speak out on the Current Controversy in Macroeconomics* (Lanham: Rowman and Littlefield, 1984).

16. See Pujol, *Feminism and Anti-Feminism in Early Economic Thought.*

17. Nancy Folbre, "The Unproductive Housewife: Her Evolution in British Economic Thought," *Signs* 16 (spring 1991): 463–84.

18. See Pujol, *Feminism and Anti-Feminism in Early Economic Thought.*

19. Economists were also strong advocates of the laws that instituted racial apartheid in the U.S. South. Through the decades of the 1880s and 1890s, the American Economic Association and many of its members provided active support for the Jim Crow laws that so profoundly affected every sphere of African-American life and death. Though most economists don't know this, and the few who do would like to sweep it under the rug, racism and sexism are an integral part of the "repressed history" of the discipline. See William Darrity Jr., ed., *Economics and Discrimination* (Cheltenham and Northhampton: Edward Elgar, 1995). See also

Mark Haller, *Eugenics: Hereditarian Attitudes in American Thought* (New Brunswick, NJ: Rutgers University Press, 1984). Haller discusses the role of Irving Fisher, a prominent American economist, as the head of the propaganda of the American Eugenics Association.

20. Donna Haraway's essay "Situated Knowledges: The Science Question in Feminism and the Privilege of Partial Perspective," *Feminist Studies* 14 (fall 1988): 579–99, articulates this position.

21. See Cheris Kramarae and Paula A. Treichler, *A Feminist Dictionary* (Champaign: University of Illinois Press, 1997).

22. Holism, in its strict philosophical sense, refers to the epistemology engendered by the work of W. V. O. Quine and Thomas Kuhn. Kuhn recognized that evidence is always seen through the lens of theory. Quine realized that the same evidence can support a number of theories. These insights fatally undermined the foundationalist epistemology associated with positivism and its later variants. Our use of the term *holism* is informed by these insights. See Drucilla K. Barker, "From Feminist Empiricism to Feminist Poststructuralism: Philosophical Questions in Feminist Economics," in *The Elgar Companion to Economics and Philosophy* (Cheltenham and Northhampton: Edward Elgar, 2004), for further discussion of holism in its philosophical sense. See also Steve Cohn, "Telling Other Stories: Heterodox Critiques of Neoclassical Micro Principles Texts," Global Development and Environment Institute Working Paper 00–06, 2000.

23. William Ernest Henley, "Invictus," in *The Oxford Book of English Verse: 1250–1900,* edited by Arthur Quiller-Couch (1919). Available at http://www.bartleby.com/101/842.html (accessed November 23, 2003).

24. A fine example of this process is described in the now famous work by educational sociologist Jean Anyon in her essay "Social Class and the Hidden Curriculum of Work," *Journal of Education* 162 (winter 1980): 67–92. Available at http://www.pipeline.com/~rgibson/hiddencurriculum.html (accessed November 23, 2003). The concept of "the hidden curriculum" is further developed in Eric Margolis, Michael Soldatenko, Sandra Acker, and Marina Gair, "Peekaboo: Hiding and Outing the Curriculum," in *The Hidden Curriculum of Higher Education,* edited by Eric Margolis (London and New York: Routledge, 2001), 1–20.

25. John Donne, "Meditation 17" (1623–24), *Devotions upon Emergent Occasions,* http://www.mrbauld.com/donnebell.html (accessed November 23, 2003).

26. The movie *The Truman Show* is a metaphor for the ways that people can be thoroughly deceived about the conditions of their lives and yet be able to discover the inauthentic nature of their reality.

27. We are indebted to feminist economist Nancy Folbre for her work developing the important concept of social structures of constraint. *Who Pays for the Kid: Gender and the Structures of Constraint* (London and New York: Routledge, 1994).

28. Collins, "Defining Black Feminist Thought."

29. Margaret Thatcher, quoted in *Woman's Own*, London, October 31, 1987. Available at http://briandeer.com/social/thatcher-society.html (accessed November 23, 2003).

30. Martin Luther King Jr. *Letter from a Birmingham Jail* (1964; reprint, San Francisco: Harper, 1994). Available at http://www.stanford.edu/group/King/popular_requests/ (accessed November 23, 2003).

Chapter 2

1. Heidi I. Hartmann, "The Family as the Locus of Gender, Class, and Political Struggle: The Example of Housework," in *Feminism and Methodology*, edited by Sandra Harding (Bloomington and Indianapolis: Indiana University Press, 1987), 109–34.

2. See Marilyn Yalom, *History of the Wife* (New York: HarperCollins, 2001).

3. "This saying is as old as the basic concepts of English common law." William Morris and Mary Morris, *Morris Dictionary of Word and Phrase Origins* (New York: HarperCollins, 1988). Other variants are "You are the boss in your own house and nobody can tell you what to do there. No one can enter your home without your permission. The proverb has been traced back to 'Stage of Popish Toys' (1581). In 1644, English jurist Sir Edward Coke (1552–1634) was quoted as saying: 'For a man's house is his castle, et *domus sua cuique tutissimum refugium*' ('one's home is the safest refuge for all'). First attested in the United States in 'Will and Doom' (1692). In England, the word 'Englishman' often replaces man." Gregory Y. Titelman, *The Random House Dictionary of Popular Proverbs and Sayings* (New York: Random House, 1996).

4. See Yalom, *History of the Wife*, 188–89.

5. Susan Donath, "The Other Economy: A Suggestion for a Distinctively Feminist Economics," *Feminist Economics* 6 (March 2000): 115–23.

6. Naomi Gertsel and Harriet Engel Gross, "Gender and Families in the United States: The Reality of Economic Dependence," in *Women: A Feminist Perspective*, edited by Jo Freeman (Mountain View: Mayfield, 1995), 92–127.

7. Ibid.

8. See Maurice Dobb, *Studies in the Development of Capitalism* (New York: International, 1964).

9. Ibid.

10. Jane Humphries, "Enclosures, Common Rights, and Women: The Proletarianization of Families in the Late Eighteenth and Early Nineteenth Centuries," *Journal of Economic History* 50 (March 1990): 17–42.

11. Peter Dorman, Nancy Folbre, Donald McCloskey, and Tom Weisskopf, "Debating Markets," edited by Tom Weisskopf and Nancy Folbre, *Feminist Economics* 2 (spring 1996) : 69–85. Note that Donald McCloskey is now Deirdre McCloskey.

12. Nancy Folbre, "The Unproductive Housewife."

13. There is a large literature on "the cult of domesticity." For one interesting discussion see Rosenberg-Smith, *Disorderly Conduct: Visions of Gender in Victorian America* (New York: Alfred A. Knopf, 1985).

14. Nancy Folbre, "Socialism, Feminist and Scientific," in *Beyond Economic Man: Feminist Theory and Economics,* edited by Marianne A. Ferber and Julie A. Nelson (Chicago: University of Chicago Press, 1993): 94–110.

15. This is ably depicted in the 2001 movie *Gosford Park.*

16. Gertsel and Gross, "Gender and Families in the United States."

17. Among the noteworthy documents expressing outrage at the reigning gender order are Mary Wollstonecraft's *A Vindication of the Rights of Woman,* first published in 1792, and *The Declaration of Sentiments* by Elizabeth Cady Stanton and Lucretia Mott, a report of the Seneca Falls Women's Rights Convention in 1848. These, and others, are available in Alice S. Rossi, ed., *The Feminist Papers: From Adams to de Beauvoir* (New York: Columbia University Press, 1973).

18. Yalom, *History of the Wife,* 188–89.

19. Folbre, "Socialism, Feminist and Scientific." Seeing that these demands were too much for even the most radical men, feminist leaders backed off and focused instead on the much narrower demand for women's formal legal equality with men as represented by the right to vote.

20. For Marshall's views on women, see Pujol, *Feminism and Anti-Feminism in Early Economic Thought.* Also see Jane Humphries, "Female Headed Households in Early Industrial Britain: The Vanguard of the Proletariat?" *Labor History Review* 63 (spring 1998): 31–65.

21. Deborah M. Figart, Ellen Mutari, and Marilyn Power, *Living Wages, Equal Wages: Gender and Labor Market Policies in the United States* (New York: Routledge, 2002), chap. 5, 67–90.

22. Ibid.

23. Ibid.

24. For further discussion see Eric Hobsbawm, *Industry and Empire: The Birth of the Industrial Revolution* (New York: New Press, 1999); Barbara L. Solow and Stanley L. Engerman, *British Capitalism and Caribbean Slavery: The Legacy of Eric Williams* (New York: Cambridge University Press, 1988); and Eric Williams, *Capitalism and Slavery* (Chapel Hill: University of North Carolina Press, 1994).

25. See Dorman et al., "Debating Markets."

26. For further discussion see Hartmann "The Family as the Locus of Gender, Class, and Political Struggle." Also see Harriet Fraad, Stephen Resnick, and Richard Wolff, *Bringing It All Back Home: Class, Gender, and Power in the Household* (London: Pluto Press, 1994); and Arlie R. Hochschild and Ann Machung, *The Second Shift* (New York: William Morrow, 1990).

27. Hochschild and Machung, *The Second Shift.*

28. Hartmann, "The Family as the Locus of Gender, Class, and Political Struggle."

29. Myra H. Strober, "Two-Earner Families," in *Feminism, Children, and the New Families,* edited by Sanford M. Dornmbush and Myra H. Strober (New York: Guilford Press, 1988): 161–90; and Man-yee Kan, "Gender Asymmetry in the Division of Domestic Labor," paper presented at the British Household Panel Survey, 2001, Institute for Social and Economic Research, University of Essex, http://www.iser.essex.ac.uk/activities/conferences/bhps-2001/docs/pdf/papers/ kan.pdf (accessed November 23, 2003).

30. Suzanne M. Bianchi, "Maternal Employment and Time with Children: Dramatic Change or Surprising Continuity?" *Demography* 37 (November 2000): 401–14.

31. Barbara Ehrenreich, *Nickel and Dimed: On (Not) Getting by in America* (New York: Henry Holt, 2002).

32. In 1900 44 percent of African-American women worked in private household service, and another 44 percent worked in agriculture. See Teresa Amott and Julie Matthaei, *Race, Gender, and Work: A Multicultural Economic History of Women in the United States,* rev. ed. (Boston: South End Press, 1996), 157.

33. Joni Seager, *The State of Women in the World Atlas* (London: Penguin, 1997), 65.

34. This expression originated with Karl Marx and Friedrich Engels in *The Communist Manifesto* (1848; reprint, London: Verso, 1998).

35. Nancy Fraser, *Justice Interruptus: Critical Reflections on the "Postsocialist" Condition* (London and New York: Routledge, 1997), 41–68.

36. United Nations Statistics Division, "The World's Women, 2000: Trends and Statistics" (New York: United Nations, 2000). Available at http: //unstats.un.org/unsd/demographic/ww2000/table2b.html (accessed November 23, 2003).

37. This conception of the family was originally articulated by Gary S. Becker, *A Treatise on the Family* (Cambridge: Harvard University Press, 1991).

38. Simone de Beauvoir, *The Second Sex* (1949; reprint, New York: Alfred A. Knopf, 1993), xxvi.

39. This is a classic essentialist understanding of the modern gender division of labor. To appreciate how deeply this essentialism has penetrated our consciousness, one need only think about the enduring children's cartoons *The Flintstones* and *The Jetsons.* We are indebted to Professor Ulla Grapard for pointing this out to us.

40. Barbara Bergmann, "Feminism and Economics," *Academe,* September–October 1983, 25.

41. Bina Agarwal, "'Bargaining' and Gender Relations: With and beyond the Household," *Feminist Economics* 3 (spring 1997): 1–50; Notburga Ott, "Fertility and Division of Work in the Family: A Game Theoretic Model of Household Decisions," in *Out of the Margin: Feminist Perspectives on Economics,* edited by Edith Kuiper and Jolande Sap (New York and London: Routledge, 1995), 80–99.

42. Notburga Ott, "Fertility and Division of Work in the Family."

43. M. V. Lee Badgett, "Gender, Sexuality, and Sexual Orientation: All in the Feminist Family?" *Feminist Economics* 1 (spring 1995): 121–40.

44. Gary S. Becker, *A Treatise on the Family*, enl. ed. (Cambridge: Harvard University Press, 1993).

45. This idea is developed in Diane Elson, "Male Bias in Macro-economics: The Case of Structural Adjustment," in *Male Bias in the Development Process*, edited by Diane Elson (Manchester and New York: Manchester University Press, 1991), 164–90.

46. Jeff Madrick, "Why Mainstream Economists Should Take Heed," *Feminist Economics* 3 (spring 1997): 143–49.

47. See Diane Elson, ed., *Progress of the World's Women, 2000* (New York: United Nations Development Fund for Women, UNIFEM, 2000), chap. 1, 16–36. See also Iulie Aslaksen, "Gross Domestic Product," in *Elgar Companion to Feminist Economics*, edited by Janice Peterson and Margaret Lewis (Cheltenham and Northampton: Edward Elgar, 1999), 411–17.

48. Kathleen Cloud and Nancy Garrett, "Inclusion of Women's Household Human Capital Production in Analyses of Structural Transformation," *Feminist Economics* 2 (fall 1996): 93–120.

49. Australian Bureau of Statistics, "Income—Income Distribution: The Value of Unpaid Work," in *Australian Social Trends, 1995*, updated November 18 2002, http://www.abs.gov.au/Ausstats/abs@.nsf/0/24e9a783f4f225bbca256bcd 0082558a?OpenDocument (accessed June 3, 2004).

Chapter 3

1. See Susan Himmelwhite, "Domestic Labor," *The Elgar Companion to Feminist Economics*, edited by Janice Peterson and Margaret Lewis (Cheltenham and North Hampton: Edwin Elgar, 1999), 126–35; and Maxine Molyneux, "Beyond the Domestic Labor Debate," *New Left Review* 116 (1979): 3–27.

2. Molyneux, "Beyond the Domestic Labor Debate."

3. Himmelwhite, "Domestic Labor."

4. Gary Becker and the "new home economics" uncritically appropriate these categories of analysis and use them to rationalize the existing gender division of labor, as well as women's economic subordination.

5. See Nancy Folbre, "'Holding Hands at Midnight': The Paradox of Caring Labor," *Feminist Economics* 1 (spring 1995): 73–92, and *The Invisible Heart: Economics and Family Values* (New York: New Press, 2001).

6. Guy Standing, "Care Work: Overcoming Insecurity and Neglect," in *Care Work: The Quest for Security*, edited by Mary Daly (Geneva: International Labour Office, 2001), 15–31.

7. Ibid., 21.

8. See Folbre, *Who Pays for the Kid.*

9. Bernard Mandeville, "The Fable of the Bees: Or, Private Vices," in *Publick Benefits,* edited by F. B. Kaye, 2 vols. (Oxford: Clarendon Press, 1924; reprint, Indianapolis: Liberty Fund, 1988).

10. Barbara Bergmann, "Watch out for Family Friendly Policies," *Dollars and Sense* 215 (January–February 1998): 10–11.

11. Tamar Levin, *New York Times,* October 24, 2000, data from the U.S. Census Bureau.

12. Stephanie Coontz, *The Way We Never Were: American Families and the Nostalgia Trap* (New York: Basic Books, 2000). It is also worth pointing out that even in the 1950s, at the height of female exclusion from the paid workforce, 40 percent of women between the ages of twenty-four and forty-four were employed.

13. Ann Crittenden, *The Economic Consequences of Motherhood: Why the Most Important Job in the World Is Still the Least Valued* (New York: Henry Holt, 2000), 5, 87–108.

14. Michelle J. Budig and Paula England, "The Wage Penalty for Motherhood," *American Sociological Review* 66 (April 2001): 204–25.

15. These are 1990 dollars. See Janet Gornick and Marcia Meyers, "Support for Working Families," *American Prospect* 12 (January 1, 2001): 3–7. Available at http://www.prospect.org/print/V12/1/gornick-j.html (accessed November 23, 2003).

16. Ibid.

17. Amott and Matthaei, *Race, Gender, and Work,* 173.

18. Arlie Hochschild, "The Nanny Chain," *American Prospect* 11 (January 3, 2000), 32–36. Available at http://www.prospect.org/print/V11/4/hochschild-a.html (accessed November 23, 2003).

19. Quoted in Arlie Russell Hochschild, "Love and Gold," in *Gobal Woman: Nannies, Maids, and Sex Workers in the New Economy,* edited by Barbara Ehrenreich and Arlie Russell Hochschild (New York: Henry Holt, 2002), 15–30.

20. Jean L. Pyle, "Sex, Maids, and Export Processing: Risks and Reasons for Gendered Global Production Networks," *International Journal of Politics, Culture, and Society* 15 (September 2001): 55–76.

21. Robert Espinoza, "Migration Trends: Maps and Charts," in *Global Woman: Nannies, Maids, and Sex Workers in the New Economy,* edited by Barbara Ehrenreich and Arlie Russell Hochschild (New York: Henry Holt, 2002), 275–80.

22. Ibid.

23. The video *Chains of Love* (1999), First Run/Icarus Films, does an excellent job with the emotional and economic dimensions of these migrant flows.

24. Joan Williams, *Unbending Gender: Why Family and Work Conflict and What to Do about It* (New York: Oxford University Press, 2001).

25. Catalyst, University of Michigan Business School and Center for the Edu-

cation of Women, "Women and the MBA: Gateway to Opportunity," 2000, http://www.umich.edu/~cew/mbafacts.pdf (accessed November 23, 2003).

26. Betty Friedan, *The Feminine Mystique* (New York: W. W. Norton, 1963).

27. Ibid.

28. Bergmann, "Watch out for Family Friendly Policies."

Chapter 4

1. Figart, Mutari, and Power, *Living Wages, Equal Wages*.

2. Amott and Matthaei, *Race, Gender, and Work*.

3. Claudia Koonz, *Mothers in the Fatherland: Women, the Family, and Nazi Politics* (New York: St. Martin's Press, 1988).

4. Becky Pettit and Jennifer Hook, "The Structure of Women's Employment in Comparative Perspective," Luxembourg Income Study Working Paper 330, September 2002. Available at http://www.lisproject.org/publications/liswps/330.pdf (accessed October 23, 2003).

5. Howard N. Fullerton Jr., "Labor Force Participation: 75 Years of Change, 1950–98 and 1998–2025," *Monthly Labor Review* (1999), http://www.bls.gov/opub/mlr/1999/12/art1full.pdf (accessed November 23, 2003).

6. U.S. Department of Labor, Bureau of Labor Statistics (BLS), *Report on the American Workforce, 1999,* http://www.bls.gov/opub/rtaw/pdf/rtaw1999.pdf (accessed November 23, 2003).

7. Barbara Bergmann, *The Economic Emergence of Women* (New York: Basic Books, 1986).

8. Claudia Goldin, *Understanding the Gender Gap: An Economic History of American Women* (New York: Oxford University Press, 1990).

9. Randy Albelda and Chris Tilly, *Glass Ceilings and Bottomless Pits* (Cambridge: South End Press, 1997); and Seager, *The State of Women in the World Atlas*.

10. Friedan, *The Feminine Mystique*.

11. The term *wage gap* is somewhat of a misnomer. Technically, if a woman earns $.75 for every $1 a man earns, the wage ratio is 75 percent, and the wage gap is 25 percent. However, in order to be consistent with nontechnical usage, we refer to the wage ratio as the wage gap.

12. U.S. Department of Labor, BLS, "Highlights of Women's Earnings in 2001," Report 960. May 2002. Available at http://www.bls.gov/cps/cpswom2001.pdf (accessed November 23, 2003).

13. When doing international comparisons, the numbers may not be exactly comparable due to the use of different definitions. It should be noted, for example, that in the United States the wage gap is calculated using the earnings of full-time workers. Other countries, however, may include both part-time and full-time workers.

14. United Nations Statistics Division, "The World's Women 2000," table 5.B.

15. International Labour Organization, "Facts on Women at Work," http://www.ilo.org/public/english/bureau/inf/download/women/pdf/factssheet.pdf (accessed June 2, 2004).

16. Deborah M. Figart, "Wage Gap," in *The Elgar Companion to Feminist Economics*, edited by Janice Peterson and Margaret Lewis (Cheltenham and Northhampton: Edward Elgar, 1999), 746–49.

17. U.S. Department of Labor, BLS, "Highlights of Women's Earnings in 2001."

18. Ibid.

19. Ibid.

20. Richard Anker, "Theories of Occupational Segregation by Sex: An Overview," in *Women, Gender, and Work*, edited by Martha Fetherolf Loutfi (Geneva: International Labour Office, 2001), 129–56.

21. Unfortunately the definitions of occupational categories used by the ILO and the BLS are slightly different. This difference does not detract from our main point.

22. Amott and Matthaei, *Race, Gender, and Work*.

23. Mary C. King, "Black Women's Labor Market Status: Occupational Segregation in the United States and Great Britain," *Review of Black Political Economy* 24 (summer 1995): 23–40. King points out that in Great Britain the term *black* refers to people of Indian, Pakistani, and Bengali ancestry as well as those of African descent from Africa or the Caribbean. King uses black in the American sense to refer to people of African descent.

24. Jean L. Pyle points this out in her discussion of the differences in natalist policies directed toward ethnic Malay women and ethnic Chinese women in Singapore. Jean L. Pyle, "Women, the Family, and Economic Restructuring: The Singapore Model?" *Review of Social Economy* 55 (summer 1997): 215–23.

25. Seager, *The State of Women in the World Atlas*, 64.

26. *Stanford Today*, September–October 1997, http://www.stanford.edu/dept/news/stanfordtoday/ed/9709/9709fea201.html (accessed November 23, 2003).

27. Mariam K. Chamberlain, "Glass Ceiling," in *The Elgar Companion to Feminist Economics*, edited by Janice Peterson and Margaret Lewis (Cheltenham and Northhampton: Edward Elgar, 1999), 396–401.

28. U.S. Department of Labor, BLS, "Highlights of Women's Earnings in 2001."

29. Ibid.

30. Ibid.

31. Joyce Jacobsen, "Human Capital Theory," in *The Elgar Companion to Feminist Economics*, edited by Janice Peterson and Margaret Lewis (Cheltenham and Northhampton: Edward Elgar, 1999), 443–48.

32. Robert Polacheck, "Human Capital and Gender Earning Gap: A Response to Feminist Critiques," in *Out of the Margin: Feminist Perspectives on Economics,* edited by Edith Kuiper and Jolande Sap (London and New York: Routledge, 1995), 61–89.

33. U.S. Department of Labor, BLS, "Highlights of Women's Earnings in 2001."

34. Joyce Jacobsen, *The Economics of Gender* (Malden: Blackwell, 1998).

35. Rhonda Williams and William E. Spriggs, "How Does It Feel to Be Free? Reflections on Black-White Economic Inequality in the Era of 'Color-Blind' Law," *Review of Black Political Economy* 1 (summer 1999): 27.

36. Jane Humphries, "Economics, Gender, and Equal Opportunities," in *The Economics of Equal Opportunities,* edited by Jane Humphries and Jill Rubery (Manchester: Equal Employment Opportunities Commission, 1995), 55–79.

37. Bergmann, *The Economic Emergence of Women.*

38. Figart, Mutari, and Power, *Living Wages, Equal Wages.*

39. Myra H. Strober and Carolyn L. Arnold, "The Dynamics of Occupational Segregation among Bank Tellers," in *Gender in the Workplace,* edited by Clair Brown and Joseph Pechman (Washington, DC: Brookings Institution, 1987), 107–58.

40. Anker, "Theories of Occupational Segregation by Sex."

41. The U.S. data is from U.S. Department of Labor, BLS, "Highlights of Women's Earnings in 2001." The data for the European Union is from European Foundation for the Improvement of Living and Working Conditions, "Gender, Jobs, and Working Conditions in the European Union," 2001, www.eurofound.eu .int/publications/files/EF0277EN.pdf (accessed November 21, 2003).

42. See Bergmann, *The Economic Emergence of Women;* and Susan Eisenberg, "Still Building the Foundation: Women in the Construction Trades," *Working USA* 2, no. 1 (1998): 23–25.

43. Paul Demko, "Burned," *City Pages* 22 (January 10, 2001). Available at http://www.citypages.com/databank/22/1049/article9281.asp. (accessed November 23, 2003).

44. Figart, Mutari, and Power, *Living Wages, Equal Wages.*

45. Ibid.

46. *Automobile Workers v. Johnson Controls,* 499 US. 187 (1991).

47. Bergmann, *The Economic Emergence of Women.*

48. Minnesota Department of Employee Relations, "Guide to Understanding Pay Equity Compliance and Computer Reports," October 2000, http: //www.doer.state.mn.us/lr-peqty/resource.htm (accessed November 23, 2003).

49. For just one statement of the principles and strategies behind the living wage movement, see the Acorn Living Wage Resource Center, http://www.living-wagecampaign.org/ (accessed November 23, 2003).

50. Figart, Mutari, and Power, *Living Wages, Equal Wages.*

Chapter 5

1. Susan F. Feiner and Bruce B. Roberts, "Hidden by the Invisible Hand: Neoclassical Economic Theory and the Textbook Treatment of Race and Gender," *Gender & Society* 4 (June 1990): 159–81.

2. Diana M. Pearce, "The Feminization of Poverty: Women, Work, and Welfare," *Urban and Social Change Review* 11 (1978): 28–36.

3. "Innocenti Report Card 1," UNICEF Innocenti Research Centre, Florence, 2000, http://www.unicef-icdc.org/publications/pdf/repcard1e.pdf (accessed November 23, 2003).

4. Jonah Goldberg, "Impoverished Ideas: Being Poor Ain't All That Great," *National Review Online,* February 8, 2002. Available at http://www.national review.com/goldberg/goldberg020802.shtml (accessed November 23, 2003).

5. Susan L. Thomas, "Race, Gender, and Welfare Reform: The Anti-Nationalist Response," *Journal of Black Studies* 28 (July 1998): 419–46.

6. See Martin Gilens, *Why Americans Hate Welfare: Race, Media, and the Politics of Antipoverty Policy* (Chicago: University of Chicago Press, 1999).

7. Susan L. Thomas, "From the Culture of Poverty to the Culture of Single Motherhood: The New Poverty Paradigm," *Women and Politics* 14, no. 2 (1994): 65–97.

8. Ibid.

9. Robert Kuttner, "The Market for Labor," in *Everything for Sale: The Virtues and Limits of Markets* (New York: Knopf, 1997), 68–109.

10. James Crotty, "Why Is There Chronic Excess Capacity: The Market Failures Issue," *Challenge* 45 (November–December 2002), 21–24.

11. See Robert D. Cherry, *Who Gets the Good Jobs: Combating Race and Gender Disparities* (Piscataway: Rutgers University Press, 2001).

12. "Innocenti Report Card 1."

13. Ibid.

14. Timothy M. Smeeding, Lee Rainwater, and Gary Burtless, "United States Poverty in a Cross-National Context," Luxembourg Income Study Working Paper 244, September 2000. Available at http://www.lisproject.org/publications/liswps/244.pdf (accessed November 23, 2003).

15. Gøsta Esping-Andersen, *The Three Worlds of Welfare Capitalism* (Princeton: Princeton University Press, 1990).

16. See Ann Schola Orloff, "Gender and the Social Rights of Citizenship," *American Sociological Review* 58 (1993): 303–28; Ruth Lister, *Feminist Perspectives* (London: Macmillan, 1997); and Diane Sainsbury, *Gender, Equality, and Welfare States* (Cambridge: Cambridge University Press, 1996).

17. See Sainsbury, *Gender, Equality, and Welfare States,* and "Gender and Social Democratic Welfare States," in *Gender and Welfare State Regimes,* edited by Diane Sainsbury (Oxford: Oxford University Press, 1999), 75–116.

18. Janet Gornick, Marcia K. Myers, and Katherine E. Ross, "Public Policies and the Employment of Mothers: A Cross-National Study," *Social Science Quarterly* 79 (1998): 35–54.

19. Karen Christopher, "Welfare State Regimes and Mothers' Poverty," *Social Politics: International Studies in Gender, State, and Society* 9 (spring 2002): 60–86.

20. In 2001, median household income was $42,228, so relative poverty begins at half that, or $21,114, a figure well above the U.S. absolute poverty thresholds. See "Money Income in the United States: 2001," Current Population Reports, Consumer Income, September 2002, http://www.census.gov/prod/2002pubs/p60–218.pdf (accessed November 23, 2003).

21. Robert E. Rector, "The Size and Scope of Means-Tested Welfare Spending," Heritage Foundation, August 1, 2001, http://www.heritage.org/Research/Welfare/Test080101.cfm (accessed November 23, 2003).

22. Rector's facts, on the other hand, are quite difficult to verify.

23. Eugene T. Lowe, "A Status Report on Hunger and Homelessness in America's Cities, 2001: A 27-City Survey," U.S. Conference of Mayors, December 2001, http://www.usmayors.org/uscm/hungersurvey/2001/hungersurvey2001.pdf (accessed November 23, 2003).

24. Ibid.

25. Barbara Bergmann and Trudi Renwick, "A Budget-Based Definition of Poverty with an Application to Single-Parent Families," *Journal of Human Resources* 29 (winter 1993): 1–24.

26. See also Constance F. Citro and Robert T. Michael, eds., *Measuring Poverty: A New Approach* (Washington, DC: National Academies Press, 1995).

27. In Western Europe this question is answered by defining the poverty line as 50 percent of median income. Thus a decent standard of living is one that enables people to be a part of the middle class.

28. The interested reader might want to take the poverty tour presented on the Web page of the U.S. Catholic bishops, http://www.nccbuscc.org/cchd/povertyusa/tour2.html (accessed November 23, 2003).

29. The data on poverty thresholds is from "Poverty in the United States, 2001," Current Population Reports, Consumer Income, September 2002, http://www.census.gov/prod/2002pubs/p60–219.pdf (accessed November 23, 2003). The calculation for the basic needs budget is from Economic Policy Institute, "Hardships in America, 2003," http://www.epinet.org/content.cfm/issueguides_poverty_poverty (accessed November 23, 2003). Basic needs budgets vary by state and region.

30. See Albelda and Tilly, *Glass Ceilings and Bottomless Pits,* 79–106.

31. In 1939 the Social Security Act was amended to add dependents and survivors benefits for widows and children of breadwinners.

32. Linda Gordon, "Welfare and Public Relief," in *The Reader's Companion to*

U.S. Women's History, edited by Barbara Smith, Marysa Navarro, Wilma Mankiller, Gloria Steinem, and Gwendolyn Mink (New York: Houghton Mifflin, 1999). Available at http://college.hmco.com/history/readerscomp/women/html/wh_039000_welfareandpu.htm (accessed November 23, 2003).

33. Ibid.

34. Albelda and Tilly, *Glass Ceilings and Bottomless Pits,* appendix B, 189–200. Albelda and Tilly show that AFDC as a share of spending was only 1.5 percent of federal spending in 1975 and only 1 percent in 1994.

35. Janice Peterson, Xue Song, and Avis Jones-deWeaver, "Life after Welfare Reform: Low Income Single Parent Families, Pre- and Post- TANF," in *Research in Brief,* Institute for Women's Policy Research Publication D446, May 22, 2002.

36. Randy Albelda, "Fallacies of Welfare-to-Work Policies," *Lost Ground: Welfare Reform, Poverty, and Beyond,* edited by Randy Albelda and Ann Withhorn (Cambridge: South End Press, 2002), 79–94.

37. Stephanie Mencimer, "Children Left Behind: Why We Need a National Child-Care Program, Now More Than Ever," *American Prospect* 13 (December 30, 2002): 29–31. Available at http://www.prospect.org/print/V13/23/mencimers.html (accessed November 23, 2003).

38. David Ross, "Child Poverty in Canada: Recasting the Issue," Canadian Council on Social Development, April 1998, http://www.ccsd.ca/pubs/recastin.htm (accessed November 23, 2003).

39. Gøsta Esping-Andersen, Duncan Gallie, Anton Memerijck, and John Myles, "A New Welfare Architecture for Europe?" report submitted to the Belgian presidency of the European Union, final version, executive summary, September 2001, http://vangool.fgov.be/Europe%20conf2%20report%20summ.htm (accessed November 23, 2003).

40. For further discussion see John Micklewright, "Social Exclusion and Children: A European View for a U.S. Debate," UNICEF Innocenti Research Centre, 90, Florence, Februrary 2002, http://www.unicef-icdc.org/publications/pdf/iwp90.pdf (accessed November 23, 2003).

41. Catherine Howarth and Peter Kenway, "Monitoring Poverty and Social Exclusion: Why Britain Needs a Key Indicators Report," New Policy Institute, London, 1998, iv, http://www.npi.org.uk/reports/mpse%20-%20Why%20Britain%20Needs%20a%20KIPS.pdf (accessed November 23, 2003).

42. Jürg K. Siegenthaler, "Poverty among Single Elderly Women under Different Systems of Old-Age Security: A Comparative Review," *Social Security Bulletin* 59 (fall 1996): 31–44.

43. See Christina Smith FitzPatrick and Joan Entmacher, "Increasing Economic Security for Elderly Women by Improving Social Security Survivor Benefits," National Women's Law Center, paper prepared for presentation at the Twelfth Annual Conference of the National Academy of Social Insurance, Wash-

ington, DC, January 27, 2000, http://www.nwlc.org/pdf/NASIwidows2.pdf (accessed November 23, 2003).

44. Ibid.

Chapter 6

1. Globalization has cultural and social aspects as well. In this chapter we focus only on its economic aspects. We recommend the video *The Global Assembly Line* for a hard-hitting look at this topic, particularly its gender dimensions.

2. For example, the terms East and West also have political and cultural connotations. They emerged during the encounters between Europeans and other regions and cultures beginning with the Crusades. In time, West came to differentiate and define the cultural legacies of Europe in contrast to the cultures and societies of both Asia and Africa. The cultures of the West were considered "civilized" and superior to the "uncivilized" or "barbaric cultures" of the colonized world. These terms were also common during the Cold War era. West denoted countries with democratic governments and primarily market economies, for example, the United States, Canada, Western Europe, and Japan. East denoted the countries with centrally planned economies and Communist forms of government, for example, Russia and the other countries in the Soviet Union as well as the Eastern European countries in the Communist bloc. These countries are now commonly referred to as transition economies. Today, the term West, or Western, denotes both the legacies of European culture and presence of democracy and markets.

3. The commonalities evaporated as the oil-producing nations of the Middle East earned huge incomes from the sale of crude petroleum (revenues from these sales are referred to as petrodollars) and as the nations of Southeast Asia switched to a development strategy based on switching resources from producing goods for domestic consumption to producing goods for sale in export markets (called export substitution policies).

4. Eric Schlosser, *Fast Food Nation: The Dark Side of the All-American Meal* (New York: HarperCollins, 2002).

5. In an influential essay Chandra Mohanty demonstrates the tendency among feminists to posit an essentialized, subjugated, Third World woman in contrast to emancipated Western women. See Chandra Mohanty, "Under Western Eyes: Feminist Scholarship and Colonial Discourses," *Feminist Review* 30 (autumn 1988): 61–88.

6. Roger Burbach, Orlando Núñez, Boris Kagarlitsky, *Globalization and Its Discontents: The Rise of Postmodern Societies* (London and Chicago: Pluto Press, 1997), 75.

7. World Bank, *World Development Report, 2000/2001,* updated April 5, 2001, http://www.worldbank.org/poverty/wdrpoverty/ (accessed November 23, 2002).

8. See United Nations Development Programme (UNDP), "Human Development in this Age of Globalization," in *Human Development Report, 1999: Globalization with a Human Face* (Oxford: Oxford University Press, 1999). Available at http://hdr.undp.org/reports/global/1999/en/pdf/hdr_1999_ch1.pdf (accessed November 22, 2003).

9. Moreno-Fontes, "The Importance of Considering Gender Issues in Migration," International Labour Organization, June 14, 2002, http://www.ilo.org/public/english/protection/migrant/projects/gender/ (accessed November 23, 2003).

10. The United States is an interesting case because it too began as a colony of England. However, European settlers colonized the indigenous peoples.

11. Hobsbawm, *Industry and Empire.*

12. See Ester Boserup, *Women's Role in Economic Development* (London: Allen and Unwin, 1970), for a discussion of the African case; and Bina Agarwal, *A Field of One's Own* (Cambridge: Cambridge University Press, 1998), for a discussion of South Asia. These books provide ample evidence of the problems created by the imposition of Western norms on African and Asian agricultural communities.

13. Sunil Kukreja, "The Two Faces of Development," in *Introduction to International Political Economy,* 2d ed., edited by David N. Balaam and Michael Veseth (Upper Saddle River: Prentice Hall, 2001), 320–45.

14. For example, in 1953 the democratic government of Guatemala was brought down when it attempted to redistribute some of the land of the United Fruit Company to landless peasants. Also in 1953 the United States supported Mohammed Reza Pahlavi, Shah of Iran, in order to prevent the nationalization of Iran's oil industry.

15. For a good overview of the history of development, see the History of Economics Web site, http://cepa.newschool.edu/het/schools/develop.htm (accessed November 23, 2003).

16. See Irene Tinker, "The Making of a Field: Advocates, Scholars, and Practitioners," in *Persistent Inequalities: Women and World Development,* edited by Irene Tinker (New York and Oxford: Oxford University Press, 1990), 27–53.

17. Lucille Mathurin Mair, secretary-general of the Copenhagen conference, quoted in Tinker, "The Making of a Field," 31.

18. See Ester Boserup, *Women's Role in Economic Development,* and "Economic Change and the Roles of Women," in *Persistent Inequalities: Women and World Development,* edited by Irene Tinker (New York and Oxford: Oxford University Press, 1990), 14–24.

19. Boserup, "Economic Change and the Roles of Women," 16, emphasis in the original. Female farming systems are characterized by shifting cultivation, allowing portions of the land to lie fallow in order to replenish nutrients, and hoe cultivation rather than plow cultivation.

20. Lourdes Benería and Gita Sen, "Accumulation, Reproduction, and Women's Roles in Economic Development," *Signs* 7 (winter 1981): 279–98.

21. V. Spike Peterson and Anne Sisson Runyan, *Global Gender Issues* (Boulder: Westview Press,1993), chap. 4, 115–64.

22. Lourdes Benería, "Structural Adjustment Policies," in *The Elgar Companion to Feminist Economics,* edited by Janice Peterson and Margaret Lewis (Cheltenham and Northhamption: Edward Elgar, 1999), 687–95.

23. The loans were made by official lenders such as the World Bank and other government development banks, as well as private commercial banks.

24. See David Malin Roodman, "Still Waiting for the Jubilee: Pragmatic Solutions for the Third World Debt Crisis," Worldwatch Paper 155, Worldwatch Institute, April 2001.

25. Ibid.

26. Juan Antonio Morales and Jeffrey D. Sachs, "Bolivia's Economic Crisis," in *Developing Country Debt and the World Economy,* edited by Jeffrey D. Sachs (Chicago: University of Chicago Press, 1989), 57–65, cited in Roodman, "Still Waiting for the Jubilee."

27. Shelley Feldman, "Crises, Poverty, and Gender Inequality: Current Themes and Issues," in *Unequal Burden: Economic Crises, Persistent Poverty, and Women's Work,* edited by Lourdes Benería and Shelley Feldman (Boulder: Westview Press, 1992), 1–25.

28. Elson, "Male Bias in Macro-economics."

29. "Oxfam International Submission to the Heavily Indebted Poor County (HIPC) Debt Review, Executive Summary," 1999, http://www.oxfam.org.uk/ what_we_do/issues/debt_aid/oi_hipc.htm (accessed September 19, 2004).

30. This is the doctrine of comparative advantage. It is important to note that costs refer not only to the explicit dollar costs of production but to opportunity costs. The opportunity cost of producing one good is the most highly valued alternative foregone. In other words, the opportunity cost of producing steel is in the value of the labor resources and manufacturing resources taken from other activities.

31. Bangladesh Export Processing Zones Authority Web site, http: //www.bangladesh-epz.com/prologue.htm (accessed November 22, 2003). Emphasis added.

32. Zimbabwe Export Processing Zones Authority Web site, http: //www.epz.co.zw/about.html (accessed November 22, 2003). Emphasis added.

33. Specifically, during the postwar period the developed countries were the source of 95 percent of FDI and the hosts of 85 percent of FDI. See David N. Balamm and Michael Veseth, *Introduction to Political Economy,* 2d ed. (Upper Saddle River, NJ: Prentice-Hall, 2001).

34. According to Guy Standing, all countries that have successfully industri-

alized have done so by mobilizing large pools of women workers. See Guy Standing, "Global Feminization through Flexible Labor: A Theme Revisited," *World Development* 27 (March 1999): 583–602.

35. Ruth Pearson, "'Nimble Fingers' Revisited: Reflection on Women and the Third World Industrialisation in the Late Twentieth Century," in *Feminist Visions of Development: Gender Analysis and Policy,* edited by Cecile Jackson and Ruth Pearson (London and New York: Routledge, 1998), 171–88.

36. Standing, "Global Feminization through Flexible Labor."

37. Pearson, "'Nimble Fingers' Revisited."

38. See ibid.; Standing, "Global Feminization through Flexible Labor"; and the introduction to the special issue on engendering development, edited by Caren Grown, Diane Elson, and Nilufer Cagatay, *World Development* 28, no. 7 (2000): 1145–55.

39. Laurie Nisonoff, "Men, Women, and the Global Assembly Line," in *Curricular Crossings: Women's Studies and Area Studies: A Web Anthology for the College Classroom,* Five Colleges Women's Research Center, October 2000, http://women crossing.org/nisonoff.html (accessed November 22, 2003).

40. Standing, "Global Feminization through Flexible Labor."

41. For a fascinating account of the relationship between work and education, see Jean Anyon, "Social Class and the Hidden Curriculum of Work," in *Rereading America,* edited by Gary Colombo, Robert Cullen, and Bonnie Lisle (Boston: Bedford Books, 1998), 186–201. Available at http://www.pipeline.com/~rgibson/ hiddencurriculum.htm (accessed November 22, 2003).

42. This term was invented by John Williamson in "What Washington Means by Policy Reform," in *Latin American Adjustment: How Much Has Happened?* edited by John Williamson (Washington, DC: Institute for International Economics, 1990). Updated November 2002, http://www.iie.com/publications/papers/ williamson1102–2.htm (accessed June 3, 2004).

43. This phrase can be attributed to the International Gender and Trade Network.

44. Women's Environment and Development Organization, "WEDO Primer: Women and Trade," November 1999, http://www.wedo.org/global/wedo_ primer.htm (accessed November 23, 2003).

45. William Greider, "The Right and U.S. Trade Law: Invalidating the 20th Century," *The Nation,* October 15, 2001, 21–29.

46. Marjorie Griffin Cohen, "Macho Economics: Canadian Women Confront Free Trade," *Dollars and Sense* 202 (November–December 1995): 18–22.

47. Gil Yaron, "The Final Frontier: A Working Paper on the Big Ten Water Corporations and the Privatization and Corporatization of the World's Last Public Resource," Polaris Institute, 2000, http://www.polarisinstitute.org/pubs/pubs_ final_ frontier.html (accessed November 23, 2003).

48. Marjorie Griffin Cohen, "Macho Economics," 18–22.

49. Farah Fosse, "An Introduction to the General Agreement on Trade in Services (GATS) for Gender Advocates," International Gender and Trade Network—Secretariat, June 2001, http://www.genderandtrade.net/EconoLit/Literacy.html (accessed November 23, 2003).

50. Susanne Soederberg, "On the Contradictions of the New International Financial Architecture: Another Procrustean Bed for Emerging Markets?" *Third World Quarterly* 23 no. 4 (2002): 607–20.

51. The term casino capitalism can be attributed to Susan Strange, *Casino Capitalism* (Oxford: Blackwell, 1986).

52. John Maynard Keynes, *The General Theory* (London: Macmillan, 1936), 159

53. World Bank, *World Development Report, 2000/2001.*

54. UNDP, "The Invisible Heart—Care and the Global Economy," *Human Development Report, 1999: Globalization with a Human Face* (Oxford: Oxford University Press, 1999). Available at http://hdr.undp.org/reports/global/1999/en/pdf/hdr_1999_ch3.pdf "Global Economy" (accessed November 23, 2003).

55. Victor George and Paul Wilding, *Globalization and Human Welfare* (New York: Palgrave, 2002), 113–38.

Chapter 7

1. Marjo-Riitta Liimatainen, "Training and Skills Acquisition in the Informal Sector: A Literature Review," IFP/Skills—Informal Economy Series, ILO, Geneva, 2002, http://www.ilo.org/public/english/employment/infeco/download/literature.pdf (accessed November 23, 2003).

2. Ibid.

3. Friedrich Schneider, "Size and Measurement of the Informal Economy in 110 Countries around the World," paper presented at workshop of Australian National Tax Center, ANU, Canberra, Australia, July 17, 2002, http://rru.worldbank.org/documents/informal_economy.pdf (accessed November 23, 2003). These estimates include illegal as well as legal activities.

4. She also includes the fact that the growth of high-income financial services bids up the price of real estate in urban areas, which makes it more difficult for small, formal enterprises to function. Saskia Sassen, "The Informal Economy: Between New Developments and Old Regulations," *Globalization and Its Discontents: Essays on the New Mobility of People and Money* (New York: New Press, 1998), 153–74.

5. The term sex worker was invented by Carol Leigh, a sex worker herself. See Carol Lee (aka Scarlot Harlot), "Inventing Sex Work," in *Whores and Other Feminists,* edited by Jill Nagle (New York: Routledge, 1997), 223–31.

6. Wendy Chapkis, *Live Sex Acts: Women Performing Erotic Labor* (London and New York: Routledge, 1996).

7. Pyle, "Sex, Maids, and Export Processing."

8. Richard J. Estes, "The Sexual Exploitation of Children: A Working Guide to the Empirical Literature," University of Pennsylvania, August 2001, http://caster.ssw.upenn.edu/~restes/CSEC_Files/CSEC_Bib_August_2001.pdf (accessed November 23, 2003).

9. ILO, "Sex as a Sector: Economic Incentives and Hardships Fuel Growth," *Magazine of the ILO: World of Work* 26 (September–October 1998). Updated November 5, 1998, http://www.ilo.org/public/english/bureau/inf/magazine/26/sex.htm (accessed June 4, 2004).

10. Ibid.

11. Kamala Kempadoo, "Introduction: Globalizing the Sex Worker's Rights," in *Global Sex Workers: Rights, Resistance, and Redefinition,* edited by Kamala Kempadoo and Jo Doezema (New York and London: Routledge, 1998), 204–9.

12. See Londa Schiebinger's historical analysis of the simultaneous emergence of gender and race ideology in *Nature's Body* (Boston: Beacon Press, 1995).

13. Leah Platt, "Regulating the Global Brothel," *American Prospect* 12 (July 2–26, 2001): 10–14. Available at http://www.prospect.org/print/V12/12/platt-l.html (accessed November 23, 2003).

14. Jo Doezema and Cheryl Overs, "Internal Activism: Jo Doezema Interviews NWSP Coordinator Cheryl Overs," in *Global Sex Workers: Rights, Resistance, and Redefinition,* edited by Kamala Kempadoo and Jo Doezema (New York and London: Routledge, 1998), 204–9.

15. Human Rights Watch, "Trafficking, 2003," http://www.hrw.org/women/trafficking.html (accessed November 23, 2003).

16. Moreno-Fontes, "The Importance of Considering Gender Issues in Migration."

17. Pyle, "Sex, Maids, and Export Processing."

18. Moreno-Fontes, "The Importance of Considering Gender Issues in Migration."

19. Pyle, "Sex, Maids, and Export Processing."

20. Ibid.

21. Leslie Salzinger, "A Maid by Any Other Name: The Transformation of 'Dirty Work' by Central American Immigrants," in *Ethnography Unbound: Power and Resistance in the Modern Metropolis,* edited by Michael Burawoy (Berkeley: University of California Press, 1991), 139–52.

22. Ibid.

23. Information from the Grameen Bank Web site, 2003, http://www.grameen-info.org/index.html.

24. See the World Bank Policy Research Report, *Engendering Development through Gender Equality in Rights, Resources, and Voice* (Oxford: Oxford University Press, 2001); and Naila Kabeer, "Conflicts over Credit: Re-Evaluating the

Empowerment Potential of Loans to Women in Rural Bangladesh," *World Development* 29, no. 1 (2001): 63–84.

25. Norman MacIsaac, "The Role of Microcredit in Poverty Reduction and Promoting Gender Equity," discussion paper, South Asia Partnership Canada, Strategic Policy and Planning Division, Asia Branch CIDA, June 12, 1997, http://www.acdi-cida.gc.ca/index-e.html (accessed November 23, 2003).

26. World Bank, *Engendering Development through Gender Equality in Rights, Resources, and Voice.* See also S. M. Hashemi, S. R. Schuler, and A. P. Riley, "Rural Credit Programs and Women's Empowerment in Bangladesh," *World Development* 24, no. 4 (1996): 635–53.

27. MacIsaac, "The Role Of Microcredit in Poverty Reduction and Promoting Gender Equity."

28. A. M. Goetz and Gupta R. Sen, "Who Takes the Credit? Gender, Power, and Control Over Loan Use in Rural Credit Programmes in Bangladesh," *World Development* 24, no. 1 (1994): 45–63.

29. Kabeer, "Conflicts over Credit."

30. Gina Neff, "Microcredit, Microresults," *Left Business Observer* 74 (October 1996). Available at http://www.leftbusinessobserver.com/Micro_summit.html (accessed November 23, 2003).

31. Pyle, "Sex, Maids, and Export Processing."

32. ILO, Global Employment Forum, summary, "Informal Economy: Formalizing the Hidden Potential and Raising Standards," November 19, 2001, http://www-ilo-mirror.cornell.edu/public/english/employment/geforum/informal.html (accessed November 23, 2001).

Chapter 8

1. See especially Pujol, *Feminism and Anti-Feminism in Early Economic Thought.*

2. At one time economists actually believed that sunspots caused business cycles. One of the founding fathers of modern economics, W. Stanley Jevons, espoused this notion.

3. Cheryl Miller and Salome Chasnoff, eds., *Beyond Beijing: The International Women's Movement, the Handbook* (Chicago: Beyondmedia, 1997).

4. Saskia Sassen, *Globalization and Its Discontents: Essays on the New Mobility of People and Money* (New York: New Press, 1998).

5. Our principle of inclusion is informed by the discussion of social exclusion. See ILO, "Social Exclusion and Antipoverty Strategies," July 6, 1998, http://www.ilo.org/public/english/bureau/inst/papers/synth/socex/ch1.html (accessed November 23, 2003).

6. Ibid.

7. See Fourth World Conference on Women, "Platform for Action,"

http://www.un.org/womenwatch/daw/beijing/platform/plat1.htm#concern (accessed November 23, 2003).

8. See Peggy Sanday-Reeves, "The Socio-Cultural Context of Rape," *Journal of Social Issues* 37 (1981): 5–27, for a discussion of the interplay of environmental factors and violence against women.

9. CEDAW, United Nations, October 28, 2003, http://www.un.org/womenwatch/daw/cedaw/ (accessed November 23, 2003). It is worth noting that the United States is the only industrialized nation that has not endorsed CEDAW. At this writing San Francisco County is the only jurisdiction in the United States that is in compliance with this important international treaty.

10. Miller and Chasnoff, *Beyond Beijing,* 93.

11. The precise ratios are 5.64 for the United States in 1997 and 2.59 for Sweden in 1995. Looking only at households with children, the ratios are 5.91 and 2.19 respectively. See Timothy M. Smeeding, "The Gap between Rich and Poor: A Cross-National Perspective for Why Inequality Matters and What Policy Can Do to Alleviate It," National Institute of Population and Social Security Research, Tokyo, Japan, March 21, 2001, http://www.sprc.unsw.edu.au/seminars/japan.pdf (accessed November 23, 2003).

12. Christopher, "Welfare State Regimes and Mothers' Poverty."

13. See Daniel H. Weinberg, "A Brief Look at Postwar U.S. Income Inequality," U.S. Census Bureau, August 22, 2002, http://www.census.gov/hhes/income/incineq/p60asc.html (accessed November 23, 2003).

14. See Marilyn Waring, *If Women Counted: A New Feminist Economics* (San Francisco: Harper, 1989).

15. See Juliet B. Schor, *The Overspent American: Why We Want What We Don't Need* (New York: HarperCollins, 1999).

16. A copy of this memo from December 12, 1991 can be found at the Whirled Bank Group Web site, 2001, http://www.whirledbank.org/ourwords/summers.html (accessed November 23, 2003).

17. Fourth World Conference on Women, "Platform for Action: Women and the Environment," October 28, 2003, http://www.un.org/womenwatch/daw/beijing/platform/environ.htm (accessed November 22, 2003).

18. See Richard Anker, "Theories of Occupational Segregation by Sex: An Overview," *International Labor Review* 136, no. 3 (1997). Available at http://www.ilo.org/public/english/support/publ/revue/articles/ank97-3.htm (accessed November 23, 2003).

19. *The Life and Times of Rosie the Riveter* is a documentary film about the lives of women in the defense industry during World War II.

Select Bibliography

Books and Articles

Agarwal, Bina. *A Field of One's Own.* Cambridge: Cambridge University Press, 1998.

Albelda, Randy, and Chris Tilly. *Glass Ceilings and Bottomless Pits.* Cambridge: South End Press, 1997.

———. "Fallacies of Welfare-to-Work Policies." In *Lost Ground: Welfare Reform, Poverty, and Beyond,* edited by Randy Albelda and Ann Withhorn, 79–94. Cambridge: South End Press, 2002.

Amott, Teresa, and Julie Matthaei. *Race, Gender, and Work: A Multicultural Economic History of Women in the United States.* Rev. ed. Boston: South End Press, 1996.

Anker, Richard, "Theories of Occupational Segregation by Sex: An Overview." In *Women, Gender, and Work,* edited by Martha Fetherolf Loutfi, 129–56. Geneva: International Labour Office, 2001.

Anyon, Jean. "Social Class and the Hidden Curriculum of Work." *Journal of Education* 162 (winter 1980): 67–92.

Argawal, Bina. "'Bargaining' and Gender Relations: With and beyond the Household." *Feminist Economics* 3 (spring 1997): 1–50.

Aslaksen, Iulie. "Gross Domestic Product." In *Elgar Companion to Feminist Economics,* edited by Janice Peterson and Margaret Lewis, 411–17. Cheltenham and Northampton: Edward Elgar, 1999.

Badgett, M. V. Lee. "Gender, Sexuality, and Sexual Orientation: All in the Feminist Family?" *Feminist Economics* 1 (spring 1995): 121–40.

Balamm, David N., and Michael Veseth. *Introduction to International Political Economy.* 2d ed. Upper Saddle River, NJ: Prentice-Hall, 2001.

Barker, Drucilla K. "From Feminist Empiricism to Feminist Poststructuralism: Philosophical Questions in Feminist Economics." In *The Companion to Economics and Philosophy.* Cheltenham and Northhampton: Edward Elgar, 2004.

Barker, Drucilla K., and Edith Kuiper, eds. *Toward a Feminist Philosophy of Economics.* New York and London: Routledge, 2003.

Select Bibliography

Becker, Gary S. *A Treatise on the Family.* Enl. ed. Cambridge: Harvard University Press, 1993.

Benería, Lourdes. "Towards a Greater Integration of Gender in Economics." *World Development* 23 (November 1995): 1839–50.

———. "Structural Adjustment Policies." In *The Elgar Companion to Feminist Economics,* edited by Janice Peterson and Margaret Lewis, 687–95. Cheltenham and Northhampton: Edward Elgar, 1999.

Benería, Lourdes, and Gita Sen. "Accumulation, Reproduction, and Women's Roles in Economic Development." *Signs* 7 (winter 1981): 279–98.

Bergmann, Barbara. "Feminism and Economics." *Academe* (September–October 1983): 22–26.

———. *The Economic Emergence of Women.* New York: Basic Books, 1986.

———. "Watch out for Family Friendly Policies." *Dollars and Sense* 215 (January–February 1998): 10–11.

Bergmann, Barbara, and Trudi Renwick. "A Budget-Based Definition of Poverty with an Application to Single-Parent Families." *Journal of Human Resources* 29 (winter 1993): 1–24.

Bianchi, Suzanne M. "Maternal Employment and Time with Children: Dramatic Change or Surprising Continuity?" *Demography* 37 (November 2000): 401–14.

Boserup, Ester. *Women's Role in Economic Development.* London: Allen and Unwin, 1970.

———. "Economic Change and the Roles of Women." In *Persistent Inequalities: Women and World Development,* edited by Irene Tinker, 14–26. New York and Oxford: Oxford University Press, 1990.

Budig, Michelle J., and Paula England. "The Wage Penalty for Motherhood." *American Sociological Review* 66 (April 2001): 204–25.

Burbach, Roger, Orlando Núñez, and Boris Kagarlitsky. *Globalization and Its Discontents: The Rise of Postmodern Societies.* London and Chicago: Pluto Press, 1997.

Chamberlain, Mariam K. "Glass Ceiling." In *The Elgar Companion to Feminist Economics,* edited by Janice Peterson and Margaret Lewis, 396–401. Cheltenham and Northhampton: Edward Elgar, 1999.

Chapkis, Wendy. *Live Sex Acts: Women Performing Erotic Labor.* London and New York: Routledge, 1996.

Cherry, Robert D. *Who Gets the Good Jobs: Combating Race and Gender Disparities.* Piscataway: Rutgers University Press, 2001.

Christopher, Karen. "Welfare State Regimes and Mothers' Poverty." *Social Politics: International Studies in Gender, State, and Society* 9 (spring 2002): 60–86.

Citro, Constance F., and Robert T. Michael, eds. *Measuring Poverty: A New Approach.* Washington, DC: National Academies Press, 1995.

Cloud, Kathleen, and Nancy Garrett. "Inclusion of Women's Household Human Capital Production in Analyses of Structural Transformation." *Feminist Economics* 2 (fall 1996): 93–120.

Cohn, Steve. "Telling Other Stories: Heterodox Critiques of Neoclassical Micro Principles Texts," Global Development and Environment Institute Working Paper 00–06, 2000.

Collins, Patricia Hill. *Black Feminist Thought: Knowledge, Consciousness, and the Politics of Empowerment.* New York: Routledge, 1990.

Coontz, Stephanie. *The Way We Never Were: American Families and the Nostalgia Trap.* New York: Basic Books, 2000.

Crittenden, Ann. *The Economic Consequences of Motherhood: Why the Most Important Job in the World Is Still the Least Valued.* New York: Henry Holt, 2000.

Crotty, James. "Why Is There Chronic Excess Capacity: The Market Failures Issue." *Challenge* 45 (November–December 2002): 21–24.

Darrity, William, Jr., ed. *Economics and Discrimination.* Cheltenham and Northhampton: Edward Elgar, 1995.

de Beauvoir, Simone. 1949. Reprint, *The Second Sex.* New York: Alfred A. Knopf, 1993.

Dobb, Maurice. *Studies in the Development of Capitalism.* New York: International Publishing Co., 1964.

Donath, Susan. "The Other Economy: A Suggestion for a Distinctively Feminist Economics." *Feminist Economics* 6 (March 2000): 115–23.

Dorman, Peter, Nancy Folbre, Donald McCloskey, and Tom Weisskopf. "Debating Markets." Edited by Tom Weisskopf and Nancy Folbre. *Feminist Economics* 2 (spring 1996): 69–85.

Ehrenreich, Barbara. *Nickel and Dimed: On (Not) Getting by in America.* New York: Henry Holt, 2002.

Ehrenreich, Barbara, and Arlie Hochschild, eds. *Global Woman: Nannies, Maids, and Sex Workers in the New Economy.* New York: Henry Holt, 2002.

Eisenberg, Susan. "Still Building the Foundation: Women in the Construction Trades." *Working USA* 2, no. 1 (1998): 23–25.

Elson, Diane. "Male Bias in Macro-economics: The Case of Structural Adjustment." In *Male Bias in the Development Process,* edited by Diane Elson, 164–90. Manchester and New York: Manchester University Press, 1991.

———, ed. *Progress of the World's Women,* 2000. New York: United Nations Development Fund for Women, UNIFEM, 2000.

Esping-Andersen, Gøsta. *The Three Worlds of Welfare Capitalism.* Princeton: Princeton University Press, 1990.

Espinoza, Robert. "Migration Trends: Maps and Charts." In *Global Woman: Nannies, Maids, and Sex Workers in the New Economy,* edited by Barbara Ehrenreich and Arlie Hochschild, 275–80. New York: Henry Holt, 2002.

Feiner, Susan F., ed. *Race and Gender in the American Economy: Views from across the Spectrum.* New York: Prentice-Hall, 1994.

Feiner, Susan F., and Bruce B. Roberts. "Hidden by the Invisible Hand: Neoclassical Economic Theory and the Textbook Treatment of Race and Gender." *Gender & Society* 4 (June 1990): 159–81.

Select Bibliography

Feldman, Shelley. "Crises, Poverty, and Gender Inequality: Current Themes and Issues." In *Unequal Burden: Economic Crises, Persistent Poverty, and Women's Work*, edited by Lourdes Benería and Shelley Feldman, 1–25. Boulder: Westview Press, 1992.

Ferber, Marianne A., and Julie A. Nelson. "Introduction: The Social Construction of Economics and the Social Construction of Gender." In *Beyond Economic Man: Feminist Theory and Economics*, edited by Marianne A. Ferber and Julie A. Nelson, 1–22. Chicago: University of Chicago Press, 1993.

Figart, Deborah M. "Wage Gap." In *The Elgar Companion to Feminist Economics*, edited by Janice Peterson and Margaret Lewis, 746–49. Cheltenham and Northhampton: Edward Elgar, 1999.

Figart, Deborah M., Ellen Mutari, and Marilyn Power. *Living Wages, Equal Wages: Gender and Labor Market Policies in the United States*. New York: Routledge, 2002.

Folbre, Nancy. "The Unproductive Housewife: Her Evolution in British Economic Thought." *Signs* 16 (spring 1991): 463–84.

———. "Socialism, Feminist and Scientific." In *Beyond Economic Man: Feminist Theory and Economics*, edited by Marianne A. Ferber and Julie A. Nelson, 94–110. Chicago: University of Chicago Press, 1993.

———. *Who Pays for the Kid: Gender and the Structures of Constraint*. London and New York: Routledge, 1994.

———. "'Holding Hands at Midnight': The Paradox of Caring Labor." *Feminist Economics* 1 (spring 1995): 73–92.

———. "Accounting for Care in the United States." In *Care Work: The Quest for Security*, edited by Mary Daly, 175–91. Geneva: International Labour Office, 2001.

———. *The Invisible Heart: Economics and Family Values*. New York: New Press, 2001.

Fraad, Harriet, Stephen Resnick, and Richard Wolff. *Bringing It All Back Home: Class, Gender, and Power in the Household*. London: Pluto Press, 1994.

Fraser, Nancy. *Justice Interruptus: Critical Reflections on the "Postsocialist" Condition*. London and New York: Routledge, 1997.

Friedan, Betty. *The Feminine Mystique*. New York: W. W. Norton, 1963.

George, Victor, and Paul Wilding. *Globalization and Human Welfare* (New York: Palgrave, 2002).

Gertsel, Naomi, and Harriet Engel Gross, "Gender and Families in the United States: The Reality of Economic Dependence." In *Women: A Feminist Perspective*, edited by Jo Freeman, 92–127. Mountain View: Mayfield, 1995.

Gilens, Martin. *Why Americans Hate Welfare: Race, Media, and the Politics of Antipoverty Policy*. Chicago: University of Chicago Press, 1999.

Gilman, Nils. "Thorstein Veblen's Neglected Feminism." *Journal of Economic Issues* 33, no. 3 (fall 1999): 689–712.

Goetz, A. M., and Gupta R. Sen. "Who Takes the Credit? Gender, Power, and Control over Loan Use in Rural Credit Programmes in Bangladesh." *World Development* 24, no. 1 (1994): 45–63.

Goldin, Claudia. *Understanding the Gender Gap: An Economic History of American Women.* New York: Oxford University Press, 1990.

Gornick, Janet, and Marcia Meyers. "Support for Working Families." *The American Prospect* 12 (January 1, 2001), 3–7.

Gornick, Janet, Marcia K. Myers, and Katherine E. Ross. "Public Policies and the Employment of Mothers: A Cross-National Study." *Social Science Quarterly* 79 (1998): 35–54.

Grapard, Ulla. "Robinson Crusoe: The Quintessential Economic Man." *Feminist Economics* 1 (spring 1995): 33–52.

Greider, William. "The Right and US Trade Law: Invalidating the 20th Century." *The Nation* (October 15, 2001): 21–29.

Haller, Mark. *Eugenics: Hereditarian Attitudes in American Thought.* New Brunswick, NJ: Rutgers University Press, 1984.

Hankison-Nelson, Lynn. *Who Knows: From Quine to a Feminist Empiricism.* Philadelphia: Temple University Press, 1994.

Haraway, Donna. "Situated Knowledges: The Science Question in Feminism and the Privilege of Partial Perspective." *Feminist Studies* 14 (fall 1988): 579–99.

Harding, Sandra. "Can Feminist Thought Make Economics More Objective?" *Feminist Economics* 1 (spring 1995): 7–32.

Hartmann, Heidi I. "The Family as the Locus of Gender, Class, and Political Struggle: The Example of Housework." In *Feminism and Methodology,* edited by Sandra Harding, 109–34. Bloomington and Indianapolis: Indiana University Press, 1987.

Hashemi, S. M., S. R. Schuler, and A. P. Riley, "Rural Credit Programs and Women's Empowerment in Bangladesh." *World Development* 24, no. 4 (1996): 635–53.

Himmelwhite, Susan. "Domestic Labor." In *The Elgar Companion to Feminist Economics,* edited by Janice Peterson and Margaret Lewis, 126–35. Cheltenham and Northhampton: Edwin Elgar, 1999.

Hobsbawm, Eric. *Industry and Empire: The Birth of the Industrial Revolution.* Harmondsworth: Penguin, 1969.

Hochschild, Arlie. "The Nanny Chain." *The American Prospect* 11 (January 3, 2003): 32–38.

Hochschild, Arlie R., and Ann Machung. *The Second Shift.* New York: Morrow, William, and Co., 1990.

Humphries, Jane. "Enclosures, Common Rights, and Women: The Proletarianization of Families in the Late Eighteenth and Early Nineteenth Centuries." *Journal of Economic History* 50 (March 1990): 17–42.

———. "Economics, Gender, and Equal Opportunities." In *The Economics of Equal*

Select Bibliography

Opportunities, edited by Jane Humphries and Jill Rubery, 55–79. Manchester: Equal Employment Opportunities Commission, 1995.

————. "Female Headed Households in Early Industrial Britain: The Vanguard of the Proletariat?" *Labor History Review* 63 (spring 1998): 31–65.

Jacobsen, Joyce. *The Economics of Gender.* Malden: Blackwell, 1998.

————. "Human Capital Theory." In *The Elgar Companion to Feminist Economics,* edited by Janice Peterson and Margaret Lewis, 443–48. Cheltenham and Northhampton: Edward Elgar, 1999.

Kabeer, Naila. "Conflicts over Credit: Re-evaluating the Empowerment Potential of Loans to Women in Rural Bangladesh." *World Development* 29, no. 1 (2001): 63–84.

Kempadoo, Kamala, and Jo Doezema, ed., *Global Sex Workers: Rights, Resistance, and Redefinition.* New York and London: Routledge, 1998.

Keynes, John Maynard. *The General Theory.* London: Macmillan, 1936.

King, Mary C. "Black Women's Labor Market Status: Occupational Segregation in the United States and Great Britain." *Review of Black Political Economy* 24 (summer 1995): 23–40.

Klamer, Arjo. *Conversations with Economists: New Classical Economists and Opponents Speak out on the Current Controversy in Macroeconomics.* Lanham: Rowman and Littlefield, 1984.

Koonz, Claudia. *Mothers in the Fatherland: Women, the Family, and Nazi Politics.* New York: St. Martin's Press, 1988.

Kramarae, Cheris, and Paula A. Treichler. *A Feminist Dictionary.* Champaign: University of Illinois Press, 1997.

Kuiper, Edith, and Drucilla K. Barker, eds. *Feminist Economics and the World Bank.* New York and London: Routledge, forthcoming.

Kuiper, Edith, Jolande Sap, Susan Feiner, Notburga Ott, and Zafris Tzannatos, eds. *Out of the Margin: Feminist Perspectives on Economics.* New York and London: Routledge, 1995.

Kukreja, Sunil. "The Two Faces of Development." In *Introduction to International Political Economy,* 2d ed., edited by David N. Balaam and Michael Veseth, 320–45. Upper Saddle River: Prentice Hall, 2001.

Kuttner, Robert. *Everything for Sale: The Virtues and Limits of Markets.* New York: Knopf, 1997.

Lister, Ruth. *Feminist Perspectives.* London: Macmillan, 1997.

Longino, Helen. *Science as Social Knowledge: Values and Objectivity in Scientific Inquiry.* Princeton: Princeton University Press, 1990.

Madrick, Jeff. "Why Mainstream Economists Should Take Heed." *Feminist Economics* 3 (spring 1997): 143–49.

Mandeville, Bernard. "The Fable of the Bees: Or, Private Vices." In *Publick Benefits,* edited by F. B. Kaye, 2 vols. Oxford: Clarendon Press, 1924; reprint, Indianapolis: Liberty Fund, 1988.

Margolis, Eric, Michael Soldatenko, Sandra Acker, and Marina Gair. "Peekaboo: Hiding and Outing the Curriculum." In *The Hidden Curriculum of Higher Education,* edited by Eric Margolis, 1–20. London and New York: Routledge, 2001.

Marx, Karl, and Friedrich Engels. *The Communist Manifesto.* 1848; reprint, London: Verso, 1998.

Mencimer, Stephanie. "Children Left Behind: Why We Need a National Child-Care Program, Now More Than Ever." *The American Prospect* 13 (December 30, 2002): 29–31.

Miller, Cheryl, and Salome Chasnoff, eds. *Beyond Beijing: The International Women's Movement, the Handbook.* Chicago: Beyondmedia, 1997.

Mohanty, Chandra. "Under Western Eyes: Feminist Scholarship and Colonial Discourses." *Feminist Review* 30 (autumn 1988): 61–88.

Molyneux, Maxine. "Beyond the Domestic Labor Debate." *New Left Review* 116 (1979): 3–27.

Morales, Juan Antonio, and Jeffrey D. Sachs. "Bolivia's Economic Crisis." In *Developing Country Debt and the World Economy,* edited by Jeffrey D. Sachs, 57–65. Chicago: University of Chicago Press, 1989.

Nagle, Jill, ed. *Whores and Other Feminists.* New York: Routledge, 1997.

Nelson, Julie A. *Feminism, Objectivity, and Economics.* New York: Routledge, 1996.

Orloff, Ann Schola. "Gender and the Social Rights of Citizenship." *American Sociological Review* 58 (1993): 303–28.

Ott, Notburga. "Fertility and Division of Work in the Family: A Game Theoretic Model of Household Decisions." In *Out of the Margin: Feminist Perspectives on Economics,* edited by Edith Kuiper and Jolande Sap, 80–99. New York and London: Routledge, 1995.

Pearce, Diana M. "The Feminization of Poverty: Women, Work, and Welfare." *Urban and Social Change Review* 11 (1978): 28–36.

Pearson, Ruth. "'Nimble Fingers' Revisited: Reflection on Women and the Third World Industrialization in the Late Twentieth Century." In *Feminist Visions of Development: Gender Analysis and Policy,* edited by Cecile Jackson and Ruth Pearson, 171–88. London and New York: Routledge, 1998.

Peterson, Janice, Xue Song, and Avis Jones-deWeaver. "Life after Welfare Reform: Low Income Single Parent Families, Pre- and Post-TANF." In *Research in Brief,* Institute for Women's Policy Research Publication Number D446, May 22, 2002.

Peterson, V. Spike, and Anne Sisson Runyan. *Global Gender Issues.* Boulder: Westview Press, 1993.

Platt, Leah."Regulating the Global Brothel." *The American Prospect* 12 (July 2–26, 2001): 10–14.

Polacheck, Robert. "Human Capital and Gender Earning Gap: A Response of Feminist Critiques." In *Out of the Margin: Feminist Perspectives on Economics,* edited by Edith Kuiper and Jolande Sap, 61–89. London and New York: Routledge, 1995.

Pujol, Michèle A. *Feminism and Anti-Feminism in Early Economic Thought.* Aldershot: Edward Elgar, 1992.

Pyle, Jean L. "Women, the Family, and Economic Restructuring: The Singapore Model." *Review of Social Economy* 55 (summer 1997): 215–23.

———. "Sex, Maids, and Export Processing: Risks and Reasons for Gendered Global Production Networks." *International Journal of Politics, Culture, and Society* 15 (September 2001): 55–76.

Roodman, David Malin. "Still Waiting for the Jubilee: Pragmatic Solutions for the Third World Debt Crisis," Worldwatch Paper 155, Worldwatch Institute, April 2001.

Rosenberg-Smith, Carroll. *Disorderly Conduct: Visions of Gender in Victorian America.* Oxford: Oxford University Press, 1986.

Rossi, Alice S., ed. *The Feminist Papers: From Adams to de Beauvoir.* New York: Columbia University Press, 1973.

Sainsbury, Diane. *Gender, Equality, and Welfare States.* Cambridge: Cambridge University Press, 1996.

———. "Gender and Social Democratic Welfare States." In *Gender and Welfare State Regimes,* edited by Diane Sainsbury, 75–116. Oxford: Oxford University Press, 1999.

Salzinger, Leslie. "A Maid by Any Other Name: The Transformation of 'Dirty Work' by Central American Immigrants." In *Ethnography Unbound: Power and Resistance in the Modern Metropolis,* edited by Michael Burawoy, 139–52. Berkeley: University of California Press, 1991.

Sanday-Reeves, Peggy. "The Socio-Cultural Context of Rape." *Journal of Social Issues* 37 (1981): 5–27.

Sassen, Saskia. *Globalization and Its Discontents: Essays on the New Mobility of People and Money.* New York: New Press, 1998.

Schiebinger, Londa. *Nature's Body.* Boston: Beacon Press, 1995.

Schlosser, Eric. *Fast Food Nation: The Dark Side of the All-American Meal.* New York: HarperCollins, 2002.

Schor, Juliet B. *The Overspent American: Why We Want What We Don't Need.* New York: HarperCollins, 1999.

Seager, Joni. *The State of Women in the World Atlas.* London: Penguin, 1997.

Shaw, Susan M., and Janet Lee. *Women's Voices, Feminist Visions: Classic and Contemporary Readings,* 2d ed. New York: McGraw-Hill, 2004.

Siegenthaler, Jürg K. "Poverty among Single Elderly Women under Different Systems of Old-Age Security: A Comparative Review." *Social Security Bulletin* 59 (fall 1996): 31–44.

Smeeding, Timothy M., Lee Rainwater, and Gary Burtless. "United States Poverty in a Cross-National Context," Luxembourg Income Study Working Paper 244, September 2000.

Soederberg, Susanne. "On the Contradictions of the New International Financial Architecture: Another Procrustean Bed for Emerging Markets?" *Third World Quarterly* 23, no. 4 (2002): 607–20.

Solow, Barbara L., and Stanley L. Engerman. *British Capitalism and Caribbean Slavery: The Legacy of Eric Williams.* New York: Cambridge University Press, 1988.

Standing, Guy. "Global Feminization through Flexible Labor: A Theme Revisited." *World Development* 27 (March 1999): 583–602.

———. "Care Work: Overcoming Insecurity and Neglect." In *Care Work: The Quest for Security,* edited by Mary Daly, 15–31. Geneva: International Labour Office, 2001.

Strange, Susan. *Casino Capitalism.* Oxford: Blackwell, 1986.

Strassmann, Diana. "Not a Free Market: The Rhetoric of Disciplinary Authority in Economics." In *Beyond Economic Man: Feminist Theory and Economics,* edited by Marianne A. Ferber and Julie A. Nelson, 54–68. Chicago: University of Chicago Press, 1993.

Strober, Myra H. "Two-Earner Families." In *Feminism, Children, and the New Families,* edited by Sanford M. Dornmbush and Myra H. Strober, 161–90. New York: Guilford Press, 1988.

Strober, Myra H., and Carolyn L. Arnold. "The Dynamics of Occupational Segregation among Bank Tellers." In *Gender in the Workplace,* edited by Clair Brown and Joseph Pechman, 107–58. Washington, DC: Brookings Institution, 1987.

Thomas, Susan L. "From the Culture of Poverty to the Culture of Single Motherhood: The New Poverty Paradigm." *Women and Politics* 14, no. 2 (1994): 65–97.

———. "Race, Gender, and Welfare Reform: The Anti-Nationalist Response." *Journal of Black Studies* 28 (July 1998): 419–46.

Tinker, Irene. "The Making of a Field: Advocates, Scholars, and Practitioners." In *Persistent Inequalities: Women and World Development,* edited by Irene Tinker, 27–53. New York and Oxford: Oxford University Press, 1990.

Tucker, Robert C., ed. *The Marx-Engels Reader.* New York: Norton, 1978.

Waring, Marilyn. *If Women Counted: A New Feminist Economics.* San Francisco: Harper, 1989.

Williams, Eric. *Capitalism and Slavery.* Chapel Hill: University of North Carolina Press, 1994.

Williams, Joan. *Unbending Gender: Why Family and Work Conflict and What to Do about It.* New York: Oxford University Press, 2001.

Williams, Rhonda. "Race, Deconstruction, and the Emergent Agenda of Feminist Economic Theory," In *Beyond Economic Man: Feminist Theory and Economics,* edited by Marianne A. Ferber and Julie A. Nelson, 144–52. Chicago: University of Chicago Press, 1993.

Select Bibliography

Williams, Rhonda, and William E. Spriggs. "How Does It Feel to Be Free? Reflections on Black-White Economic Inequality in the Era of 'Color-Blind' Law." *Review of Black Political Economy* 1 (summer 1999): 27.

World Bank Policy Research Report. *Engendering Development through Gender Equality in Rights, Resources, and Voice.* Oxford: Oxford University Press, 2001.

Yalom, Marilyn. *A History of the Wife.* New York: HarperCollins, 2001.

Internet Sources

Acorn Living Wage Resource Center. http://www.livingwagecampaign.org/ (November 23, 2003).

Anker, Richard. "Theories of Occupational Segregation by Sex: An Overview." *International Labor Review* 136, no. 3 (1997), http://www.ilo.org/public/ english/support/publ/revue/articles/ank97–3.htm (accessed November 23, 2003).

Australian Bureau of Statistics. "Income—Income Distribution: The Value of Unpaid Work." In *Australian Social Trends, 1995.* Updated November 18, 2002. http://www.abs.gov.au/Ausstats/abs@.nsf/0/24e9a783f4f225bbca256 bcd0082558a?OpenDocument (accessed June 3, 2004).

Bangladesh Export Processing Zones Authority Web site. http://www.bangladesh-epz.com/prologue.htm (accessed November 23, 2003).

Catalyst, University of Michigan Business School and Center for the Education of Women. "Women and the MBA: Gateway to Opportunity." 2000. http: //www.umich.edu/~cew/mbafacts.pdf (accessed November 23, 2003).

Convention on the Elimination of All Forms of Discrimination against Women. United Nations, October 28, 2003. http://www.un.org/womenwatch/ daw/cedaw/ (accessed November 23, 2003).

Estes, Richard J. " The Sexual Exploitation of Children: A Working Guide to the Empirical Literature," University of Pennsylvania, August 2001. http://caster.ssw.upenn.edu/~restes/CSEC_Files/CSEC_Bib_August_2001 .pdf (accessed November 23, 2003).

FitzPatrick, Christina Smith, and Joan Entmacher. "Increasing Economic Security for Elderly Women by Improving Social Security Survivor Benefits." National Women's Law Center, paper prepared for presentation at the Twelfth Annual Conference of the National Academy of Social Insurance, Washington, DC, January 27, 2000. http://www.nwlc.org/pdf/NASIwidows2.pdf (accessed June 4, 2004).

Fosse, Farah. "An Introduction to the General Agreement on Trade in Services (GATS) for Gender Advocates" International Gender and Trade Network— Secretariat, June 2001. http://www.genderandtrade.net/EconoLit/Literacy .html (accessed November 23, 2003).

Fourth World Conference on Women. "Platform for Action." http://www.un.org/

womenwatch/daw/beijing/platform/plat1.htm#concern (accessed November 23, 2003).

———. "Platform for Action: Women and the Environment." October 28, 2003. http://www.un.org/womenwatch/daw/beijing/platform/environ.htm (accessed November 23, 2003).

Fullerton, Howard N., Jr. "Labor Force Participation: 75 Years of Change, 1950–98 and 1998–2025." *Monthly Labor Review* (1999), http://www.bls .gov/opub/mlr/1999/12/art1full.pdf (accessed November 23, 2003).

Goldberg, Jonah. "Impoverished Ideas: Being Poor Ain't All That Great." *National Review Online,* February 8, 2002, http://www.nationalreview.com/ goldberg/goldberg020802.shtml (accessed November 23, 2003).

Gordon, Linda. "Welfare and Public Relief." In *The Reader's Companion to U.S. Women's History,* edited by Barbara Smith, Marysa Navarro, Wilma Mankiller, Gloria Steinem, and Gwendolyn Mink (New York: Houghton Mifflin, 1999). Available at http://college.hmco.com/history/readerscomp/women/html/ wh_ 039000_welfareandpu.htm (accessed November 23, 2003).

Howarth, Catherine, and Peter Kenway. "Monitoring Poverty and Social Exclusion: Why Britain Needs a Key Indicators Report." New Policy Institute, 1998, London. http://www.npi.org.uk/reports/mpse%20-%20Why%20 Britain%20Needs% 20a%20KIPS.pdf (accessed November 23, 2003).

Human Rights Watch. "Trafficking." http://www.hrw.org/women/trafficking .html (accessed November 23, 2003).

"Innocenti Report Card 1." UNICEF Innocenti Research Centre, Florence, 2000. http://www.unicef-icdc.org/publications/pdf/repcard1e.pdf (accessed November 23, 2003).

International Labour Organization. "Social Exclusion and Antipoverty Strategies." July 6, 1998. http://www.ilo.org/public/english/bureau/inst/papers/synth/ socex/ch1.htm (accessed November 23, 2003).

———. "Facts on Women at Work." http://www.ilo.org/public/english/bureau/ inf/download/women/pdf/factssheet.pdf (accessed June 2, 2004).

International Labour Organization, Global Employment Forum. Summary. "Informal Economy: Formalizing the Hidden Potential and Raising Standards." November 19, 2001. http://www-ilo-mirror.cornell.edu/public/ english/employment/geforum/informal.htm (accessed November 23, 2003).

Jesuit, David, and Timothy Smeeding. "Poverty Levels in the Developed World," Luxembourg Income Study Working Paper 321, July 2002. http://www .lisproject.org/ publications/liswps/321.pdf (accessed November 23, 2003).

Kan, Man-yee. "Gender Asymmetry in the Division of Domestic Labor." Paper presented at the British Household Panel Survey, 2001, Institute for Social and Economic Research, University of Essex. http://www.iser.essex.ac.uk/ activities/conferences/bhps-2001/docs/pdf/papers/kan.pdf (accessed November 23, 2003).

Liimatainen, Marjo-Riitta. "Training and Skills Acquisition in the Informal Sector: A Literature Review." IFP/Skills—Informal Economy Series, International Labour Organization, Geneva, 2002. http://www.ilo.org/public/english/employment/infeco/download/literature.pdf (November 23, 2003).

Lowe, Eugene T. "A Status Report on Hunger and Homelessness in America's Cities, 2001: A 27-City Survey." U.S. Conference of Mayors, December 2001. http://www.usmayors.org/uscm/hungersurvey/2001/hungersurvey2001.pdf (accessed November 23, 2003).

MacIsaac, Norman. "The Role of Microcredit in Poverty Reduction and Promoting Gender Equity." Discussion paper, South Asia Partnership Canada, Strategic Policy and Planning Division, Asia Branch Canada International Development Agency, June 12, 1997. http://www.acdi-cida.gc.ca/index-e.htm (accessed November 23, 2003).

Minnesota Department of Employee Relations. "Guide to Understanding Pay Equity Compliance and Computer Reports." October 2000. http://www.doer.state.mn.us/lr-peqty/resource.htm (accessed November 23, 2003).

"Money Income in the United States: 2001," Current Population Reports, Consumer Income, September 2002. http://www.census.gov/prod/2002pubs/p60–218.pdf (accessed November 23, 2003).

Moreno-Fontes, Gloria. "The Importance of Considering Gender Issues in Migration." International Labour Organization, June 14, 2002. http://www.ilo.org/public/english/protection/migrant/projects/gender/ (accessed November 23, 2003).

Neff, Gina. "Microcredit, Microresults." *Left Business Observer* 74 (October 1996), http://www.leftbusinessobserver.com/Micro_summit.html (accessed November 23, 2003).

Nisonoff, Laurie. "Men, Women, and the Global Assembly Line." *Curricular Crossings: Women's Studies and Area Studies: A Web Anthology for the College Classroom,* from the Five Colleges Women's Research Center, updated October 2000. http://womencrossing.org/nisonoff.html (November 22, 2003).

"Oxfam International Submission to the Heavily Indebted Poor County (HIPC) Debt Review, Executive Summary." 1990. http://www.oxfam.org.uk/policy/papers/hipc/hipcreview/hipc.ZIP (accessed November 23, 2003).

Pettit, Becky, and Jennifer Hook. "The Structure of Women's Employment in Comparative Perspective," Luxembourg Income Study Working Paper 330, September 2002. http://www.lisproject.org/publications/liswps/330.pdf (accessed November 23, 2003).

Rector, Robert E. "The Size and Scope of Means-Tested Welfare Spending." Heritage Foundation, August 1, 2001. http://www.heritage.org/Research/Welfare/Test080101.cfm (accessed November 23, 2003).

Schneider, Friedrich. "Size and Measurement of the Informal Economy in 110

Countries around the World." Paper presented at Workshop of Australian National Tax Centre, ANU, Canberra, Australia. July 17, 2002, http://rru.worldbank.org/documents/informal_economy.pdf (accessed November 23, 2003).

Smeeding, Timothy M. "The Gap between Rich and Poor: A Cross-National Perspective for Why Inequality Matters and What Policy Can Do to Alleviate It." National Institute of Population and Social Security Research, Tokyo, Japan, March 21, 2001. http://www.sprc.unsw.edu.au/seminars/japan.pdf (accessed November 23, 2003).

United Nations Development Programme. "Human Development in This Age of Globalization." In *Human Development Report, 1999: Globalization with a Human Face.* http://hdr.undp.org/reports/global/1999/en/pdf/hdr_1999_ch1.pdf (accessed November 23, 2003).

———. "Poverty Reduction." March 22, 2002. http://www.undp.org/mainundp/propoor/index.html (accessed November 23, 2003).

United Nations Statistics Division. "The World's Women, 2000: Trends and Statistics." New York: United Nations, 2000. Statistical tables (updated January 27, 2004) available at http://unstats.org/unsd/demographic/ww2000/tables.htm.

U.S. Department of Labor, Bureau of Labor Statistics. "Highlights of Women's Earnings in 2001." Report 960, May 2002. http://www.bls.gov/cps/cpswom2001.pdf (accessed November 23, 2003).

———. *Report on the American Workforce, 1999.* http://www.bls.gov/opub/rtaw/pdf/rtaw1999.pdf (November 23, 2003).

Weinberg, Daniel H. "A Brief Look at Postwar U.S. Income Inequality." U.S. Census Bureau, August 22, 2002. http://www.census.gov/hhes/income/incineq/p60asc.html (accessed November 23, 2003).

Whirled Bank Group Web site, 2001. http://www.whirledbank.org/ourwords/summers.html (accessed November 23, 2003).

World Bank. *World Development Report, 2000/2001.* Updated April 5, 2001. http://www.worldbank.org/poverty/wdrpoverty/ (accessed November 23, 2003).

Yaron, Gil. "The Final Frontier: A Working Paper on the Big Ten Water Corporations and the Privatization and Corporatization of the World's Last Public Resource," *Polaris Institute,* 2000, http://www.polarisinstitute.org/pubs/pubs_final_frontier.html (November 23, 2003).

Zimbabwe Export Processing Zones Authority Web site. http://www.epz.co.zw/about.html (accessed November 23, 2003).

Index

affirmative action, 72, 115
Africa, 50, 96, 99, 109, 119
African-Americans, 86, 87, 141–42
African-American women, 25, 27, 32,
    49–50; as domestic workers, 65;
    elderly, 93; and gender wage gap,
    62–63; and Social Security, 86. *See
    also* race/racism
Agarwal, Bina, 36
age, 63, 91. *See also* eldercare
agrarian communities, 21–22, 99,
    101–2. *See also* farming
agribusiness, 97
agriculture, subsistence, 99, 101–4. *See
    also* farming
Aid to Dependent Children (ADC), 87
Aid to Families with Dependent Chil-
    dren (AFDC), 87, 88
Albelda, Randy, 52, 90
American Enterprise Institute, 83–84
American South, 65, 146n. 19
Anker, Richard, 70
antipoverty programs, 75, 77, 80, 88.
    See also poverty, feminization of
aristocracy of labor, 29–30, 111
Asia, 96, 98, 99, 115–16. *See also
    specific country*
atomism, 12–14
Australia, 39, 40, 62, 64, 92

Badgett, M. V. Lee, 36–37
Bangladesh, 109, 124–25

banking, 70. *See also* World Bank
bank loans, 115, 124–26, 127
basic needs budgets, 84–85
Becker, Gary S., 38
Beijing: Fourth World Conference on
    Women, 133; Plus 5 conference,
    135
Benería, Lourdes, 102–3, 107
Bergmann, Barbara, 36, 45, 54, 60,
    73, 84; crowding hypothesis of,
    69
Betty Good Wife, 52–53
Bianchi, Suzanne M., 32
biology, 35. *See also* human nature;
    women's nature
birthrate, 60–61
blue-collar occupations, 71–72. *See also*
    working class
Boserup, Ester, 101–3
bourgeoisie, 23–24, 30
Brave New World (Huxley), 52
Budig, Michelle J., 46
Butler, Josephine, 16, 40

Canada, 73, 92, 113
Canadian Council for Social Develop-
    ment (CCSD), 90–91
Canadian International Development
    Agency (CIDA), 125
capitalism, 7, 23–24, 93, 115; and
    globalization, 96, 98–99, 102, 111;
    industrial, 30

care, dependent, 1, 33. *See also* caring labor

career advancement, 51–52, 142

caring and earning, 130, 140

caring labor, 16–17, 41–55, 133; and career advancement, 51–52, 54; and globalization, 96, 116–17; and migrant women, 49–50; and parental leave, 46–47, 48, 54; and reciprocity, 42, 43–44; and reproduction, 103, 107, 112; and "the nanny chain," 49–51; unpaid, 41–42; work-family divide, 51–54; working conditions of, 43; and working parents, 45–49. *See also* childrearing

Chapkis, Wendy, 120

Chicago School, 35

childbearing, 46, 59, 72. *See also* motherhood

childcare, 1, 29, 41, 44, 51; national policies toward, 39, 47, 77, 81, 103; as paid labor, 33, 47, 88, 124; social responsibility for, 46, 49; subsidized, 75, 88, 90

childrearing, 30, 54, 60–61, 67, 80; social benefits to, 55. *See also* caring labor

children, 35–36; as economic assets/burdens, 47, 91, 102; poverty of, 77, 90–92, 125; prostitution of, 120

choice, science of, 4–5. *See also* individual agency/choice

Christopher, Karen, 81

cigarette packaging, 113

citizenship, 133

civil rights, 54. *See also* human rights; women's rights

Civil Rights Act (1964), 56, 71–72; Title VII, 71–72

civil unions, 34. *See also* marriage

Civil War, U.S., 25, 122

class, 7, 30. *See also* social hierarchies; status

Clinton, Bill, 89

Cloud, Kathleen, 39

Cohen, Marjorie Griffin, 114

Cold War, 96, 99–100

colonialism, 29–30, 98–99, 101–2, 121

commodification, 102, 103, 112

commodities, 3–4, 22, 23–24, 116

communities, 130, 136–37

Conference of Mayors, U.S., 83

Conley, Frances, 66

conservatives, 34, 88–89, 93, 129, 135

Constitution, U.S., 34

constrained optimization, 5

constraints, nature of, 14

consumer price index, 82

consumption, 20, 22, 23, 64, 119

Convention on the Elimination of All Forms of Discrimination against Women, 134–35

Copenhagen, women's conference in, 100

corporations, 66, 133, 137. *See also* transnational corporations

cost-benefit calculations, 67

craft skills, 111

Crittenden, Ann, 46

currency devaluation, 105, 115–16, 121

Czech Republic, 77

daily bread, 3, 23

de Beauvoir, Simone, 8, 35

debt, 114, 116, 124, 138; Third World, 104–6, 107–8, 115

Decade for Women (1976–86), 100

decision making, 34–35, 37, 40, 134

Denmark, 48–49

dentistry, 67, 69

Department of Agriculture, U.S., 82
Department of Health and Human
  Services, U.S., 90
deregulation, 76, 105
devaluation, 131–32. *See also* inclusion
developing countries, 46, 56, 109,
  111, 112; and income inequality,
  129; and informal economy, 118;
  and portfolio investment, 115;
  poverty rates in, 125. *See also* global
  South; Third World
discrimination, 34, 56, 68, 86, 96; and
  economic waste, 141–42; and gender, 68, 70, 72–73, 129, 134. *See
  also* race/racism
division of labor, 3–4, 7, 56, 111,
  129–31, 136; egalitarian, 130, 131,
  132; in families/households, 20,
  35–38. *See also* gender (sexual) division of labor
divorce, 61, 80. *See also* marriage
domesticity: cult of, 23–26, 27, 28,
  30–31, 40; full-time, 60, 61
domestic labor/work, 23, 46, 48;
  debates on, 41–42; and gender
  inequality, 1, 39; and migrant
  women/ethnic groups, 32–33, 50,
  97

Eastern Europe, 49, 77
economic development/growth, 75,
  76, 78, 138–39, 141; and globalization, 96, 97–98, 100–103, 106,
  108, 109, 112, 118; and women,
  100, 101, 135
Economic Policy Institute (EPI),
  84–85
economic policymakers, 105, 106,
  139–40. *See also* structural adjustment policies
economics, 3, 22–23, 75; feminist
  project, 6–11; home, 35–38, 42

economics, mainstream, 67, 78, 103,
  108, 128, 135; family economy and,
  30, 35; household labor, 41–42;
  neoclassical, 4–5, 14, 71; and quality of life, 139
economic status, 33, 75, 92–93, 99,
  101
economic system, 135; fairness of, 2,
  18, 136–38; inclusive, 132; and
  meaningful work, 2, 18, 142–43;
  and quality of life, 2, 18, 138; and
  security, 2, 74, 86, 139–40; wastefulness of, 2, 18, 140–42
economic well-being, 1, 39, 41–42,
  120, 132, 135
economists, 135. *See also specific individuals*
economy, 76, 80, 93, 102
economy food plan, 82
education: early childhood, 53, 138; of
  women, 68, 100, 133
eldercare, 41, 44, 103, 124
elderly poverty, 90, 91–93
Elizabeth I, queen of England, 95
Elson, Diane, 107
emancipation, 6, 50
emergency food and shelter, 83, 84
employment, 32, 51, 56, 76, 100,
  115. *See also* labor; unemployment
empowerment of women, 6, 125–26,
  135
Engels, Friedrich, 6, 27
England, 22. *See also* Great Britain
England, Paula, 46
English East India Company, 95
Enlightenment, 11
environmental degradation, 134,
  140–41
equality: economic, 27–28, 62, 87,
  137, 143; educational, 100, 133; in
  opportunity, 131. *See also* inequality
Equal Pay Act (U.S., 1963), 71

Index

Esping-Andersen, Gøsta, 79, 91
Espinoza, Robert, 50
ethnic groups, 29, 63, 64–65, 86
Europe, 21–22, 25, 26, 103; Eastern,
    49, 77; poverty in, 78; social poli-
    cies in, 91; Western, 28, 48; work-
    ing women in, 57, 62. *See also specific
    country*
exclusion, 131–32. *See also* inclusion
exploitation, 1–2, 30, 33; and global-
    ization, 96; and natural environ-
    ment, 140; racial, 50; of women,
    102
export-led development, 108, 109,
    112, 118
export-processing zones (EPZs), 109

"Fable of the Bees, The" (Mandeville),
    44
factory work, 27, 30, 109–10, 120
fairness of economic systems, 2, 18,
    136–38. *See also* equality; social jus-
    tice
family business, 102
family economy, 4, 16, 19–40, 50,
    101; alternative, 36–37, 61;
    cooperation and conflict in, 34–40;
    cult of domesticity, 23–26, 27, 28,
    30–31, 40; egalitarian, 33; liveli-
    hood of, 26; male breadwinner–
    female caretaker model, 86–87,
    88; middle-class, 28, 30; models
    of, 33; and negotiation, 36; and
    patriarchy, 19–20, 21–22; and
    policy, 34, 53; and power, 31–34;
    transitional, 32; wages, 21–24,
    27–31, 46. *See also* children;
    motherhood
family leaves, 33, 46–47, 48, 54, 88
Family Medical Leave Act (U.S.), 47
farming, 46, 97, 101–2, 104, 116–17.
    See also agrarian communities

female-dominated occupations, 67–69,
    71, 73, 79, 102
female-headed household. *See* lone
    mothers
Feminine Mystique, The (Friedan), 61
feminism, 7–8, 129
feminist economics project, 6–11
feminization of labor, 57, 111, 129
feminization of poverty. *See* poverty,
    feminization of
feudal economy, 22
Figart, Deborah M., 27, 53–54, 62, 69
financial speculation, 115–16
Finland, 48–49, 92
firefighting, 70–71
First World, 96–97, 103, 109. *See also*
    industrialized nations; *specific coun-
    tries*
Folbre, Nancy, 42
food production, 101. *See also* farming
food stamps, 82, 85
foreign capital, 109, 112
foreign debt, 124. *See also* debt
foreign direct investment (FDI), 109
foreign occupation, 133
Fosse, Farah, 114
Fourth World Conference on Women
    (1995), 133
France, 81, 92
Fraser, Nancy, 33
free market/trade, 35, 49, 96, 105,
    108; and national policy, 132, 136;
    and poverty, 76, 79. *See also* neolib-
    eralism
free trade zones (FTZs), 109
Friedan, Betty, 52, 61
full-time work, 43, 44, 68, 77, 79

Gallie, Duncan, 91
Garrett, Nancy, 39
gender, 3, 69, 77, 80; and bias, 10,
    129; coding of, 7, 129, 142; and

development, 106–7, 116; dualisms of, 16; and globalization, 95; and hierarchy, 40, 94, 102; ideology of, 41, 45, 80, 88, 101, 143; and poverty, 82–85; and racism, 27; and roles, 7–8, 9, 25, 40, 70; and society, 11–14; traditional view of, 37
gender equality/equity, 1, 10–11, 33, 59, 62, 101; and globalization, 112, 114; and human rights, 35; and labor market, 71, 74; and poverty, 80, 94; and unregulated markets, 127
gender (sexual) division of labor, 7, 9, 20, 21, 99; caring labor, 16–17, 43, 45, 50–51; and family economy, 31, 33–34, 35, 40, 45; and globalization, 96, 102–3, 106–7; and Swedish childrearing policies, 54
gender wage gap, 6, 9, 14, 61–63, 64, 73; and discrimination, 68; and feminization of poverty, 75; and globalization, 110; and human capital differences, 68–69; and Latina women, 62–63; measuring, 61; and occupational segregation, 66–67
General Agreement on Tariffs and Trade (GATT), 100
genuine progress indicator (GPI), 139
Germany, 57–58, 81, 92
Gilman, Charlotte Perkins, 16, 25, 40, 42
glass ceiling, 1, 66
globalization, 14–15, 17, 56, 95–127, 133; and debt, 104–8; and division of labor, 96, 102–3, 106–7, 111; and economic development, 96, 97–98, 100–103, 106, 108, 109, 112, 118; and economic structural changes, 119; and factory work, 95, 109–11, 120; and free trade,

108–12; and gender, 95; and informal economy, 118–27; and marketization of governance, 112–16; and privilege, 98–100; taxonomy of, 96–98
global South, 78, 95, 97, 109, 111; and environmental degradation, 113–14, 141; and fairness, 138; and GAD, 106; and informal sector, 118; and policy interventions, 138. See also developing countries; Third World
Goldin, Claudia, 61
Gordon, Linda, 88
Gornick, Janet, 80
governance, marketization of, 112–16, 136
government, 43, 137; and globalization, 96, 103, 112. See also policy
Grameen Bank, 124–26
Great Britain, 27, 28, 65, 91. See also England; United Kingdom
Great Depression, 78, 85–86
Great Society, 88
Green Revolution, 104
gross domestic product (GDP), 40, 48–49, 139

healthcare, 77, 133, 138
heavily indebted poor countries (HIPCs), 107–8. See also debt
Henley, William Ernest, 13
hierarchies, 7, 96, 130; gender, 40, 94, 102; social, 2, 24, 32, 56, 102, 128, 131
Hispanic women, 92–93
HIV/AIDS, 98, 122
Hobsbawm, Eric, 98–99
Hochschild, Arlie R., 31–32, 49
holism, 12–14
home, 9, 11
home economics, 35–38, 42

Index

homemaking, 45, 60. *See also* domestic labor/work; household labor/work

home production, 22, 23, 24

Homo economicus (Economic Man), 5

hookers, 122. *See also* sex work(ers)

household labor/work, 21, 35, 37–40, 54, 80, 126–27; pay, 32–33; and SAP-imposed conditions, 106, 107; unpaid, 1, 24, 29, 39, 41, 42, 102

households, 37, 61, 82, 84, 99, 126; dual-earner, 34; production in, 20–21, 23, 61; traditional, 31–32

househusband, 52

housewives, 70, 101

housing, 77, 83, 84

human capital, 67–69, 70, 111, 140–42

human costs, 112

Human Development Index (HDI), 98

human nature, 4, 11, 128, 137

human reproduction, 52, 102, 135

human resources, 74. *See also* human capital; labor market

human rights, 123, 132. *See also* women's rights

Human Rights Watch, 123

Humphries, Jane, 42, 68–69

Hungary, 77

Huxley, Aldous, 52

ideal workers, 51

ideology, 18, 20, 27; of domesticity, 23–26, 27, 28, 30–31, 40; of equal rights, 80; of family wage, 28–31, 46; gender, 41, 45, 80, 88, 101, 143

immigrants, 49–50, 57, 133; and informal economy, 119, 121, 123. *See also* migrants/migration

imperialism, 30, 99, 101–2

inclusion, 129–32, 135, 136, 138, 143

income, 76, 84, 98, 137; inequality in, 119, 129, 137; low market, 81; median, 78; national, 39. *See also* wages/wage labor

India, 50, 95

indigenous peoples, 99, 121

individual agency/choice, 13, 15, 35, 131

industrialization, 103, 108, 110, 140

industrialized nations, 46, 56, 62, 71, 98, 129; economies of, 104–5; First World, 96–97, 103, 109; G8 countries, 107–8; and informal economy, 118, 119; North, 97, 100

industrial revolution, 21, 28, 30, 44, 45

Industry and Empire (Hobsbawm), 98–99

inequality: and division of labor, 131; economic, 1–2, 133–34; gender, 7, 23, 38, 99, 141; global, 98; income, 119, 129, 137; and policy decisions, 138. *See also* equality

informal economy, 17–18, 118–27; domestic work in, 123–24; and globalization, 118–27; and legality, 33, 119; and microcredit, 124, 126, 127; sex work in, 119–23; and subcontracting, 127

institutionalism, 41, 42

institutions, 130–31

International Association for Feminist Economics (IAFFE), 133

International Bank for Reconstruction and Development. *See* World Bank

international finance, liberalization of, 115. *See also* globalization; neoliberalism

International Gender and Trade Network, 114

international interventions, 132–35

International Labor Review, 141

International Labour Organization

(ILO), 43, 73, 118, 120
International Monetary Fund (IMF),
   100, 106, 108, 112, 116; and water
   privatization, 114
Islamic states, 135
Italy, 75

Japan, 62
job evaluation systems, 73
Johnson, Lyndon Baines, 87
Johnson Controls (battery manufacturer), 72
Jubilee 2000, 108
justice, 14, 75. See also social justice

Kabeer, Naila, 126
Kempadoo, Kamala, 121
Keynes, John Maynard, 115
King, Martin Luther, Jr., 14
King, Mary, 65
Kuwait, 50
Kyrk, Hazel, 42

labor, 21, 22, 23, 110–11, 130, 138;
   feminization of, 58, 111, 129; manual vs. mental, 111; productive, 91,
   103; reproductive, 42, 103, 139. See
   also women's labor/work; work
labor force, 23, 54, 79, 103, 111; and
   caring labor, 107; and free trade,
   108; and Social Security, 91;
   women's participation in, 48,
   57–61, 67–68, 88, 116
labor market, 56–74, 111, 122; gender equality in, 64, 68, 71, 74, 75
labor organizations/unions, 28, 29, 65,
   77, 111, 137
land ownership, 22, 99, 101
Latin America, 96, 119
Latina women, 62–63
legal equality for women, 26–28, 100.
   See also equality; women's rights

legality in informal sector, 33, 119
Life and Times of Rosie the Riveter, The
   (Weikal), 143
literacy, 98. See also education
livelihood, traditional, 17–18. See also
   agrarian communities
living standards, 14–15, 30, 74, 83
loans, 104, 115, 124–26, 127
local entrepreneurs, 110
lone mothers, 61, 75, 79–82, 87, 137;
   poverty of, 88–89, 90
lone-parent household, 34, 43

macroeconomics, 43, 107, 139
Madrick, Jeff, 39
male breadwinner–female caretaker
   model, 45–46, 88, 143; family
   economy and, 28, 31, 35, 40; and
   Social Security, 86–87
male-dominated occupations, 67,
   68–70, 73
male-headed households, 79, 88
male prejudice, 66
male privilege, 19–20, 71. See also
   patriarchy
male skills, 69
male superiority, 8
Mandeville, Bernard, 44
maquiladoras (free trade zones), 109
market, 4, 9, 41, 43, 61; and family
   economy, 20; forces of, 137; and
   globalization, 103, 104; and household labor, 33, 126; spread of, 30.
   See also free market/trade; labor market
market "insiders," 111
marketization of governance, 112–16,
   136
marriage, 34, 36–37; and divorce, 61,
   80
Married Women's Property Act
   (U.K.), 26

Index

Marshall, Alfred, 27
Martineau, Harriet, 16, 26, 40
Marx, Karl, 6, 27
Marxism, 5–6, 41, 42, 97, 103, 132
Massachusetts Supreme Court, 34
mass production, 21, 22. *See also* factory work
maternal love, 51. *See also* caring labor; lone mothers; motherhood
McCloskey, Deirdre, 30
media, 76, 89, 134
Medicaid, 85
medical leave, 47, 53
medical profession, 66
Memerijck, Anton, 91
men's work, 1, 7, 45, 56, 62. *See also under* gender; male; patriarchy
Methanex v. United States, 113
Mexico, 104, 111, 113
microcredit, 124–26
middle class, 28, 30
Middle East, 96. *See also specific country*
migrants/migration, 49–50, 97–98, 112, 121, 133. *See also* immigrants
Mill, Harriet Taylor, 26
minimum wage, 137
misery, global, 98–100. *See also* globalization
Mohun, Simon, 42
money managers, 115
moral code, 86–87
Morales, Juan Antonio, 106
motherhood, 27, 44, 46, 52. *See also* childbearing; family economy; lone mothers
Mott, Lucretia, 40
Mutari, Ellen, 27, 53–54, 69
Myles, John, 91

Nairobi, women's conference in, 100
natural resources, 140–42
Nazi Germany, 57–58

Nelson, Julie A., 4
neoclassical economics, 4–6, 14, 71
neoliberalism, 105, 116, 126, 136, 141; and national policy, 132, 133, 135
Netherlands, 81, 92, 121–22
New Deal, 86, 88
new home economics, 35–38
newly industrializing countries (NICs), 108, 110
New Policy Institute (Great Britain), 91
nongovernmental organization (NGO), 133
nonincome transfers, 82, 84
North, 97, 100. *See also* industrialized nations; *specific countries*
North American Free Trade Association (NAFTA), 108–9, 113
Norway, 48–49, 77

occupational segregation, 6, 72, 110, 141; and feminism, 69–71; and gender wage gap, 17, 66–67; horizontal, 65–66; and human capital theory, 68–69; and law, 66; vertical, 66
O'Connor, Kathleen, 70–71
oil prices, 104
oppression, gender, 7. *See also* gender; patriarchy
Organization for Economic Cooperation and Development (OECD), 62, 64
Origins of the Family, Private Property, and the State, The (Engels), 6
Orwell, George, 113
Ott, Notburga, 36
Oxfam (charity), 108

paid labor, 1, 6, 31–33, 42, 107, 142; caregiving, 43; childcare, 50; and community responsibility, 140; demands of, in families, 24, 26, 28, 29, 43; employment leaves, 33, 48; household, 32; and inclusion, 132; and occupational segregation, 16–17; and sex work, 121; and women, 39, 51, 56, 59, 129. *See also* unpaid labor; wages/wage labor

paid labor force, 56, 80

parental leaves, 33, 46–47, 48, 54, 88

parental responsibility, 52. *See also* childrearing; motherhood

part-time work, 46, 62, 68, 77, 79

patriarchy, 6–7, 70, 77, 87, 99, 135; and authority/power, 19–20, 31–32; and family, 21–22

pay equity, 54, 72–74. *See also* gender wage gap

Pearce, Diana M., 75

people of color, 76; women, 27, 49, 57, 72, 121. *See also specific group*

Personal Responsibility and Work Opportunity Reconciliation Act (U.S.), 89

Philippine domestic workers, 50

pieceworkers, 117, 126–27

Platform for Action (UN document), 133–35

Poland, 77

policy, 45, 113–14; and egalitarian division of labor, 131, 132, 135, 136; and family economy, 34, 39, 40; and gender equity, 71–74. *See also* economic policymakers; social policy

pollution, 113–14, 141

Polo, Marco, 95

poor communities, 76

poor countries, 107–8, 123, 141. *See also* developing countries; Third World

poor women, 32, 50, 51; and caring labor, 55; of color, 65; and conditions in nineteenth century, 57; exploitation of as caregivers, 55; and microcredit, 125. *See also* poverty, feminization of

poverty, feminization of, 15–16, 17, 75–94, 127, 133, 137; absolute, 77–78, 84; antipoverty programs, 75, 77, 80, 88; and children, 77, 90–92; costs of, 93; deserving vs. undeserving, 87, 90; and economic policy, 76–77, 78, 85–90, 138; and elderly, 90, 91–93; and families, 83; and globalization, 96, 98; and income, 78, 84; international comparisons in, 77–82; and lone mothers, 79–82, 88–89, 90; measurement of, in U.S., 78, 82–85; media on, 76, 89; microcredit and, 124–26, 127; in middle-income countries, 108; national rates, 78, 81, 98, 125; and nonincome transfers, 82, 84; and race coding, 89, 94; reduction of, 83, 88; scapegoating of, 82; social responsibility for, 76

poverty, rural, 22

Power, Marilyn, 27, 69

private firms, 103, 140. *See also* transnational corporations

private virtues, 44

privatization, 76, 105, 114

privilege, 7, 96, 98–100, 129; male, 19–20, 71

production, 6, 19, 30, 142; agricultural, 22, 101, 103, 104; and consumption, 16, 22–23; and environmental costs, 140–41; and globalization, 101, 103, 108–9; household, 22, 23, 24, 39; industrial, 23; subsistence, 99, 101–4, 103

productive work, 11, 67, 103, 130,
132
property rights/land ownership, 22,
26, 99, 101
prostitution, 27, 120, 122. See also sex
work(ers)
provisioning, 4, 9
public policy. See policy
public sector, 107
public services, 81
public transportation, 77
public vices, 44
Pyle, Jean L., 120

quality of life, 2, 18, 138–39

race/racism, 27, 29, 64–65, 77; Jim
Crow laws, 25, 65, 86, 146n. 19;
and poverty, 89, 94; and segregation, 25, 50, 141
rational choice, 4–5, 14–15. See also
individual agency/choice
Reagan, Ronald, 89
Rector, Robert, 83
redistribution, 4, 19, 34
Red Thread (sex industry lobby),
122
regulations, national, 113. See also
globalization
Reid, Margaret, 39, 42
Renwick, Trudi, 84
representation, 130, 131, 143
reproduction, 8–9, 19, 31, 42, 139;
division of labor, 107, 129; human,
52, 102, 135; and productive
labor/work, 103, 130, 132
resources, 4, 20
restaurant workers, 66–67
retail sales force, 66
retirement pensions, 86, 91, 92
Roosevelt, Franklin D., 86
Rosie the Riveter, 57

Sachs, Jeffrey, 106
safe sex and sex work, 122
Sainsbury, Diane, 80
St. Paul Fire Department, 70–71
same-sex couples, 34, 36–37
San Francisco Bay area, 139
Sassen, Saskia, 119
Saudi Arabia, 50
Scandinavia, 48–49, 77. See also Sweden
Seager, Joni, 32
Second World, 96. See also Third
World
segregation, racial, 25, 50, 141
self-interest, 4, 5, 14, 61
self-sufficiency, 21–22
Sen, Gita, 102–3
service workers, 114
sexism, 70
sexual harassment, 70
sexually transmitted diseases (STDs),
98, 122
sex work(ers), 117, 118, 120; and
globalization, 119–23; prostitution,
27, 122; rights of, 123; working
conditions of, 121
shopping, 57. See also consumption
Siegenthaler, Jürg K., 92
single mothers, 80–81, 87. See also
lone mothers
Smith, Adam, 3–4
social division of labor, 129, 136. See
also division of labor
social good, 4. See also social policy
social hierarchies, 2, 56, 102, 128,
131; and family, 24, 32. See also
social status
socialist movements, 26
social justice, 14, 75, 132, 137, 139;
and feminist economics, 7, 10, 11,
14
social location, 130

social norms/values, 34, 136
social policy, 18, 20, 92, 131; for adequate caring labor, 43; for adequate childcare, 44; and childrearing, 45, 48; and globalization, 96; progressive, 132–33; welfare, 87, 89, 91, 103, 138
social reformers, 30
social reproduction, 42, 43, 99, 112
social rights, 80
social science research, 6
Social Security, 86–87, 91–92
social services, 41, 107, 124
social status, 24, 99, 134. *See also* social hierarchies; status
society, gender roles in, 11–14
South. *See* American South; global South
South Asia, poverty in, 98
Soviet Union, 96, 99
specialization, 35, 103, 111
Spriggs, William, 68
Sri Lankan domestic workers, 50
standard of living, 14–15, 30, 74, 83
Standing, Guy, 43, 111
Stanton, Elizabeth Cady, 40
status: class, 7, 30; economic, 33, 75, 92–93, 99, 101; gender, 102; social, 24, 99, 134; of women, 2, 25, 101, 106, 107, 111, 128
street vendors, 117
structural adjustment policies (SAPs), 105–6, 112, 120; conditions of adjustments, 107–8; gendered effects of, 106; hidden costs of, 107; and privatization, 105, 114
subcontracting, 127
subsistence agriculture, 99, 101–4
subsistence wages, 111
Summers, Lawrence, 141
Supplemental Security Income, 86
supply and demand, 20, 35, 38

Supreme Court, U.S., 72
suspicion, hermeneutics of, 8
sweatshops, 118
Sweden, 48–49, 53–54, 77, 92, 137
Swiss bank accounts, 106

taxes, 80, 137
technology, 22
Temporary Assistance to Needy Families (TANF, U.S.), 89
Thailand, 120–21
Thatcher, Margaret, 13
Theory of the Leisure Class, The (Veblen), 6
Third World, 96–97, 100; debt crisis, 104–6, 107–8, 115
Thomas, Susan, 76
Tilly, Chris, 52
Tossey, Julie, 70–71
trade agreements, 95, 108–9, 112–13, 115
trade barriers, nontariff, 113, 114–15
trade liberalization, 77, 112. *See also* free market/trade
trafficking of women, 123
training for women, 68. *See also* education
transitional economies, 118–19
transnational capital, 111
transnational corporations, 17, 56, 95, 108–10, 112; and pollution, 113–14; rights of, 116; subcontracting by, 127
Truth, Sojourner, 40

unemployment, 22, 86, 98, 124. *See also* employment
unions. *See* labor organizations/unions
United Auto Workers v. Johnson Controls, 72
United Kingdom, 64, 75, 92. *See also* Great Britain

United Nations, 39, 98, 103, 114;
Children's Fund (UNICEF), 120;
Commission on the Status of
Women, 100; Declaration on the
Rights of the Child, 49–50; Development Programme (UNDP), 98;
Platform for Action, 133
universal suffrage, 54
unpaid labor, 4, 9, 17, 42, 54, 107;
household, 1, 24, 29, 39, 41, 42,
102; and inclusion, 132; of women,
39–40
utility-maximizing behavior, 5
utopian vision, 132

Veblen, Thorstein, 6, 42
Victorian era, 9, 24, 25, 30; ideology
of, 10, 25, 40, 75, 99, 101. See also
domesticity, cult of
violence against women, 133
voluntary exchange, 4, 9

wages and gender. See gender wage
gap
wages/wage labor, 33, 39, 57, 60;
equity, 54, 72–74; family, 21–24,
27–31, 46; and globalization, 95,
102, 109–11, 116–17; minimum,
137; setting of, 69–70; women's,
27, 29. See also paid labor
Washington consensus, 112
water, privatization of, 114
wealth and poverty, extremes of, 137
Weikal, Lola, 143
welfare policies, 87, 89, 91, 103, 138
welfare state regimes, 48, 78–82
Wells, Ida B., 40
Western Europe, 28, 48. See also
Europe
Western hegemony, 18
white male privilege, 71. See also patriarchy

white man's burden, 10
Williams, Joan, 51
Williams, Rhonda, 68
wives, 26, 52–53; housewives, 70,
101. See also marriage
women, and law, 26–28
women in development (WID), 106
women of color, 27, 49, 57, 72, 121
women's earnings, 27, 34, 35, 46, 54,
55; pin money, 29. See also gender
wage gap
women's labor/work, 1, 56, 107, 111,
129; domesticity, 23, 24, 39; economic status, 33, 75, 101; occupational segregation, 69, 70, 74; participation rate, 57–59, 80; and
protective legislation, 27, 31. See
also caring labor; childcare
women's movement, 61, 100
women's nature, 28, 35, 69
women's power, 1, 36, 125–26, 135
women's rights, 25, 72, 134
Women's Role in Economic Development
(Boserup), 101
women's roles, 27, 63, 69, 101.
See also childbearing;
motherhood
women's status, 25, 106, 107, 111,
128; economic, 33, 75, 101
women's well-being, 23
work: factory, 27, 30, 57, 109–11,
120; full-time, 43, 44, 68, 77, 79;
meaningful, 2, 18, 142–43; non-
market, 36, 39, 67, 138; part-time,
46, 62, 68, 77, 79; productive, 11,
67, 103, 130, 132; unskilled, 69.
See also labor; women's labor/work
worker's compensation, 86
working class, 28–30
working conditions, 121, 126, 142
working families, 19, 53. See also family economy

working parents, 46–49, 52

World Bank, 100, 103–4, 108, 112, 119, 141; and microcredit, 125–26; and water privatization, 114

World Trade Organization (WTO), 100, 108–9, 112, 114

World War I, 57

World War II, 42, 49, 57, 58, 78, 99

Year of the Woman (1975), 100

Yellow Wallpaper, The (Gilman), 25

Zimbabwe, 109

HQ 1381 .B365 2004
Barker, Drucilla K., 1949-
Liberating economics